Mario Baldassarri, Luigi Paganetto and Edmund S. Phelps (*editors*)
THE 1990s SLUMP: CAUSES AND CURES

Mario Baldassarri, Luigi Paganetto and Edmund S. Phelps (*editors*)
WORLD SAVING, PROSPERITY AND GROWTH

Mario Baldassarri, Luigi Paganetto and Edmund S. Phelps (*editors*)
INTERNATIONAL DIFFERENCES IN GROWTH RATES: MARKET
  GLOBALIZATION AND ECONOMIC AREAS

Mario Baldassarri and Paolo Roberti (*editors*)
FISCAL PROBLEMS IN THE SINGLE-MARKET EUROPE

The Privatization of Public Utilities

The Case of Italy

Edited by

Mario Baldassarri
Professor of Economics
University of Rome 'La Sapienza'
Italy

Alfredo Macchiati
Head of Economic Research Department
CONSOB, Rome

and

Diego Piacentino
Associate Professor of Public Finance
University of Urbino

in association with
Rivista di Politica Economica, SIPI, Rome
and
CEIS, University 'Tor Vergata', Rome

First published in Great Britain 1997 by
MACMILLAN PRESS LTD
Houndmills, Basingstoke, Hampshire RG21 6XS and London
Companies and representatives throughout the world

A catalogue record for this book is available from the British Library.

ISBN 0-333-68898-8

 First published in the United States of America 1997 by
ST. MARTIN'S PRESS, INC.,
Scholarly and Reference Division,
175 Fifth Avenue, New York, N.Y. 10010

ISBN 0-312-17258-3

Library of Congress Cataloging-in-Publication Data
The privatization of public utilities : the case of Italy / edited by
Mario Baldassarri, Alfredo Macchiati, Diego Piacentino.
  p.   cm.
Includes bibliographical references and index.
ISBN 0-312-17258-3 (cloth)
1. Public utilities—Italy.   2. Privatization—Italy.
3. Privatization.   I. Baldassarri, Mario, 1946–   .   II. Macchiati,
Alfredo, 1951–   .   III. Piacentino, Diego.
HD2768.I84P74   1997
338.4'73636'0945—dc21   96–46621
                                                            CIP

This book is printed on paper suitable for recycling and made from fully managed and sustained forest sources.

10   9   8   7   6   5   4   3   2   1
06   05   04   03   02   01   00   99   98   97

Printed in Great Britain by
The Ipswich Book Company Ltd
Ipswich, Suffolk

Contents

List of Contributors

Mario Baldassarri	Professor of Economics, University of Rome 'La Sapienza'
M. Gabriella Briotti	Confindustria, Rome
Guido Cervigni	Bocconi University, Milan and EUI, Florence
Massimo G. Colombo	University of Pavia
Vincenzo Visco Comandini	Istituto di Studi sulle Regioni – CNR, Rome
Paola Garrone	Polytechnic of Milan
Franco A. Grassini	LUISS 'Guido Carli', Rome
Peter M. Jackson	University of Leicester
Alfredo Macchiati	Head of Economic Research Department, CONSOB
Elena Notarangelo	Istao, Ancona
Francesco Lo Passo	Italian Treasury, Rome
Alberto Pera	Autorità Garante della Concorrenza e del Mercato, Rome
Andrea Pezzoli	Autorità Garante della Concorrenza e del Mercato, Rome
Diego Piacentino	Associate Professor of Public Finance, University of Urbino
Michele Polo	Bocconi University, Milan
Gian Cesare Romagnoli	University of Florence
Carlo Scarpa	University of Bologna

Preface

1. - The privatisation of public utilities raises several, complex issues. The privatisation decision involves not only the transfer of ownership from the public to the private sector, and thus the design of appropriate selling procedures (with regard to valuation of assets, flotation of shares, etc.), but also, and most importantly, it appears to require the adjustment of significant features of the industrial organisation and the regulatory framework.

In Italy, and generally in the European experience, public utilities have operated in relation to an array of government measures: they have been granted wide and at times all-comprehensive monopolistic franchises; their pricing policies have been controlled and constrained; and finally, they have often received substantial subsidies.

This can be easily interpreted as the consequence of a concern, neither minor nor passing, for the behaviour of public utilities, and in particular for the need to ensure that this complies with what is required by the collective interest. In this respect, it is unlikely that privatisation per se *can provide an adequate response* vis à vis *that concern.*

It is also worth noting that a similar perspective seems to underline the recent development of the debate over privatisation. Indeed, on the one hand, growing attention has been directed at the aims and methods of regulation: on the other, there has been a convergence with the concerns typical of the American debate over public utilities and deregulation, in particular the market conditions and the organisational structure of firms and industries.

2. - *This volume approaches the theme of the privatisation of public utilities in this perspective, and then focuses on the two related questions of why and how to proceed to privatisation.*

While the volume is addressed to the Italian situation, the perspective taken is more general. On the one hand, in recent years, the theoretical debate over privatisation has undergone considerable progress; on the other hand, actual experience with privatisation has widened greatly, embracing a large number of countries and a variety of production activities: these were developments of considerable saliency, which had to be considered, and taken advantage of.

3. - *The present volume is divided into three parts. The first includes studies wich deal with privatisation in general terms; they discuss, and in several cases, offer specific conclusions as to the normative bases, economic constraints, and technical formulas of the privatisation of public utilities.*

In the second part, contributions of a different nature are collected. They deal with two highly relevant aspects of the international experience. On the one hand, the British privatisation experiment is considered, being the most important which has taken place in the industrial countries, and whose effects (and lessons) are yet to be fully understood; on the other hand, consideration is given to the development of the stance and actions of the European Union with respect to the organisation of public utilities.

Lastly, the third part comprises sectorial studies, with reference to the activities which have been traditionally regarded as belonging to the realm of public utilities, and which, in Italy (as in a great number of countries) have been performed by public enterprises with wide monopoly franchises: telecommunications, electricity, natural gas, the mail and the railway systems.

4. - *In Italy, consideration of the issue of privatisation is suggested, first of all, by the important, high-priority place that the privatisation option is accorded by the current trends in policy making and reform.*

There is, however, another and perhaps more critical reason for considering the privatisation issue, namely the (relative) scarcity of, or in any case lack of impulse and tension in the debate.

For some time now, privatisation of public utilities has attracted widespread support, not only at the level of theoretical analysis and discussion, but also, most remarkably, at that of public opinion and political debate. At the same time, however, not many in-depth analyses have been conducted, and fewer firm conclusion reached, as to concrete steps and practical arrangements.

This seems to be apparent in the case of the privatisation of Enel, the public enterprise which is in control of a very large part of the electricity industry. Recently, two subsequent governments have unreservedly endorsed the privatisation option: but the government currently in power has taken stand in favour of the straightforward sale of a fraction of the shares of the company as it is, while its predecessor favoured, on the contrary, privatisation cum structural reform in the spirit of albeit not necessarily on the model as of the British experiment. These two differing positions, and especially the intervening switch, have largely escaped analysis and assessment.

5. - The resort to privatisation policies has rapidly developed into a large-scale phenomenon. On the one hand, it has extended to many countries; on the other, it has involved numerous activities carried out by the public sector, well beyond those performed by public utilities, which are presently of concern.

It would be difficult, however, to claim that this process has originated and taken shape over time, in relation to clear-cut principles, and consistently chosen practical moves.

In general, it would appear that the privatisation movement is not an organic process, the outcome of planned decisions, but rather an experimental process, indeed the outcome of the dynamic interaction of widely differing strands of thought in governments, far from unanimous persuasions among economists, and — often and not less importantly — unforeseen market reactions (especially capital market friction).

Perhaps even the most important European experience, the British privatisation experiment, is not, after all, the coherent expression of a unitary policy, as it has been presented and often believed to be; to keen observers it appears, on the contrary, to be the (evolving) result of a number of reasons, some more political than economic in nature, and some more important than others at different times or with respect to different sectors (Johnson [2]).

6. - *When approaching the Italian case, it can be useful to start with a consideration of the objectives (benefits) which are usually referred to as premises for a privatisation programme: reducing the public sector borrowing requirement, improving the efficiency (both allocative and internal) of operation, widening and strengthening the stock market.*

Which of these objectives can be seen as driving forces of the Italian privatisation process? Even a cursory examination of the relevant official documents is sufficient to bring out significant uncertainty in orientation. The early Scognamiglio Commission's report (1990) endorsed the objectives listed above, and, in addition, that of increasing the confidence of the international business community in the Italian economy. Subsequently, however, the concern for the improvement of efficiency became overriding. In this respect, the Government's official paper on economic and financial planning for 1995-1997, presented by the Berlusconi government in August 1994, typifies the trend, by stating that the primary objective of the privatisation programme is "an overall increase in efficiency". The Dini government was similarly inclined: «The privatisation process is a unique opportunity to improve the efficiency of the economy as a whole, reduce the cost of services, improve their quality and thus improve the competitiveness of the productive system as a whole, and ensure that productivity gains are transferred to the final consumers» (From Prime Minister Dini's initial statement delivered to Italy's Chamber of Deputies, January 23, 1995).

Other objectives appear to have lost of appeal, at least in part, with time — those, in particular, of redressing public deficits and improving the reputation of the Italian economy; also, an initial emphasis on the need to introduce competition into the privatised industries has waned. On the other hand, the development of the stock market has remained a recurring theme of concern.

7. - *There are of course well-founded reasons for viewing privatisation as instrumental to the objective of efficiency, both in general and with reference to the Italian situation.*

Italian public enterprises do not offer a uniform picture, but it can be claimed that inefficiency problems are ubiquitous. Allocative inefficiency is plausibly a general phenomenon, given the presence and extent of subsidisation and cross-subsidisation; while productive inefficiency is more specific to — or more pronounced in — those industries where organisational and technical progress have been slower, i.e. the mail and the rail.

Text-book formulations indicate that remedial policy for allocative inefficiency should be based on the dismantling of entry barriers and monopoly franchises; this policy would require, as accompanying measures, the separation and unbundling of naturally-monopolistic and competitive activities, and the prohibition, for monopoly franchises holding firms, to enter the adjacent liberalised markets. If no measures are taken with respect to vertical structure, in such a way that separation is first enacted and then maintained, privatisation could even turn out to be a counterproductive policy: a privatised company, strongly motivated towards profit, will be driven to fully exploit its monopoly position, so as to realise the monopoly rents, those which the public management in part failed to seize, and in part deployed in socio-political objectives. Recourse to regulation is, then, the obvious preventive policy, albeit its lines, and real possibilities are, as will be seen below, subject to a number of questions.

This should not be taken as acceptance of the primacy of the competition over ownership argument in its extreme version (as sketched, e.g. in Vining-Boardman [4]). This holds that where competition is sustainable and operating, it acts as a sufficient condition for ensuring efficiency, and thus no difference exists, in this respect, between publicly and privately owned firms. In fact, it is difficult to imagine that a public enterprise can be completely freed of political interference, or that the markets — including the labour and capital markets — are so strongly competitive as to forbid it.

However, when there is internal management inefficiency, privatisation could be instead the most appropriate policy choice.

In conclusion, with respect to public utilities, no simple prescription is at hand, for example of the type summarised in the formula, to privatise for productive efficiency, to liberalise for allocative efficiency. The two policies can interact in a variable manner, depending on cost functions and the degree of market integration and competition; liberalisation, in any case, poses the question of the need and contents of new forms of regulation.

8. As to the goal of strengthening the stock market, it is no coincidence that it has received constant attention. One important consequence of public ownership is that the public sector performs the two functions of capital allocation and risk bearing. Privatisation implies transferring these functions to the stock market, and thus the performance of this market assumes paramount importance.

Here, however, it is also possible to note some circularity between the goal and the instrument. The success (or feasibility) of privatisation depends on the performance of the stock market: the capacity for absorption is influenced, not only by the size of the company, but also by the characteristics of demand and the market microstructure. The objectives of developing the stock market and broadening shareholding are therefore conditioned to some extent by the immediately preceding situation.

9. - Perhaps to these considerations another, which also relates to the objectives of privatisation, can be added.

Privatisation can be seen as instrumental in reducing the involvement of the public sector — and political decision making — in the management of the economy. In a stronger version, the view is that in this way economic activities can be removed from the politicians' sphere of control; in a weaker version, the view is instead that in this way public sector decision-making can be relieved of difficult responsibilities and tasks.

10. - *Designing (and implementing) a privatisation programme requires a number of choices with regard to both procedure and final goals. Here, the main issues — and inescapably controversial ones — are likely to be* (i) *the structure — vertical, horizontal and possibly regional — of the privatised industries, and the entry conditions;* (ii) *the ownership structure and the divestiture process and* (iii) *the regulatory framework and competition policy.*

As regards the first issue, it is possible to note that the debate has expressed converging opinions on the issue of the actual presence of natural monopoly conditions in the sectors where public utilities operate: such conditions are less far-reaching than was traditionally believed, and can be assumed, with reasonable confidence, to be present perhaps only in the supply of networks, in particular local distribution networks.

At the same time, however, attempts to empirically establish the border lines between naturally monopolistic and (potentially) competitive activities have led to only limited successes.

Of course, this is a situation which makes in difficult to draw firm conclusions and prescriptions.

Perhaps the main observation that can be advanced here is that the reasons of principle would appear to be strongly in favour of the separation of companies and the unbundling of activities. In the first place, merely transferring the present monopolies to the private sector would only repropose — in more complicated terms — the question of regulation (legal framework and controlling agency); from this viewpoint, markets with some degree of competition would appear to be an essential condition for obtaining efficiency gains and to make regulation easier and more effective.

In the second place, it should be taken into account that, within any reasonable time horizon, privatisation operations can be carried out only once. From this point of view, the separation of companies to be privatised would leave room for subsequent adjustment processes, in the form of acquisitions, mergers and diversifications;

while selling the present monopolies as they stand would produce market situations which could only be modified with difficulty and very slowly.

In the third place, it is not difficult to think of separation policies which do not entail (very) high reversibility costs: that is policies which would not aim at a thorough, in depth restructuring of industries, but instead would limit themselves to the separation of specific, relatively circumscribed activities. This has been the case, for example, in the UK, with the establishment of a second and much smaller company in the telecommunications industry, Mercury, alongside British Telecom.

Finally, in the fourth place, it is also possible to raise arguments in support of recource to the formula of regional separation, which is much easier to implement, as compared with the other formulas of separation — vertical and horizontal. The municipal utilities are well established examples of resorting to such a formula, while more recent ones are those of the mixed companies in which regional governments typically hold a stake operating in the field of natural gas distribution.

11. - As regards the second set of issues — relating to divestiture and the resulting ownership structure — there are (at least) two issues worth mentioning.

Firstly, privatisation operations usually take considerable time, and this means that in the interim period the public sector is called upon to perform two functions, those of the owner (shareholder) and the regulator; but those functions imply different sets of objectives and behaviour rules, and thus their balancing, while necessary, is likely to be difficult, as well as controversial.

Secondly, the change in ownership, from the public to the private sector, is bound to interact with the important liberalisation processes to which the various public utility services are subject, although in a far from homogeneous manner. This interaction should be carefully taken into account: in a country such as Italy, where large companies and institutional investors are few, competitive market arrangements represent a unique opportunity for signi-

ficantly modifying the structure of incentives for the managers of monopolistic companies.

12. - As to the specific theme of regulation, it is necessary to give explicit consideration to the objectives, and especially to the alternative between regulation for the plan and regulation for the market, radically posed by Hayek [1].

Also, in the light of Italy's limited experience of independent regulatory agencies, another aspect worth considering is the articulation of the institutional system that will take charge of the regulatory tasks, particularly with reference to the legal arrangements for the review of the decisions taken by the regulatory body. This aspect is linked to the other, somewhat controversial, one of the proper role of discretionary power. Discretionary power tends to be viewed with suspect or hostility by traditional liberal thinking, for which the agents' behaviour, and thus also the regulators' can be traced almost exclusively to motivations of individual advantage; this view leaves little room for the influence of ideas and ideals, and the possibility that a regulatory agency can count on the dedication, as Kahn ([3], p. 11) put it, of "vigorous, imaginative and enthusiastic protagonists of the public interest".

13. - Another critical aspect of the privatisation of public utilities is the resulting distributional impact. There are two channels in operation, which are distinct as regards both time and logic: they relate respectively to the selling price of the firm and the price of the goods and services which are sold and bought.

It is very difficult to determine the selling price of a public enterprise, and this makes room for political judgement and influence. These can take on greater weight when price-fixing is carried out by means of either negotiation (as in the case of direct sale), or relational contracting with the banks entrusted with the placement of shares.

For the second of these channels, privatisation can be expected to be neutral — i.e. of no consequence for the prices of the goods and services both bought and sold — in the presence of a competitive market. But where monopoly conditions are present, as in the case of public utilities, and they are left unchanged by privatisation, no similar expectation can be obtained. In this case, regulation comes to play a crucial role, being the source of a determining influence from the viewpoint of the overall effect of privatisation on the revenues of customers and suppliers. The change in ownership, per se, *is likely to bring about some improvement in internal efficiency; if there is aslo a capable and authoritative regulator, the consumers may share the benefits of cost reduction. But the most important consequence (albeit an uncertain one as regards direction) is that which may derive from modification of pricing policies. Current pricing policies, as practised by public utilities, tend to be constrained by distributional considerations; small, low income consumers are (implicitly) subsidised, while large consumers, typically firms, bear the costs of such subsidies.*

In general, it can be expected that privatisation will engender difficulties and tensions with regard to the practice of cross-subsidisation.

In the present situation, the existence of cross-subsidies can only be presumed, and their actual magnitude left to conjecture. There are no conditions which can make cross-subsidies visible, just as (or because) there are no incentives for eliminating or reducing them: in reality, on the one hand, the profit motive can only make itself felt in a weakened manner over public enterprises which currently operate in a monopoly regime; while, on the other hand, full legal protection exists from entry threats of other companies, whether actual or potential.

*But privatisation, by changing these circumstances, will uncover possibilities and establish incentives in an opposite direction. In essence, privatisation will bring attention to, and scrutiny of, both profitability of underpricing and defensibility (*vis à vis competition*) of overpricing.*

In addition, at the level of policy principles, the practice of cross-subsidisation would appear to have gradually lost its appeal. In part, the reasons traditionally given to justify redistribution via *low tariffs appear to be weakened, but on the other hand, and perhaps more conclusively, if there are valid distributional objectives in this field, they may be better served by explicit and visible subsidy policies, namely by public budgeting and funding.*

14. - Privatisation, which several successive Italian governments first endorsed and then started to concretely implement with the sale of a number of banking, insurance and industrial companies, is about to enter into a more delicate phase with the sale of public utilities.

It is difficult to avoid the impression that this phase is being tackled on the basis of an approach which is largely open-ended, and thus exposed, in its development, to experimental choices and uncertain turns.

The purpose of the studies collected in this volume is to single out and summarize the issues, and to contribute to building a structured framework for reflection.

M. BALDASSARRI
A. MACCHIATI
D. PIACENTINO

I - CENTRAL ISSUES

Privatisation, Liberalisation and the Orientation of Regulation

Alberto Pera *

Autorità Garante della Concorrenza e del Mercato, Roma

The purpose of this paper is to present some very general thoughts concerning the interaction between privatisation of public enterprises, the changes in the regulation of public utilities and market competition. Aside from their mere simultaneity, there is a close relationship between the privatisation processes which have taken place in a large number of countries from the beginning of the 1980s and the changes in the structure of regulation of public utility sectors in which many privatised companies operate.

Such relation stems in part from the need to face old issues in a new context. Traditionally, state-owned enterprises have played a dual role in public utility services, acting both as providers of services and as regulators. Their privatisation has required a clear separation of the two functions. This has led to a reconsideration of the efficiency of pre-existing regulation models, often considered as characterized by undesired distortive effects and administrative inertia [1]. Consequently, new methods aimed at fostering less distortive behaviours have been determined.

Yet, the relation between the two processes depends also on the fact that privatisation has permitted to question not only the methods,

---

* The author is Secretary General of the Italian Competition Authority. The opinions expressed in this paper are the Author's personal views and are not necessarily shared by the Italian Competition Authority.

N.B.: the numbers in square brackets refer to the Bibliography at the end of the paper.

[1] See KAHN A.E. [12]; JOSKOW P. - NOLL R. [11]; PERA A. [20].

but also the appropriateness of regulation regimes. In particular, privatisation has often led to liberalisation processes whose objective is the complete establishment of market conditions. Examples are provided by the development of competitive markets in air transportation, telecommunication services, electric power production and supply, in many countries. Such examples are likely to become more numerous in the future as technical and organisational innovations enable competition to extend to other public utility sectors. In these cases, the economic regulation of the market, implying the administrative determination of prices and supply conditions, can be only a temporary status, and is intended to guarantee the passage from a monopolistic situation to a free market [2].

It is important to underline that in such cases it is the very nature of the regulation that changes. The traditional aim of regulation is to protect defenceless consumers from the abuse of power of a monopoly, the existence of which is however deemed to be necessary because of either the technical and economic features of the market or the «social» needs whose satisfaction is held essential. From this point of view, regulation necessarily implies that the structure of the industry is «frozen» to some degree: its development is dictated not by market incentives but rather by the regulator's evaluation. The introduction of more flexible and efficient intervention procedures does not change the situation.

On the contrary, whenever the regulation aims at facilitating the transition towards competition, we should not seek to fix in detail the behaviours of enterprises, but rather to create the conditions needed to foster competition. Actually, as soon as full competition is established on the market, regulation itself should disappear. Ordinary antitrust legislation should then be sufficient to guarantee that the firms do not threaten the competitive order of the market.

However, the transition from the present to the new situation poses delicate problems. In particular, it is not always clear that

---

[2] We are obviously referring to the regulation of prices, contractual terms and quantity. In these sectors, there will still be extensive *technical* actions, intended to determine *standards* and technical conditions, safety rules as well as to establish supply procedures that will not damage consumers in sectors in which, for instance, services are mostly supplied through subscription contracts.

regulation operates now in a different context. Thus, there is the risk that some procedures are introduced which could alter the future development of the market structure.

In order to provide some elements on the issues outlined, I shall proceed as follows. As at times some degree of antinomy is held between privatisation and competition, first I shall make some remarks about this relation; secondly, I shall analyse some directions along which regulation should move in the prospect of market liberalisation; and lastly, I shall comment upon the relation between regulation and competition protection.

1. - Privatisation and the Market

The experience of the many countries which have implemented far reaching privatisation processes shows that almost everywhere they lead to the elimination of barriers to entry, to market liberalisation processes and to the introduction of competition [3].

From the point of view of economic analysis, the relation between privatisation and competition is less clear-cut. Often, the authors that have tackled the issue admit that privatisation may give rise to benefits in terms of productive efficiency and of the reduction of X-inefficiency. They underline, however, that these very same results may stem from the system of incentives provided by the competitive environment; they may be expected also from non privatised enterprises if they operate in a competitive context and are subject to a budget constraint. These authors also argue that, should privatisation take place through the establishment of a non competitive market order, it could lead instead to situations that could be inefficient from a production standpoint, at least in terms of X-inefficiency. This would derive from the lack of incentives to «internal» control resulting from the absence of competition. Instead, there would be a strong incentive to dodge the regulator's control [4].

From these considerations one quickly concludes that the owner-

---

[3] See PERA A. [19]; OECD [18]; WORLD BANK [24] for examples.
[4] See, for instance, VICKERS J. - YARROW G. [23]; DI MAJO A. [6].

ship is not necessarily important to reach efficiency in both production and allocation and that what really counts are market conditions.
In a competitive environment even public enterprises could display an
efficient behaviour, and indeed one could not exclude *a priori* that
they will not turn out to be even more efficient that private enterprises.

Contrasting these views are the opinions of those [5] who, on the
basis of experience rather than on theory, tend to believe that the
greater efficiency of the private enterprise should be generally
assumed. Thus, these authors tend to share Pasquale Saraceno's
sincere conclusions [20], whereby «in a market economy it is not
privatisation that needs to be politically justified, but rather the lack of
privatisation». In the first place, they point out that most studies
comparing the efficiency of public and private enterprises show the
superiority of the latter [6].

Secondly, they note that improvements in the performance of
enterprises are generally reported following privatisation. In particular, studies on the privatisation of companies operating both in a
condition of regulated monopoly and in a competitive environment
demonstrate that privatisation is generally followed by improved
efficiency, increased productivity and price policies that are more
favourable to consumers [7].

Lastly, they underline that public ownership often leads to distortions not only in the pursuit of productive efficiency but also in
defining companies' competitive positions on the markets in which
they operate. This conclusion comes from considering the inevitably
strict link between the administration of public enterprises and
political power. There is strong suspicion that companies can influence political choices to ensure their privileged position on the market
by obtaining public aid and introducing distortions in the market
mechanism that can benefit them [8].

---

[5] The fact that these opinions are given especially by institutions, such as the OECD
[18] and the WORLD BANK [24] having long-standing experience in the study and the
practical application of public enterprise management reforms should make one think.

[6] See NAHMIJAS A. [15] for a review.

[7] Cited in WORLD BANK [24].

[8] See the case of FORNALCZYK A. [9]. On the other hand, as Fornalczyck pointed
out, even privatised companies may enjoy the same protection at certain conditions, if

Therefore, these analyses seem to emphasise that, far from preventing the establishment of competition, privatisation allows instead to reconsider the suitability of the market structure with a view more to public interest and less to that of the companies involved. In this light, privatisation often gives rise to liberalisation and regulatory reform processes. Nevertheless, since privatisation is seen as an indispensable element to open the market, the methods with which it is implemented and the associated regulation changes are very important. The former aspect is analysed below, whereas the latter shall be dealt with shortly.

In some sectors, such as electric power or railway transportation, competition is only possible if monopolistic and competitive areas of the industry are separated. In these sectors, although not in others, the existence of a network infrastructure that cannot be duplicated economically results both in an indivisibility and in an «essential facility» for providing the service. In this case, a company which operates at the same time in the management of the monopolistic infrastructure and in the supply of the service, may easily use its dominant position to hamper competition. Consequently, in these sectors privatisation has often been accompanied by deep structural changes, involving the separation of the network management from the provision of services on potentially competitive markets. Examples are provided by the developments which took place in the electricity industry in the United Kingdom, Argentina and more recently in Spain.

Yet, it is clear that a new order of this type would be very difficult if not impossible unless it is conceived and implemented *prior* to the privatisation of companies. Otherwise, buyers will have the impression that together with ownership of the company they have also acquired the right to a given market structure where the company plays a monopolistic role. It could be argued that this impression is not always legitimate, because monopoly is not only an exceptional economic situation but is also juridically exceptional, as we shall see further on, and as such it needs to find a justification not in itself but

---

the aims of privatisation are other than economic efficiency. See following footnote (9) on this regard.

rather in the existence of well recognised public interests. From a political point of view, however, it would be very difficult for such a change to be implemented, especially in the run-up to privatisation [9].

On these grounds, the liberalisation of the market and the establishment of a competitive order should occur prior to or at the same time as privatisation, not because there is a value prejudice regarding the possibility of private management, but because the very same procedures of privatisation risk otherwise to render successive liberalisation difficult [10].

2. - Regulation

Regulation has been in recent years one of the most fertile areas for empirical analysis, methodological suggestions and institutional changes, such as the establishment of regulatory authorities [11]. Traditionally, the analysis of regulation focused on the definition of criteria that could prod controlled companies to pursue efficiency in both production and allocation. Nevertheless, in sectors that are going to be liberalised, regulation serves one more purpose, that could even become the *leading* objective, i.e. *to promote* the creation of real competition, by ensuring appropriate access conditions to new companies.

---

[9] For this reason, in examining the options for a new order of the power sector being privatised in transitional economies, NEWBERY D. [16], suggests that it should stay public until its final order has been decided.

[10] Yet, such an outcome generally depends on the fact that different objectives are sought with privatisation. In particular, there is no doubt that the boost towards privatisation mostly derives from the contribution that it is deemed capable of giving national budget financing and/or public debt relief. The importance of these other objectives has sometimes led to a limited relation between privatisation and the opening of the market. It has been argued that the sale of companies having some degree of market power may enable these companies to acquire a higher value so that at times this may foster the option of not fully exploiting the possibility of liberalisation. There are examples of this regarding both the privatisation of public utility companies in industrialised countries (such as for instance British Gas in the case of companies) and the processes that are under way in transition economies, where sometimes the state has decided to privatise companies operating in market sectors (for example in the automobile industry), protecting the company privatised so as to increase its value.

[11] See MILANA C. - PADOA SCHIOPPA [14] and SPULBER D.F. [22].

There are two reasons why the liberalisation of sectors that were previously subject to regulation may be considered appropriate. First, because the market mechanism is thought to be able to ensure both the efficient production and the efficient allocation of products. If this is the case, there are no grounds for regulation, since it could yield at the most the same results as the market would lead to and more often it could even lead to less desirable results. Another reason is the superiority of a competitive mechanism in the timely adaptation to the modifications in market behaviours and structures resulting from technological and organisational change. Indeed, the experience of sectors such as telecommunications shows that technical and organisational innovation and the progress of contractual mechanisms make developments extremely uncertain and dynamic, allowing at the same time a high degree of competition. In this case, the competitive order is essential for agents to quickly adjust to changes by adapting strategies and behaviours, whose effects will have an impact on supply prices and terms.

The regulator's new objectives and the more traditional ones are not necessarily always compatible with one another. In fact, in the initial stages of liberalisation the industry structure is inevitably not competitive either fully or in an oligopolistic manner. Often, originally monopolistic companies continue to hold dominant positions for a long time after the market has been opened to competition. In these instances, the regulator may have to face the difficult task of choosing between immediate consumer protection and the promotion of competition.

Particularly, Burton [4] emphasises that the regulation reform which accompanied many privatisations aimed at establishing a regime of «managed competition», where the companies' behaviour and the structure of the market are largely decided by the regulator. This approach may seem inconsistent with one directed at favouring the evolution of the market in a fully competitive sense.

The following paragraphs outline a few implications of such an approach, particularly in terms of price regulation procedures, the access to network infrastructures and the treatment of the dominant enterprises.

2.1 *Price Regulation*

In order to foster competition on the markets for public utilities, the incentives to the entry of new competitors able to erode an existing dominant position should be increased. Such incentives often consist in the high margins enjoyed by the dominant firm in some of the markets on which it operates. On the other hand, consumer protection would require the reduction of the dominant company's extra profits and thus of those very margins that should foster the entry on the market.

Burton [4] observes that this apparent trade-off between the promotion of competition and consumer protection can be avoided by using *price cap* mechanisms, introduced in the United Kingdom when the large public utilitiy enterprises were privatised. In fact, *price cap* mechanisms are based on given rules, to be applied for rather long periods of time and not aimed at preestablishing a company's price structure, but only at regulating its overall evolution. Therefore, a company is allowed to adjust its price policy to changes in market conditions and possibly to obtain high margins in some markets. These margins, however, would encourage the entry of competitors, whose access is safeguarded by both the regulator and the application of general competition rules.

In Burton's opinion, this pro-competitive approach should not be weakened by the prevailing concern for the immediate consumer protection. The attempt to eliminate high margins and profits achieved on the markets for some services may lead to a frequent adjustment of efficiency standards, the establishment of different values of standards for the different services and the introduction of supplementary criteria in the regulation of prices. As a consequence, the regulator's discretional power is increased and stricter constraints are imposed on the price structure. In the meanwhile, the regulator may be led to postpone the entry of competitors on the market in order to keep a given price structure unchallenged.

Therefore, in order to promote competition, price regulation methods should be adopted that are consistent with the aim of fostering entry of new competitors on the markets. Once efficiency rules of the *price cap* type are imposed on the dominant firm, the attention should shift to access conditions on the market and to ensuring that the dominant company does not use its market power to prevent the entry of new competitors. Undoubtedly, consumer protection may be achieved better and more naturally once an effective competition has been established; the enforcement of anti-trust rules will help preserve such competition.

2.2 Access to Network Infrastructure

As has already been mentioned, in many public utility sectors firms need an access to a network infrastructure, in order to be able to provide their services. A profitable development of alternative infrastructures is possible in some sectors, such as telecommunications, but is only partially achievable in others, such as electricity, gas or railway transport. Regulation will then have to adapt to these different situations: in the first case, the development of alternative infrastructures should be fostered, whereas in the second case, level playing field conditions for all competitors should be identified. The latter objective may be pursued differently depending on whether the network management has been separated from the provision of services.

If the management of the network, for instance of the electricity transmission network or of the railway network, has been previously separated, care should be given to provide transparent and non discriminatory access conditions to all competitors [12].

Whenever the network management has not been separated from the provision of services, lacking an appropriate regulation, the enterprise in charge of the network will find itself able to shift part of its production and distribution costs on to competitors. In some cases, it may also try to prevent the access of competitors to the network.

---

[12] In this case, auctions may sometimes be appropriate. Nevertheless, an auction is not in itself a mechanism that promotes the evolution of a competitive market structure, since it only ensures the allocation of a scarce resource to those who can obtain the highest profit from it, which can often be the case of a dominant enterprise. Thus, if the aim were to promote competition, other criteria may be appropriate and a regulatory control of access conditions is often necessary.

Therefore, it is crucial that regulation defines the *rights* of use of the network and access *conditions*.

This task is complex, however. The allocation of infrastructure costs, needed to set proper access fees, is difficult due to the existence of sunk costs. Although suitable accountancy procedures may be employed, the result will often be unpredictable. On these grounds, beside accountancy aspects, substantial organisational reforms are often needed such as the separation of infrastructure operators into different organisational units [13]. In any case, the mere consideration of the extremely complex nature of these issues should suggest the appropriateness of a structural separation of the network management from the provision of services, as far as this can be accomplished.

Lastly, a different situation occurs whenever alternative infrastructures are possible, such as in the case of telecommunications. Beside the problems of granting access to the infrastructure, other issues arise concerning the connection of the various networks, essential to exploit the capacity of the entire system and, above all, to enable each competing company to achieve the wider realm of consumers. It should be evident that the solution to these problems may be the establishment of a regime of full competition [14]. In an environment where service suppliers compete on a plurality of interconnected networks, both the final prices of the services and connection fees will be determined by the market [15].

Yet, until the market is characterised by the presence of a firm who runs a largely dominating network meeting most of the traffic and is also a service supplier, a solution is unlikely to be reached through voluntary agreements, and a regulatory effort will be required [16].

---

[13] For the sector of telecommunications, see CASTELLI F. [5] and the references therein.

[14] For a suggestive representation of the trends in this sense in telecommunications, see NOAM E.M. [17].

[15] It is on the basis of such considerations, as well as of the availability of several infrastructure networks, that the plans of a thorough liberalisation of telecommunications now being discussed in the United States have been conceived.

[16] In the recent history of telecommunications, the development of competition has in some instances been possible thanks only to the regulatory bodies' decision to make

It should be noted, however, that if the regulator's objectives include fostering the development of alternative infrastructures, setting access and connection frees will be extremely complex. Such fees may vary between the marginal cost and the cost of self-production, which can vary substantially, and should cover any cost of the universal service. What is more, the regulator will have to face a difficult trade-off between the aim of enabling a wider access to the existing infrastructure and that of preserving the incentive to the establishment of alternative infrastructures.

2.3 *Asymmetric Regulation*

In the light of the previous considerations, *asymmetric* regulation methods, adopted in many countries, particularly in the sector of telecommunications, should be evaluated. Although in telecommunications remarkable competitive forces have developed, the elimination of legal monopolies led only very slowly to changes in market structure, even in those countries that have been undertaking liberalisation for many years [17];

This stems from the existence of both structural and strategic entry barriers resulting from the dominant firm's cost and commercial penetration advantages and from its ability to practice predatory and discriminatory strategies vis-à-vis its competitors.

In order to attenuate the effect of such entry barriers, it is held that the introduction of temporary asymmetric limitations to the operations of the dominant firm with respect to newcomers might be appropriate. These limits may concern price or service conditions

---

the connection mandatory. This has been the case, for instance, of the United Kingdom, where Oftel decided to force British Telecom to interconnect first to Mercury and then to cable TV operators. In telecommunications, interconnection is mandatory for a leading network operator, as explained in the text, in accordance with Community telecommunications regulation (see EUROPEAN COMMISSION [7]).

[17] In the United Kingdom, over ten years after the market was opened to competition, British Telecom still has about 90% of the domestic telephony market and 80% of the international telephony market. In Japan, ten years after telephony was liberalised, NTT is by far the leading company with a market share exceeding 70%. In the United States, at twenty years from the liberalisation of long-distance telephony, ATT still holds over 70% of the market.

aimed at avoiding the pursuit of strategic behaviours [18], may establish futher obligations of a «social» character, which are not imposed on new entrants, at least not on the smaller ones [19], and may prevent the dominant firm from providing some services or managing some infrastructures, so as to foster the development of alternative suppliers of services and infrastructures [20].

From a static standpoint, these provisions may be deemed inefficient: they prevent the exploitation of scope economies and, consequently, the pursuit of more efficient production techniques. Yet beside these costs, the advantages should be emphasised: asymmetric regulation fosters the development of independent firms and thus allows a more rapid achievement of situations where competition may determine how the market works, once regulation asymmetry has been done away with.

Of course, the double character of the effects of asymmetric regulation leads to some caution in tackling the issue. There seems to be general agreement, however, on the need, in some cases, to restrict the provision of services and the management of infrastructures by dominant enterprises in order to allow new competitors to enter a market. Such restrictions, in any case, should be limited in time, and within such time limit market conditions need to be continuously reviewed [21].

The experience of countries which have implemented an asymmetric regulation show, on the other hand, that it has fostered the development of keen competitors as well as large investments in

---

[18] In the United States, for example, the time of the liberalisation of the telecommunications industry, ATT was long forced not to reduce prices below given levels in order to prevent predatory price policies.

[19] In the United Kigdom, competitors with a market share lower than 10% do not need to contribute to the financing of the universal service provided by British Telecom.

[20] In particular, from the latter point of view the provision should be evaluated whereby the telecommunication leading company cannot supply television broadcast services, which is sometimes part of the various countries' regulations. In the United States, for example, telecommunication companies have long been excluded from the management of cable TV broadcasting networks, and in the United Kingdom British Telecom is banned from installing television cables until 1996, whereas companies supplying them may broadcast on these telecommunication services.

[21] See CASTELLI F. [5].

infrastructures, which now represent alternative channels to gain access to the utility markets [22].

3. - From Regulation to Antitrust

Whenever regulation aims at facilitating the establishment of competitive conditions, the concerns that lead it are very similar to those directing the action of competition authorities in the enforcement of antitrust rules: limitation of the dominant enterprises' market power, prevention of abuses and easing the access of competitors to the market. The difference between a regulatory body and a competition authority lies in that the former has direct powers to determine the market structure and to regulate companies' behaviours; thus, in principle, if correctly oriented, a regulatory body can contribute more effectively and more directly to *fostering* a competitive environment.

This does not mean, however, that the application of general competition rules in regulated sectors is useless. On the contrary, the enforcement of antitrust rules by the general competition authority may be necessary to identify which market area should be temporarily excluded from competition and to encourage the regulator to undertake the appropriate measures. It is worth noting that in some sectors, particularly in telecommunications, liberalisation processes went through a progressive delimitation of regulated markets following antitrust authorities' actions, which gradually reduced the area excluded from competition.

In the United States, the liberalisation of telecommunications began with the *Carterphone* judgement at the end of the Fifties,

---

[22] In particular, in the United Kingdom the ban on the creation of infrastructures imposed on British Telecom, although criticised in terms of its efficiency, led nevertheless to the establishment of alternative local infrastructures by cable TV companies who entered partnerships with international telecommunication operators. This gave rise to the creation of a second infrastructure for the access and supply of all telecommunication services. On the other hand, the experience of countries such as the United States or the United Kingdom, where asymmetric regulation went along with liberalisation, shows that it does not seem to have compromised neither the position of the dominant firm on the domestic or international markets nor its financial conditions, while contributing to the development of a competitive environment.

liberalising the use of terminal equipment that was not produced by
the monopolist network manager. The liberalisation of long-distance
telecommunications was made possible following a 1977 judgement,
applying the antitrust law, whereby ATT, which held a monopoly
position, was obliged to interconnect a competing operator, MCI. This
judgement was adopted despite the fact that the telecommunication
regulatory body (the Federal Communication Commission) had previously denied the interconnection to MCI. Lastly, the complete
liberalisation of telecommunications, with the exception of local
telephony, after the splitting up of ATT, occurred as a consequence of
a transaction between the monopolist and the judge from whom the
appeals regarding ATT's alleged abuses of dominant position were
pending [23].

In Europe, a large number of decisions issued by the European
Commission and of judgements by the Court of Justice allowed a
reduction of the area where member states' domestic legislation
hampers the development of competition on the market. As far as
Italy is concerned, a number of decisions by the Competition
Authority concerning telecommunications as well as airport services
have limited the field over which monopolistic firms enjoy exclusive
rights. These examples show how the enforcement of antitrust law by
the authority in charge of overseeing its general application, highlighting whether competition is unduly limited, ensures an effective and, in
some cases, even essential delimitation of the regulated area.

On this regard, it should be noted that competition and regulation
are not only two different economic procedures to organise the
market, but also imply two different legal systems, in relation with the
different regime of rights of the companies operating on a competitive
and on a regulated market. Indeed, in Western countries, regulation is
normally considered as an *exception*, whose acceptability is subject to
the existence of specific conditions that justify the need to correct the
operation of the market. This is certainly true in the United States,
where the possible exclusion of a sector from competition rules needs
to be legally decided by the Congress [24]. The same applies to the

---

[23] For a detailed description of regulatory developments in the United States in the
light of antitrust rulings, see v. FAULHABER G. [8].

[24] For a discussion of this subject, see HOVENKAMP H. [10], Chap. 19.

European Union, where the competition rules provided for in articles 85 and 86 of the *Treaty of Rome* [25] apply to all sectors; the second paragraph of article 90 of the *Treaty* subordinates any exception to the existence of well-defined purposes of general interest that can be assessed by the Court of Justice, and, in any case, restricts exemptions to what is strictly necessary to achieve such objectives [26]. The interpretation of this rule given by the Court of Justice has been restrictive both in terms of the evaluation of the protected general interests, which cannot clash with the European Union's integration needs, and in terms of the procedures with which these can be pursued. Hence, unnecessary restrictions are never allowed [27].

In Italy, competition rules, introduced by the Act 287 of 1990, provide, at article 8, a similar approach. This provision, however, is susceptible of an even further-reaching interpretation if it is considered in relation with the provision included in article 43 of the *Italian Constitution* regarding the conditions to which a public reserve on an activity may be established [28]. As has been observed, the conditions imposed in article 43 of the *Constitution* for the establishment of a legal reserve may be interpreted in a restrictive manner as implying that in the absence of such conditions, competition should be the rule [29].

Concluding, the above considerations indicate that in many utility sectors, regulation tends to be temporary. As the market order evolves towards a competitive structure, the question of establishing in an authoritative way the leading company's behaviour becomes increasingly less important, whereas that of allowing competition to operate

---

[25] Article 85 of the TREATY prohibits anticompetitive agreements between companies. Article 86 prohibits the abuse of a dominant position.

[26] In accordance with the same paragraph, the companies entrusted with the management of services of a general economic interest (...) are subjected to (...) competition rules, insofar as the application of such rules does not hinder the fulfilment, *de jure* or *de facto*, of the specific task that has been entrusted to them.

[27] See BELLAMY and CHILD [2], Chap. 13 and LOLLI A. [13] for an analysis.

[28] Article 43 of the *Italian Constitution* states that «With a view to general use, the State may originally reserve or transfer (...) to the State or public bodies (...) given enterprises or enterprise categories that are involved in essential services or sources of energy or monopolies and are mostly of general interest».

[29] See BOGNETTI G. [3] and LOLLI A. [13], as well the suggestive report by AMATO G. [1].

properly with the typical instruments of antitrust law represents an increasingly greater concern. An example is provided by the recent appeal by the British authority in charge of regulating telecommunications, OFTEL, to adjust Britain's antitrust rules to those of the European Community in order to eastablish a prohibition of the abuse of a dominant position, which is·thought to be more effective than regulation to curb the anti-competitive behaviour of the main operator in the telecommunication markets [30].

On this matter, it is interesting to compare the institutional developments concerning regulatory bodies in different countries. In those countries where liberalisation has been pursued only recently, it is accompanied by the establishment of regulatory authorities that are specific for each sector. In other countries, however, where liberalisation started earlier or has reached a more advanced stage, a different path is followed, by gradually doing away with regulation authorities and concentrating the economic regulation in sectors that are largely liberalised in the hands of the antitrust authority [31].

---

[30] *Financial Times*, 24 November 1995.
[31] In 1995, this has been the course of action opted for in Australia, where liberalisation processes have opened to competition sectors such as transport, telecommunications and energy.

BIBLIOGRAPHY

[1] AMATO G., «General Conclusions» Conference on *Antitrust: Rules, Institutions and International Relations*, Roma, Autorità Garante della Concorrenza e del Mercato, 1995.

[2] BELLAMY - CHILD, *Common Market Law of Competition*, London, Sweet & Maxwell, 1993.

[3] BOGNETTI G., *La costituzione economica italiana*, Milano, Giuffré, 1993.

[4] BURTON J., *The Competitive Order and Ordered Competition*, mimeo, Birmingham, University of Birmingham, 1995.

[5] CASTELLI F., *La regolamentazione delle telecomunicazioni: dal monopolio pubblico alla competizione nella rete di accesso*, mimeo, Roma, Fondazione Ugo Bordoni, 1995.

[6] DI MAJO A. (ed.), «Le politiche di privatizzazione in Italia», *Terzo rapporto CER/IRS sull'industria e la politica industriale italiana*, Bologna, il Mulino, 1989.

[7] EUROPEAN COMMISSION, *The Green Book for the Liberalisation of Telecommunication Infrastructures*, Brussels, 1994.

[8] FAULHABER G., «Deregulation and Innovation in Telecommunications» in LIBECAP G. (ed.), *Innovation in New Markets: The Impact of Deregulation on Airlines, Financial Markets, and Telecommunications*, vol. II, London, JAI, 1988.

[9] FORNALCZYK A., «How Much Privatization; How Much Liberalisation», Conference on *Antitrust: Rules, Istitutions and International Relations*, Roma, Autorità Garante della Concorrenza e del Mercato, 1955.

[10] HOVENKAMP H., *Federal Antitrust Policy: The Law of Competition and its Practice*, St Paul (Minn.), West Publishing Co., 1994.

[11] JOSKOW P. - NOLL R., «Regulation in Theory and Practice: An Overview», in FROMM G., *Studies in Public Regulation*, Boston, MIT Press., 1981.

[12] KAHN A.E., *The Economics of Regulation*, vol. I, New York, Wiley, 1970.

[13] LOLLI A., «Riserva di impresa e diritto comunitario: i monopoli elettrici», *Rivista trimestrale di Diritto Pubblico*, n. 1, 1993.

[14] MILANA C. - PADOA SCHIOPPA KOSTORIS F., *La regolamentazione dei prezzi dei servizi di pubblica utilità*, Roma, ISPE, 1995.

[15] NAHMIJAS A., «Confronti di efficienza tra imprese pubbliche e private» in MARZANO A. (ed.), *Crisi e ristrutturazione delle imprese a partecipazione statale*, Milano, F. Angeli, 1992.

[16] NEWBERY D., «Competition and Regulation in the Electricity Industry», paper written for the OECD/World Bank's Conference on *Competition and Regulation in Network Sectors*, Budapest, 1994.

[17] NOAM E.M., «Beyond Liberalization: From the Network of Networks the System of Systems», *Telecomunications Policy*, vol. 18, n. 4, 1994.

[18] OECD, *Competition, Regulation and Performance*, mimeo, Paris, Committee on Competion Law and Policy, 1995.

[19] PERA A., «Deregulation and Privatization in an Economy Wide Context», *OECD Economic Studies*, n. 12, 1989.

[20] — —, «Introduzione» in PERA A. (ed.), *Regolamentazione, efficienza, mercato*, Milano, F. Angeli, 1991.

[21] SARACENO P., «Partecipazioni statali», in *Enciclopedia del diritto*, Milano, 1982.

[22] SPULBER D.F., *Regulation and Markets*, London, MIT Press., 1989.

[23] VICKERS J. - YARROW G., *Privatization*, London, MacMillan, 1988.

[24] WORLD BANK, *Burocrats in Business*, Washington, 1995.

Some Criteria for Privatization in Italy

Gian Cesare Romagnoli *
Università di Firenze

1. - Introduction

Since 1980 the privatization issue has been the focus of a big debate on the changing role of the state and its eventual substitution by the private sector as producer of goods and services. Since then more than eighty countries, with the two important exceptions of Italy and China, have started a privatization process, albeit adopting different criteria and typologies, according to a plurality of policy objectives pursued [1]. These privatization experiences favoured by the liberist ideological and political revival induced by British public failures have aroused world-wide interest and argument for emulation but have not produced general ideal solutions to complex problems dependent on different economic, social and political situations.

This complexity makes the economics of public divestiture fundamentally different from private divestiture and may offer an explanation for the slow pace of divestiture policies in some countries, even though the disclosure of diffused corruption has weakened, among the people, the public interest motivation for politics and with it the

---

* The author is Professor of Economic Policy at the Faculty of Political Sciences «Cesare Alfieri».

N.B.: The numbers in square brackets refer to the Bibliography at the end of paper.

[1] According up to a World Bank study 6800 privatizations have taken place between 1980 and 1991, 2000 of which in less developed countries and 800 in Eastern European countries.

possible way-out to long term negative-sum-games where a majority gets immediate advantages.

Privatization certainly allows to give back to private citizens losses previously borne by the government but experience has shown that undue haste and lack of analysis in dismantling the economic mechanism of the state, as well as rent-seeking continuous postponement of the privatization process can, in a financially unbalanced public sector, lead to waste and disruption for the whole economic system.

This paper is divided into two parts. First some conclusions of the theory of privatization are restated. Second some criteria for privatization in Italy are analysed in order to evaluate whether to sell and what to sell first.

2. - Some Conclusions of the Theory of Privatization

Summarily the conceptual framework bearing on privatization in the «developed mixed economy» is one which predicts that efficiency of productive activity can be expected to improve as the organizational form shifts from protected state enterprise toward private competitive production (Wiseman [13], p. 258). But there are practically important differences in the structure and organization of national economies which make it necessary to build up the appropriate intellectual construct for the development of privatization policy. Therefore privatization is not universally defined. Under the privatization label one may find a large number of initiatives, like the sale of public firms, the change of labour relations for public employees, the abolition of legal and fiscal monopolies managed by public firms, the allowance of larger autonomy to public managers and other transitions of public firms to private forms [2]. In other words privatiz-

---

[2] These include deregulation, liberalization, incremental privatization, self-privatization, franchising (for public services sold under natural monopolies), contracting-out (for local public services easy to be controlled and distributed free), charging for the service, and eventually the property transfer bound to the fall of public interest since it is difficult to show the superiority of the private sector in terms of allocative efficiency.

ation may simply divorce ownership *per se* from the exercise of most ownership rights.

One main point here is that bringing critical research to bear on public sector decision processes does not mean that the market is perfect. In the difficult mix of two problematic forms of social organizations one has to find balances. This is precisely what we need the theory of privatization for (Paldam [8] p. 182). Rather than having to choose between public and private action and/or property, new tools of government action have made it possible to blend the two in a wide assortment of ways which tend any way to remove the state and its administrative hierarchical logics from the production of goods and services. On the other hand any public economic activity may be privatized but privatization is not sufficient, *per se*, to produce more competitive markets. Therefore the privatization process will generate a need for temporary or permanent monitoring activities, for example in sectors which are not easily made competitive.

We have a positive and a normative theory of privatization. The normative one shows the composition of private and public ownership which maximizes welfare in an economy. Consequently, the respective rules on privatization can be justified by some higher order value judgements, as formally expressed by a social welfare function. The application of a welfare function of the usual type can be challenged for various reasons, but while this observation leads to the conclusion that from the theoretical basis social welfare as the objective of a firm is more disputable than individual welfare, it does not imply that profit should always direct government intervention. In fact if it is true that in principle positive theory means the rejection of welfare based theory, in practice positive theory objectives of profit, output, revenue maximization imply an individualistic welfare function as well as a social welfare function. While it is not disputable that competitive industrial firms or commercial banks are privatized with the intention of leaving the firm to the market and the market to the firm. Since positive objectives are only a partition of normative ones it is meaningless or tautological to state that «Positive theory objectives seem to be more successful in stimulating performance than normative theory objectives», (Bös [2] p. 90).

The question is not whether and how it is possible to force

welfare arguments in positive theories since governments are, at least nominally, interested in welfare. If public utilities are privatized the welfare arguments which previously led to nationalization (economics of scale and scope, trade union influence, bureaucratic structures, excessive vertical and horizontal integration) often remain. Where public utilities' technologies of returns to scale deviate from those conducive to perfect competition, the achievement of optimality requires public utility regulation. But even when virtuous technologies of requires to scale are available, crude privatization — *cum laissez faire* — is not a feasible way of approximating optimality if there are production or consumption externalities (Samuelson [9], pp. 4-5).

Governments regulate the price of privatized monopoly firms in order to prevent consumer exploitation and firms «excess» profits because efficiency gains lower selling prices only if perfect competition prevails, and economists tend to think of low prices as correlated with higher consumer surplus. This argument is correct even if the basis of the government interest in low prices is its interest in attracting votes. If voters are attracted by what economists call higher welfare, the Buchanan-type politician is interested in welfare (Bös [2], pp. 90-1). But this is a syllogism and it is based on the assumption that the quality of the quantity of the public service produced and distributed exceeds a given minimum standard and that the consumers are able to assess this and get the same public service elsewhere at the same price should they be discontented with the former.

Principal-agent approaches show how the transition in ownership changes objectives (from rent-seeking to profit maximization) and incentives in the firm. In a public firm the government is imperfectly informed about costs or demand, typically it fails to achieve X-efficiency and allocative efficiency. In a private firm with imperfectly informed private shareholders the concept of incentive-pay can be shown to be successful in achieving X-efficiency, although it fails with respect to allocative efficiency: incentive-pay schedules typically link manager pay to profit which leads to profit-maximizing prices.

The well known distinction between production and provision may lend itself to the privatization process of public utilities, allowing either to minimize their costs or to regulate their allocation. If the privatized firm is a public utility, profit maximization implies monopoly prices, which are undesired. This eminent market failure — where the assumption of non increasing returns to scale falls and with it the existence of a Pareto-optimal equilibrium in the Arrow-Debreu model — is the basis of Boiteux government regulation of private firms (Bös [2], p. 91).

Since the potentially competitive character of the sector is to be taken into account, the quest for efficiency, grounded on the virtues of perfectly competitive markets, contrasted with the managerial inefficiences of public firms, should not «dominate» other privatization objectives, without showing that this is the market where the privatized firm will operate.

The issue that markets fail the implementation of the optimal conditions of perfect competition is either evident or crucial. Therefore one can always observe inefficiences to eliminate for which state intervention may be proposed. This condition is not anyway sufficient and public intervention should not escape the evaluation of its costs.

On the other hand public goods, externalities and relevant monopolies should not be ignored because of public deliberate resource misallocation, or because of the organizational bureaucratic behaviour, or for missing market rules, or for informational and managerial problems.

Privatizing a public utility and letting its new owners charge profit-maximizing tariffs will in practice let them be quoted at above their true social marginal costs. Much deadweight loss in the Pareto-optimality sense will ensue. Even if loose bargaining leads to discriminating-monopoly pricings, the transaction costs that impede attaining a feasible optimum will be staggering. A public utility regulated approach can, paradoxically, be thought of as the ideal-cost-sparing Coase «property» arrangement since it spares transaction costs. A *Coase Theorem* to handle natural public utilities related to increasing returns-to-scale and lumpiness is a chimera (Samuelson [9], pp. 11-2).

As an alternative to price regulation of a fully privatized firm, some countries prefer partial privatization which applies a sort of regulation from within the enterprise instead of the usual regulation from outside the enterprise. But it is not a good instrument to cope with the trade-off between efficiency gains and monopoly pricing. In the principal-agent setting partial privatization implies an informational advantage — if the government has direct access to the information, under public provision, about the firm's production possibilities — but an incentive disadvantage. Encouragement of market entry as an alternative way to control a privatized utility is otherwise contrasted by regulation (Bös [2], p. 92).

Theories and experiences point us to the view that the problems of central control in an economy can be very severe and that its record is very poor. This engenders the question of how government control can be changed in order to face problems of information and externality layered on top of those of monopoly as in the cases of public utilities.

If it is the political process in the Parliament or other territorial assemblies which is to indicate the type and optimal quantities of public goods and services and therefore their demand [3], the management activity (let alone the risk dimension which is anyway borne by the firm) may take different forms according to whom owns the capital, nominates and controls the managers (Gordon [4], pp. 16-7). If the new shareholders, in spite of all the management control problems, succeed in redesigning the incentives of privatized firms so that they maximize share values will the outcome be efficient? There are many reasons for concern. As firms restructure in response to new incentives, the presumption is that there will be massive layoffs and many firm bankruptcies if resources were allocated very badly in the past. As a result, the social opportunity cost of continuing the worker's employment is less than the wage, since the unemployed also impose negative externalities on the rest of society. Bankruptcy incentives are also normally distorted. In fact large debts induced by poor allocation decisions in the past may make continuation difficult even if the firm's current investments are profitable. This is not justified on efficiency grounds. Conversely a firm's past debt may have been wiped out by current inflation allowing the firm to borrow

---

[3] While the role of prices in the private management is aimed at profit maximization independent of the market regime, in the public management their role is only aimed at determining the quantity demanded, obviously where preferences are revealed.

substantially without risk of default, even if its current investments are of little value (Gordon [4], p. 18).

In a mixed economy, the proceeds of the sale of parts of the state sector through the capital market can be used to reduce tax burdens of citizens generally or be spent on public expenditures, or be used to reduce the public debt. Furthermore the short term financial effects of divestiture on the budget of the public sector, given by cash inlays, are to be confronted, especially in the case of a large scale privatization process, with the effects of property loss. It is also difficult that the financial gain or loss from the sale, i.e. the price paid, will be equal to the net present value of its prospective earnings because of asymmetric information and other imperfections which characterize the privatization process. The stress on the revenue effects of privatization has been increased by the practice of judging public sector performance by reference to the PSBR. This treats the proceeds of asset sales as a revenue receipt and presents cash transactions without reference to their impact on future incomings and outgoings or reference to any form of balance sheet. It is clearly erroneous to treat these receipts analogously to other items of government revenue.

What distinguishes the modes, private or public, are the differences in the transaction costs of intervention into delegated production relationships. In choosing between public and private provision it is important to consider both the expected benefits and the costs of intervention and the probability that intervention will occur if the privatized firm is not regulated. However the real problem is that it is very difficult for voters/decision makers to identify the true accounts of costs and benefits obtainable from each proposal of privatization. In this sense, to try to identify the true pay-off of any proposal is the important task for the economist (Udagawa [11], p. 149).

Two important elements of this calculation include the complexity of the task under consideration and the need for rapid adaptation to unforeseen contingencies in order to guarantee the final destination. The first element becomes relevant for large scale privatization processes where a fully-fledged approach is required that alternatively provides also for dismissal and/or novel use of the goods owned by firms gone bankrupt, leveraged-buy-out by the employees or by the managers, auction of whole firms or of parts of them, public offers of shares, sale to investment funds (Nuti [7], p. 427). The second aspect is crucial (as in the case of national defence, or justice) where ease of intervention to redirect activities and to limit the duration of negotiation may be relatively important. Under such circumstances, public provision is more likely to be the preferred mode of organization. Of course when the use of intervention is facilitated, its abuse is simultaneously made more difficult to control and efficiency gains of the public management, though suboptimal, can be achieved only by a proper incentive structure.

In fact the economic borders of the state is a question on which economists can produce decisions only as ordinary citizens. Nonetheless economists can give technical support to the political evaluation of the relative merits of alternative policies aimed at predetermined objectives.

As markets are very seldom efficient resource allocators, so governments are very seldom, or never, perfect planners. Therefore the relevant question is very pragmatic: is market failure more serious than government failure in the provision of particular goods and services? Control problems condition the measure, the structure, the form of public intervention, but the degree of competition extension, or of state intervention, aiming at efficiency gains is rather complex and varies considerably among economic sectors. Therefore the call for a general competition or privatization policy to cope with market or government failures is based on the assumption that this complexity is irrelevant and so it denies this central proposition (Helm [5], p. 74). But even if competition cannot necessarily solve market failures, it is often very useful (Vickers and Yarrow [12], p. 426). In fact competition, rather than property, may more likely achieve efficiency gains. The privatization process (like that of nationalization) share the same fundamental error of confusing them.

Sappington and Stiglitz ([10], pp. 580-1) have presented a fundamental privatization theorem which shows the conditions under which privatization is optimal. An ideal auction process «to become a regulated firm» can be applied which leads to welfare-optimal private provision without requiring government's knowledge of the production possibilities and of the cost functions. However in practice this ideal setting typically cannot be applied and privatization failures arise (if the contractor is risk averse or his liability is limited, if the government cannot achieve a correct social evaluation of the produced quantity or cannot be considered as a single principal). In short, neither public nor private provision can fully resolve the difficult incentive problems that arise when considerations of imperfect information result in delegation of authority which arise under both forms of organization.

Economic argumentation cannot dispose of the *caveats*, the assumptions and restrictions of the respective models, but problems of applied economics for political aims arise also when governments assume an increasing number of objectives some of which are either conflictual or inconsistent, causing failures unless the respective trade-offs are predetermined. Privatization policy is often caught in the conflict between competition, property, PSBR requisites, tax cuts, more diffuscd share-capital ownership. The simple fact that there may be conflict in a variety of objectives should not inhibit privatization in principle. One way to face this problem is to decrease the number of objectives pursued but then the political question arises which of them are to be left out.

3. - Some Criteria for Privatization in Italy

The result of privatization can be modelled by comparing privatized and public enterprises: analytical approaches refer to the differences in incentive structures whereas empirical studies deal with various measures of productivity in privatized and public firms, often ignoring the forms of protection offered by particular market regimes which allow for non-market cost and revenue structures.

As to the macroeconomic effects of privatization one can expect that the short term financial effects of divestiture on the budget of the public sector will be associated to the fall of public investment and to the decline of interest expenditure on public bonds. Anyway the change of the macroeconomic situation should not be measured by a price system which may be more distorted in terms of social welfare after privatization.

If, as is likely, a large scale privatization program includes natural monopolies, externalities, or activities characterized by asymmetric information or other incomplete markets, the price system which takes place without regulation may worsen social welfare. Therefore it is necessary to measure the above mentioned effects making use of a shadow price system which may take account of the potential costs associated to the privatization process. A simple rule for evaluating the decision of public divestiture is to consider the net value of the operation using shadow prices and weighting consumption with distributive coefficients. This procedure allows more precise evaluation of the efficiency gains which are required from the private sector and to the new regulations aimed at compensating the public sector.

Where the privatization process is not a large scale one, and/or does not induce a significant change in the whole economy with direct and indirect effects over all markets, the partial equilibrium cost-benefit analysis, or net efficiency benefit, achieved in the single markets, can offer adequate criteria to answer some crucial questions: whether to sell and what to sell first.

Jones, Tandon and Volgesang ([6], pp. 10-20) have tried to answer the above questions assuming that government wishes to maximize social welfare and that private firms pursue profit maximization. To maximize social welfare, the welfare change, given by the difference between the social values of the privatized and public firms plus any sale premium, must be positive. Answers to the former of the above basic questions follow directly from this procedure which, though correctly based, is politically inapplicable since the government minimum supply price for privatization is lower (negative) when the difference between the social values of the privatized and public firm is positive. Since this is the relevant condition to maximize social welfare, privatizations would generally lead to government outgoings instead of incomings unless negative prices are politically excluded for the sale of publicly-owned enterprises. Furthermore, according to Jones, Tandon and Volgesang, the government should pay any amount of money in order to privatize whenever the government is neutral between funds in public or private hands i.e. the sale premium vanishes. On the contrary, also in this case, it seems plausible that the government should privatize only if the difference between the social values of the privatized and public firms is positive. Finally, if the sale premium is negative [4], the same authors correctly conclude that the higher the price paid to the government for privatizations the lower the social welfare gain. Nonetheless one can observe that in this case a wider privatization of public production and provision should be proposed vìs-a-vìs a contraction of public incomings from privatization. Since socially desirable and undesirable private synergies may take place in the privatization process, the sale should not necessarily go to the highest bidder, but rather to the highest offer coming from the group of the best bidders, ranked through the associated welfare changes.

Another problem encountered in a privatization program is where should the priorities lie. On this issue, leaving aside political considerations, a variety of economic criteria have been recently suggested which deserve some comment. Among these the criterion suggested by Beesley and Littlechild ([1], pp. 30-7), indicates those industries where the consumer benefits of privatization are greatest. They are determined by firm turnover, lack of remedial action, competition, all of which offer large potential scope for savings. These ideas are clarified by conceiving of each public industry as located in a simple 2x2 matrix which shows demand prospects (good or bad on long run trends) and supply prospects (single or multiple ownership). Graph 1 shows our own conjectures for Italy as to the quadrant in which each industry is currently placed.

Industries in quadrant *D* are already subject to international competition which secures prices as low as can be expected. Thus consumers will gain little from privatization. They will however gain substantially, though indirectly, notably as taxpayers, because of the *X*-efficiency gains eventually associated to the sale of these firms which are financially weak, often in spite of large subsidies. So high priority of privatization is indicated in spite of the opportunity of a solid remedial action.

Industries in quadrant *C* are relatively untouched by remedial action but they presumably offer minor scope for improvement in efficiency. They have no significant problems of monopoly power and

---

[4] The negative sale premium may be associated either to systematic diversion of public funds or to suboptimal private investment level.

GRAPH 1

CLASSIFICATION OF SOME ITALIAN PUBLICLY-OWNED INDUSTRIES

		Demand prospects	
		Good	Bad
Supply prospects	Single	**A** TELECOM ITALIA ITALGAS Airports Public utilities Post ALITALIA	**B** FF.SS. (rail)
	Multiple	**C** ENEL (electricity) AGIP SNAM PROGETTI Banks SME (food)	**D** ILVA (steel) FINMARE (shipbuilding) ENICHEM (chemicals) ALUMIX

thus they are second candidates for privatization though careful attention needs to be given to their structure after privatization.

Industries in quadrant *A* do not favour multiple competing ownership since they are characterized by high sunk costs. Consumers are therefore at risk, unless restriction on new entry can be removed, since privatizing these industries will pose problems in curbing monopoly power.

Industries in quadrant *B* are technically sustainable monopolies. However social and political problems would accompany the withdrawal of services. Privatization schemes will need to be designed with careful thought to non commercial obbligations. Nonetheless, once the appropriate regulation authorities are provided and work well — a necessary condition to be satisfied before public monopolies are privatized — it seems that priority lies on privatization of firms in quadrant *B*, with respect to those in quadrant *A*, since consumers' benefits, associated to higher efficiency gains, are more likely to be achieved where demand prospects are bad.

As to the corrective actions which may be suggested for the conduct of big national monopolies, «the great enemies to good management» in Adam Smith's words, one has to consider that efficiency gains and larger competitiveness associated to privatization are bound to three criteria:

1) the privatization of all the services actually provided by public monopolies, except for their core business which guarantees the general supply of the services and respect for their public utility role;

2) a specific regulation for the control of the desired quality standard, of the adequate technological and organizational innovations, and of the price dynamics of the services considered, produced by a regulatory authority able to discourage strategic behaviour of the firms towards them;

3) breaking up the monopolies, whenever it is possible, into smaller competing firms [5].

The first requisite implies a reconsideration of state intervention in the economy where competition limitations or distortions imposed for the «general interest» are revised. The second requisite is based on the hypothesis that public interest pursual does not always imply the direct public management of the economic activity considered but also, or perhaps better, its regulation, i.e. the imposition of rules and controls which «individuate and coordinate to social aims», according to what is provided in Article 41 of the Italian Constitution, the economic activity, without impairing its economic target which remains its primary aim, once those rules and controls are respected. The third requisite derives from the observation that since modern democracies participate a delicate equilibrium made of political and economic pluralism, privatization is supposed not to reduce them.

A different ranking of what to sell first is associated to the criterion suggested by Corsetti and Rey [3], based on the economic and financial performances of public enterprises. They also use a simple 2x2 matrix which shows industries' profitability combined with financial soundness, in order to determine which industries are to be sold first and which are to be dismissed. Graph 2 shows some

---

[5] Tirole recommends doing this before a firm is privatized, given the difficulties Western countries have faced in breaking up private monopolies.

GRAPH 2

CLASSIFICATION OF SOME ITALIAN PUBLICLY-OWNED INDUSTRIES

		Financial structure	
		Sound	Unsound
Profitability	Positive	*A* TELECOM ITALIA AGIP Airports Banks Public utilities	*B* SME
	Negative	*C* IRI SNAM PROGETTI	*D* ALITALIA FF.SS. ILVA FINMARE ENICHEM ALUMIX

Italian state-owned enterprises placed into Corsetti and Rey's, [3], matrix.

Industries which are either profitable or financially sound rank first, according to these authors, because they are most interesting for private buyers. On the contrary firms which either experience losses or are financially weak should be dismissed, according to them, in order to save the funds needed for a solid remedial action. Nonetheless profitable firms which need a solid remedial action can increase their worth or decrease their risk of default if they get the funds needed. Finally non profitable industries though financially sound because of their assets, or their orders on hand or their market share, may be privatized, according to the authors, only if they can be either vertically or horizontally integrated into their buyers' activities.

Corsetti and Rey [3] caution anyway on the need to introduce regulating authorities, before selling the property rights of state-owned industries where privatization concerns legal or technically sustainable monopolies.

These authors consider two selling strategies for industries placed off the principal diagonal of their matrix. The first strategy is that of the «merchant banker» who sells firms after dismissing those which incur losses and regaining financial soundness for the rest, though showing no interest for either employment or industrial policy problems, or for the externalities associated to monopolistic positions. The second strategy follows the «mergers and acquisition approach» where the seller (the Italian Treasury) creates holdings which include firms placed in quadrants A and B, where the profits of the former are used to regain financial soundness for the latter. Within this strategy the firms placed in quadrant C are to be excluded unless they are incorporated into those of quadrant B to ease their fiscal or financial problems. Therefore the privatization ranking indicated by Corsetti and Rey [3], for Italy finds first the firms in quadrant A, followed by those in quadrant B and C, while those located in quadrant D should be dismissed.

On the contrary one can observe that the application of their criterion, where consumers' benefits are to be maximized, indicates different priorities where firms in quadrant D rank first, also considering the above mentioned three corrective actions for the conduct of big monopolies, followed by firms in quadrants C, B and eventually A [6].

---

[6] A comparison of BEESLEY M.E. - LITTLECHILD S.C. [1] criterion with that of CORSETTI G. - REY G.M. [3] is possible once that regulating authorities are provided and work well and publicly-owned industries' debt has been repaid.

BIBLIOGRAPHY

[1] BEESLEY M.E. - LITTLECHILD S.C., «Privatization: Principles, Problems and Priorities», in BEESLEY, M.E. (ed.), *Privatization, Regulation and Deregulation*, London, Routledge, 1992, pp. 23-39.

[2] BÖS D., *Privatization. A Theoretical Treatment*, Oxford, Clarendon Press, 1991.

[3] CORSETTI G. - REY G.M., «Le privatizzazioni italiane: aspetti teorici e modalità applicative», paper presented at the cycle of seminars on *L'evoluzione dell'economia italiana dall'adesione allo SME ad oggi* organised by Dipartimento di Economia Pubblica, Università «La Sapienza», Roma, 1994.

[4] GORDON R.H., «Privatization: Notes on Macroeconomic Consequences», Università di Monaco, *CES Working Paper Series*, n. 21, 1992.

[5] HELM D., «I confini economici dello Stato», in PENNELLA G. (ed.), *Regolazione e/o privatizzazione*, Bologna, il Mulino, 1992, pp. 29-83.

[6] JONES L.P. - TANDON P. - VOLGESANG I., *Selling Public Enterprises: a Cost-Benefit Methodology*, Cambridge, MIT Press, 1990.

[7] NUTI D.M., «Privatizzazione di massa: costi e benefici di un capitalismo istantaneo», *Economia Pubblica*, n. 9-10, 1994, pp. 417-30.

[8] PALDAM M., «Public Choice/More of a Branch or More of a Sect?», *Public Choice*, n. 77/1, 1993, pp. 177-84.

[9] SAMUELSON P.A., «Tragedy of the Open Road: Avoiding the Paradox by Use of Regulated Public Utilities that Charge Corrected Knightian Tolls», *Journal of International and Comparative Economics*, n. 1, 1992, pp. 3-12.

[10] SAPPINGTON D.E.M. - STIGLITZ J.E., «Privatization, Information and Incentives», *Journal of Policy Analysis and Management*, n. 6/4, 1987, pp. 567-82.

[11] UDAGAWA A., «The Next Twenty-Fire Years of Public Choice», *Public Choice*, n. 77/1, 1993, pp. 197-202.

[12] VICKERS J. - YARROW G., *Privatization: An Economic Analysis*, Cambridge, MIT Press, 1988.

[13] WISEMAN J., «Privatization in the Command Economy», in HARTLEY K. - OTT A.F. (eds.), *Privatization and Economic Efficiency*, Aldershot, E. Elgar Pub. Ltd., 1991, pp. 257-70.

[14] WITTMAN D., «Why Democracies Produce Efficient Results?», in ROWLEY C.K. (ed.), *Public Choice Theory*, III: *The Separation of Powers and Constitutional Political Economy*, Aldershot, E. Elgar Pub. Ltd., 1993, pp. 543-72.

Privatization and The Ownership Structure of Public Utilities

Francesco Lo Passo · **Alfredo Macchiati** *
Italian Treasury, Roma CONSOB, Roma

Introduction

This study analyzes some of the issues related to the ownership structure of public utilities in the process of being privatized. Firstly it examines how the structure of the market influences ownership. Secondly it examines the effects of the state as a regulator or a stockholder, though no longer sole owner.

The first section goes synthetically through the contributions on ownership structure, which are relevant to the questions raised by this study. The second and third sections look at, respectively, the effects of the permanence of the state as a regulator and as a stockholder. The final section gives some descriptive empirical evidence.

The objective of this study is to identify the efficiency conditions for the ownership structure of public utilities, where the structure of the market, regulation and public property interact. It is the aim of this study to identify when the equilibrium structure of ownership — i.e. the one which the single shareholders buy additional shares in the company up to the point where marginal benefits of control equate their costs — is efficient in maximizing the value of the company. An increase in the value of the company, however, is not per se an

* Francesco Lo Passo, member of the Council of Experts, and Alfredo Macchiati, head of the Economic Research Department, remain solely responsible for the views expressed and any errors, which do not involve the Italian Treasury or CONSOB.

N.B.: the numbers in square brackets refer to the Bibliography at the end of the paper.

indication of an increase in the welfare of the society. This is the case if the company in question operates in a competitive environment. If on the contrary the company operates in monopoly an increase in its value might imply an increase in the rents charged consumers and, consequently, a decrease in social welfare.

The primary condition for efficiency is that the structure of ownership is endogenous to the market: i.e. the ownership structure of the privatized public utilities will be concentrated or diffused as dictated by the reference market. This is consistent with the theory claiming that when sufficient market discipline is lacking, concentrated ownership is preferable. Concentrated ownership maximizes monitoring of the management and, therefore, minimizes agency costs. On the contrary, shareholding is diffuse when the market is competitive as agency costs are not relevant. Investors will diversify their portfolio by buying shares in several companies and by holding relatively small stakes in each one. Stylized empirical evidence drawn from privatized companies in the electrical energy and telecommunications industries demonstrates that in general this initial condition holds.

A second condition for efficiency requires the state regulators to enhance competition wherever this is practical and to reduce any interference in the market. The empirical evidence collected in the British market is as yet too partial to be evaluated.

A third condition for efficiency requires that large companies are placed on the market gradually, but relatively rapidly. In this way the goals of the state-as-a-seller prevail over the socio-political goals of the state-as-shareholder.

1. - Ownership Structure and Competition

Ownership structures are generally examined in a principal agent framework [1]. Monitoring of managers by the stockholders requires

---

[1] A great number of contributions concerns property rights and agency costs. We like to recall the papers of JENSEN M.C. - MECKLING W.H. [11] and FAMA E. - JENSEN M.C. [9]. For a recent synthesis which focuses on privatizations see STIGLITZ J.E. ([16], chapter X). Among the more important empirical works see YAFEH Y. - YOSHA O. [18].

appropriate incentives. Normative considerations would suggest an allocation of control such as to maximize the value of the company and, indirectly, the welfare of the society. Consequently a substantial part of managers' compensation has to come from the company income and the market for corporate control has to be competitive.

The behavior of stockholders in preparing contracts for managers and their capacity to monitor their enforcement and thus the possibility of pushing the company toward efficiency depends on the stockholders' incentives and these incentives depend on a series of variables. In the first place, we find the basic reason behind the investors' decision to invest (savings for individual stockholders; entrepeneurial activity for companies; financial intermediation for institutional investors; redistribution for the state). After that we must consider: the size of each party's investment in the company as compared to their total wealth, the presence of other investors and which investor exercises control and how concentrated ownership is.

Further specifications might lead us to look at, for example, the amount of interactivity and possible integration among companies or in the case of individual investors, whether the company's products are part of his normal consumption patterns.

Demesetz - Lehn [8] (henceforth DL) have explored some of the main variables that influence ownership structure. According to DL property rights are always allocated optimally because stockholders choose to invest up to a level at which marginal benefits of having one more share are equal to its marginal costs. DL have identified as factors that influence control: the size of the enterprise, the benefits connected with control and regulation.

With regard to size, the larger the enterprise, the smaller the percentage of the equity necessary to control it. Thus the very largest companies tend to be widely owned.

With regard to the benefits of control, these benefits — i.e. the revenue stockholders can obtain by monitoring shirking by mangement — depend on the environment where the company operates. The more uncertain the environment, the greater the benefits that the shareholders can derive from control and the greater the pressure to exercise control. When there is a very high degree of uncertainty, the shareholders must maintain an intense monitoring effort to separate

the performance connected to the managers' ability to the performance connected to the uncertainty of the environment. Therefore
property is concentrated. When there is little uncertainty in the
environment, shareholders can evaluate the performance of the management with little monitoring and ownership is widespread.

The influence of product market competition on the ownership
structure can be more complex than has been hypothesized by DL.

In fact the managers' moral hazard is often made more difficult
by the control which is freely exercised by the markets. If companies
are operating in a sufficiently competitive regime either as regards
their output or their input, and if they are not well run, the companies
are more likely to go bankrupt (Milgrom - Roberts [14] p. 285).
However the stable market prices and market shares referred to in DL
do not necessarily reflect a competitive environment.

The Coase theorem applied to DL, states that optimal ownership
structure gives an efficient allocation. This is true with two caveats
related to the existence of transaction costs and free riding (Grossman
- Hart [10]).

In the absence of transaction costs and opportunistic behavior,
full property rights give an efficient allocation. In the market for
corporate control this means that an inefficiently run company will be
purchased by third parties which, operating efficiently, will maximize
the value of the company. Thus they will be willing to pay a premium
over the market price.

The minority stockholders may ask the bidder to pay them this
premium. In addition there might be formal or informal rules which
increase takeover costs (e.g. the obligation to buy a percentage of
stock greater than that needed to acquire control). The existence of
transaction costs and the possibility of free riding mean that a
company does not always maximize its value. Changes in ownership
over time, even for physiological reasons such as inheritance, and
changes over time of objectives, such as the modification of its
productive activity, can create or increase agency costs.

We believe, however, that transaction costs and free riding do not
apply generally to privatized companies. These are normally placed on
the market using competitive bidding, whether this takes place at a
public auction or at a private placement. Investors maximize their

revenues and thus, within the constraints imposed by the existing corporate governance, they choose the most effective ownership structure for this purpose.

So, the ownership structure of privatized companies should be efficient at the margin. Competitive companies should have a more diffuse ownership structure than companies which operate as monopolies. The need for control and monitoring by the stockholders diminishes as the exposure to competition increases, because the management will find itself disciplined by the market. We want to stress, anyway, that where the privatized companies are public utilities (PU) value maximization will not necessarily correspond to welfare maximization. For this to be true, markets need to be competitive. This is not always the cause with PU. As a matter of fact in many cases where PU are no longer natural monopolies protective legislation does not allow free entry. Investors' bids therefore will incorporate monopoly rents. This will obviously imply a decrease in consumer surplus.

2. - Regulation and The Market for Corporate Control

PU companies are subjected to regulation in practically all countries. According to DL, regulation can influence ownership structure, limiting majority stockholders' control. In this way minority shareholders are protected. Regulation would require monitoring of the management whose cost would be subsidized by a third party — the regulatory agency of the state — which is not a stockholder. The presence of regulation would imply a larger number of small shareholders than if no regulation were in place.

We believe that the simplified DL world has to take into account two aspects of any regulation. First of all, whenever the purpose of regulation is to influence the industry structure (number of licenses, subsidies to new entrants, prohibition of vertical and/or horizontal integration) it can be used to modify the value of the company if this is sold in successive stages, rather than as a whole (there is a regulatory risk). There are therefore problems of coordination between the state as a stockholder and as a regulator.

Secondly regulation might have the purpose not to allow changes in control following total privatization.

The likelihood of an influence of regulation on the value of the privatized company will be higher or lower accordingly to two dimensions: the goal of regulation and its independence from political influence. The goal of regulation should be to enhance competition, where feasible, by eliminating distortions (Baumol [1]). As regards independence, the setting up of agencies, autonomous of the government and granted with limited discretionary power, is one of the least intrusive forms of regulation. As a consequence those practices such as the revision of prices before prearranged dates or the encouragement of new entrants (so-called assisted entrance) — when a privatized company is made to offer services to new operators at particularly advantageous rates, without specifying for how long this treatment will be granted — should be eliminated. However, the government can maintain some influence on those autonomous agencies. It can do so by its right to allocate funds, to confirm or to nominate management, to approve internal regulation or other important acts that influence the running of the agency.

Furthermore one has to take into account that the government can modify its regulatory system (Levy - Spiller [12]). PU are in general an effective way of achieving the socio-political objectives of the government and so, even if the state is only to remain a temporary stockholder, there is a high probability of a future influence.

The presence of the state as both a stockholder and as a regulator also poses a problem of coordination of action as there are multiple principals. The state-as-regulator, once hc tries to influence the structure of the sector, will have to cope with the state-as-shareholder. What can their relationship be?

Their objectives are not necessarily coincident. As a matter of fact we might hypothesize a decision process of this type. Let us suppose that the state-regulator and the state-shareholder meet to determine the structure of the industry of the PU and the tariffs. Tariffs up to that moment have been based on widespread cross-subsidies. The state-as-regulator pushes toward free entry and toward marginal price setting mechanisms, while the state-as-shareholder wants the PU to be a monopoly (because a monopoly maximizes the value of the company before privatization). It does not want to cut cross-subsidies because it would be politically unacceptable, i.e. it would decrease the likelihood of winning new elections, or it might decrease the value of the company.

The management of the PU can influence the bargaining process. Management might prefer the quiet life of monopoly in order to extract some of the rents. It would exercise pressure on the state-as-regulator to pursue the goals of the state-as-shareholder. On the other hand, the management is not interested in maintaining the existing tariff structure as, for example, it is not directly involved in the political arena. It might be the case that the outcome of this bargaining balances in some way the interests involved such that tariffs are changed even though free entry is not allowed.

In addition regulation has direct influence on the ownership structure after total privatization. Here the goals of regulation are crucial, particularly as regards the attitude toward vertical and horizontal integration and the criteria used in determining tariffs for services. Restrictive regulation on integration can restrict the set of efficient ownership structures. Price regulation can disincentivate takeovers. A price-cap mechanism allows bidders to gain from increases in efficiency of the companies taken over, rate of return regulation gives no incentives to bidders as gains in efficiency are transferred to consumers. The evidence from the United Kingdom and the United States is in this direction. The United Kingdom applies a price-cap mechanism to PU tariffs and there have been several takeovers. The United States have a rate of return mechanism and the market for corporate control shows fewer takeovers.

In conclusion, the normative statement of the efficiency of ownership rights of the Coase theorem does not apply to the cases where the state remains as a stockholder and opposes a free market regulation or protects the company from the threat of a takeover.

3. - Partial Privatization and Incentives

Historically the solution to the problem of the coordination between the state-as-regulator and the state-as-shareholder has been the privatization of PUs in several tranches. The state, by spreading the sale of a PU, makes its promise not to interfere in the PU business and not to redistribute its value through regulation more credible. If partial privatization represents an intermediate and temporary step toward total privatization, the objectives of the stockholding state should be almost identical to the objectives of a private enterprise. Having already determined that it will be selling its entire equity stake, the state must be interested in maximizing its revenues from this sale. So there should be no space for the socio-political objectives that are traditionally connected with companies which are partially owned by the state (Mixed Enterprises - henceforth ME) and which lower the company's value.

On the other hand the structure of incentives — to maximize value for the state and to avoid shirking by the management — can be more complex than the one described above. It is worth keeping in mind the evidence, both theoretical and empirical, that points out the weaknesses of enterprises with mixed capital (Boardman - Vining [4] and [5], Vining - Boardman [17].

Shareholders enjoy superior information in a ME as compared with the information the state has on a enterprise entirely government owned (State Owned Enterprise - henceforth SOE) as they are able to evaluate the performance of the company by looking at the changes in the market value of its shares. This however does not necessarily imply that the performance of MEs is superior to the performance of State Owned Enterprises (SOEs). The co-existence of private and public property can generate conflicts in the objectives of the company which will not allow the use of stock market information for the purpose of more efficient control.

The amount of public property together with the degree of diffusion of private ownership determine different levels of influence of the government and thus a different behavior by the ME. Depending on which interests prevail, the company will pursue profit maximization or redistribution a more opportunistic behavior by the management. MEs are exposed to agency costs related to the number of private investors and the size of their investment and to the presence of both public and private shareholders.

Specifically, management behaves very opportunisticly in the presence of widespread private property or of equal public and private shareholding (Boardman - Vining [5]). The existence in the MEs of public capital as well as private shareholders makes takeovers practically impossible and has the effect of isolating the enterprises from the market of corporate control. As management is less accountable than in private companies MEs are less efficient.

Substantially MEs are not able to achieve the government's redistributive objectives and at the same maximize profits as if they were private firms. There is no reason to believe that MEs operate more efficiently than SOEs and, obviously, than PCs.

The probability of opportunistic behavior from the state and the management in a partially privatized enterprise is higher the longer the state maintains a stake in it. The longer the period, the higher the probability that inefficient incentives such as those in MEs overcome the efficient incentives of the state-seller. Interest groups benefiting from SOEs can better organize themselves against those who promoted privatization (Becker [2]). Anyway, the placement of large blocks of shares on the market must take into account the constraint of market absorption.

Up to here, the discussion assumes that the regulatory framework is not discretional or modifiable, but constant over time. The same regulation will be in place after privatization. On the contrary regulation might be temporary or weak (i.e. it leaves room for discretionary behavior by the agency and/or the government) — for example because it is believed that the government has to be one of the investors in order to avoid the abuse of dominant position by the monopolist. In this prospective Bös [6] and Bös - Peters [7] consider partial privatization as a middle of the road solution compared to the trade-off between the benefits in terms of efficiency that come with private property and the loss of welfare that is likely to occur under an unregulated private monopoly. According to these authors, the presence of the state among the shareholders corresponds to a form of regulation within the enterprise, as opposed to the normal external regulation. From Bös's prospective, the state will remain shareholder forever.

Aside from maintaining a percentage of the company's equity, the permanence of the influence of the state can be achieved through the golden share. The golden share gives the state specific property rights such as the right to appoint directors but not the right to receive dividends. It cannot be sold on the market. The two instruments can be alternatives, but in reality they are often complementary, the golden share comes in together with the ownership of some ordinary shares and in general survives complete privatization.

From the characteristics of the golden share it is possible to infer the credibility of the state's promise to not interfere in the running of the enterprise and to not attempt to influence the future evolution of the ownership structure. In the first place, it depends on whether the golden share has a fixed term, or can be revoked, or if it is permanent. Only in the former two cases, and obviously with the substantial difference in the promise to not interfere between the first and second, can we define partial privatization as a step toward total or permanent privatization. And in addition if the golden share gives the right to participate only in shareholders' assemblies or also to appoint directors of the board (and if so how many compared to the total) and if it gives the right to vote or not. The state might have a vote on all decisions made by the board or only on those decisions concerning ownership (e.g. right to vote on new investors). It is evident that the highest level of intrusion is reached with the combination, representation on the board and right to vote on all the decisions made by the board regardless of the subject. If this prerogative is added to that of irrevocability there is no difference between a privatized company in which the state maintains its rights through a golden share and a ME with the majority of its capital public.

4. - Stylized Facts

To test if ownership of the privatized companies, which we believe efficient at the margin as hypotized by DL, varies according to the structure of the market, we look at the electric utilities of the United Kingdom and the United States (Table 1). In both countries there are companies in this sector which are exposed to different levels of competition. In addition shareholding in these two countries can be diffuse as their corporate governance allows value maximization in presence of a large number of small investors.

TABLE 1

A) OWNERSHIP STRUCTURE OF TELECOMMUNICATION COMPANIES
(1995)

Companies	% of 5 largest shareholders	% of 10 largest shareholders	Market share
Companies with a high share of the market			
— Singapore Telecom	96.4	97.4	100.0
— Telecom Crpn of New Zealand	48.0	50.0	85.0
— British Telecom	30.5	36.1	83.0
— Telecom Malaysia	75.3	83.2	70.0
Mean	62.6	66.6	
Companies with a smaller share of the market			
— AT&T	5.8	6.8	60.0
— Cable & Wircless	20.5	28.0	25.0
— MCI	33.2	44.2	20.0
— Sprint	15.8	23.6	10.0
Mean	18.8	25.6	

B) OWNERSHIP STRUCTURE OF ELECTRICAL POWER COMPANIES

Companies	% of 5 largest shareholders	% of 10 largest shareholders
Integrated companies		
— California		
Mean (3 companies)	12.00	16.30
— New York State		
Mean (6 companies)	13.25	18.30
— Scottish Power	15.97	25.82
— Scottish Hydro Electric	12.90	21.13
Mean	14.44	23.48
Power producing companies		
— National Power	13.09	18.83
— PowerGen	14.17	20.27
Mean	13.63	19.55
Power distribution companies		
— UK's RECs mean (10 companies)	21.38	31.44

Source, specialized publications.

In the United States there are a number of integrated companies which produce and distribute electricity. In the United Kingdom there are three energy producing companies. One of these uses nuclear power and still belongs to the state. It is excluded from our analysis. There are also two integrated distributors and producers of electricity. Then there are twelve regional distribution companies and a company that transmits and dispatches energy which is owned by the distribution companies.

The production companies are subject to competition, the integrated companies are subject to competition in their production activity, but the distribution companies are monopolies.

The ownership of the production companies and of the integrated companies is more widespread than that of the distribution companies. The five largest investors possess on average 14.44% of total equity of the integrated companies and 13.63% of the production companies of the United Kingdom.

The stakes of the five largest shareholders of the integrated companies of California and New York State are equal to respectively 12% and 13.25% of total equity. The stakes of the five largest shareholders of the distribution companies of the United Kingdom is significantly higher, averaging 21.3% of equity.

The tendency toward concentration in the distribution companies becomes still more evident if we look at the ten largest shareholders. Here the average of their total holdings is 31.44% of equity. The corresponding data for the integrated and production companies of the United Kingdom is 23.48% and 19.55% of equity. It is 16.30% and 18.3% for the integrated companies of California and New York State.

The analysis of the ownership structures of telecommunications companies leads us to analogous conclusions. The ownership of companies which are most exposed to competition — and so with a smaller share of the maket — have a more widespread investor base. The five largest stockholders of the competitive companies own an average of 18.8% of equity, while the five major stockholders of the monopolistic companies own an average of 62.2% of equity. The analysis of the shareholding of the ten biggest investors gives the same result.

It is well known that the stockholders' monitoring of management increases as the percentage of equity owned increases as the concentration of control determines a coincidence between efforts and benefits of monitoring. The increase in control decreases agency costs. On the other hand, we believe that the mechanism of competitive bidding by means of which privatizations are carried out, whether in a public auction or in private negotiations, determines an optimal shareholder base, i.e. it maximizes the value of the firm.

Therefore, keeping DL in mind, we interpret the positive correlation between diffuse ownership and exposure to competition in the sense that the discipline of the market is a good substitute for the monitoring of the shareholders.

In Table 2 we show that the presence of the state in PUs, even if only temporarily, is a fairly common phenomenon. Thus one of our questions — what are the effects of the presence of the state-as-stockholder during the period of a privatization — is not totally academic. In particular we see that the period during which the state remains a shareholder can be very short, but it can also stretch out indefinitely. Obviously it is not possible to quantify in the table the level of credibility of the state to complete the privatization.

The state influences the optimal allocation of shareholding through the characteristics of the golden share. The contents of the golden share point out several constants and some variables: the right to veto new investors who would purchase substantial stakes was present in all the cases we considered; the golden share can be discretionally revoked by the government in all cases but one. The right to nominate administrators is given in nine of the cases we examined (Table 3).

The recent empirical evidence of the United Kingdom supports that the optimal allocation of control is endogenous to the regulation in place. Recent modifications in regulation have determined changes in ownership of the companies distributing electricity and a subsequent increase in their value. The golden share in the distribution companies expired on 31 March 1995.

The companies which distribute electricity in the United Kingdom are at the moment being subjected to a wave of takeovers which are shown in Table 4. These takeovers are mostly hostile and they are, for the most part, being carried out by potential strategic shareholders such as the production companies and the integrated companies. The reason for these bids is the expiry on 31 March of the golden share of the distribution companies which blocked any single investor from owning more than a 15% stake in the equity. As a consequence, the producers of electrical energy are now able, through the purchase of the distribution companies, to create a territorial

TABLE 2

A) PERCENTAGE OF THE PRIVATIZED TELECOMMUNICATIONS COMPANIES WHICH HAVE REMAINED THE PROPERTY OF THE STATE

Companies	Nation	Year of privatization	% still state owned
British Telecom	United Kingdom	1984	49.8
		1991	20.0
		1993	0
NTT.........................	Japan	1987	75.0
		1988	65.4
KPN	The Netherlands	1994	65.5
		1995	0
Syaricot Telecom Malaysia	Malaysia	1990	75.0
		1992	53.4
Telefonos de Mexico	Mexico	1991	15.5
		1992	4.6
Telecom of Jamaica	Jamaica	1987	53.1
		1988	40.0
		1989	20.0
		1990	0
Cable & Wireless	United Kingdom	1981	50.6
		1983	23.1
		1985	0
Singapore Telecom	Singapore	1993	92.8
TeleDenmark.................	Denmark	1994	51.0
PTT Nederland	The Netherlands	1994	70.0
Bezek	Israel	1990	94.0
		1991	77.0
Korea Telecom...............	South Korea	1993	90.0
		1994	80.0
Telefonica	Argentina	1990	30.0
Telecom	Argentina	1990	30.0

B) PERCENTAGE OF THE PRIVATIZED ELECTRICAL POWER
COMPANIES WHICH HAVE REMAINED THE PROPERTY OF THE STATE

Companies	Nation	Year of privatization	% still state owned
National Power	United Kingdom	1991	60.0
		1995	0
PowerGen	United Kingdom	1991	60.0
		1995	0
Endesa	Spain	1988	76.0
		1994	66.0
Alicura	Argentina	1993	41.0
Chocon	Argentina	1993	41.0
Piedra del Aguilla	Argentina	1994	41.0
Edesur	Argentina	1992	49.0
Transener	Argentina	1993	49.0
Escelsa	Brazil	1995	27.0
Cesp	Brazil	1994	93.0
Tenaga	Malaysia	1991	75.0

connection with the users of the distribution companies, which will in its turn be useful when on 1 January 1998 end users will be able to choose their supplier. We should mention how for a certain period there was some doubt exactly how the government would treat vertical integration in the sector. The government, on the basis of the opinion of the regulator in the sector, decided to interest the Monopoly and Mergers Commission as regards the cited takeover operations.

In addition the US experience, started over three decades ago, seems to indicate that the market for the control of the PUs functions poorly because of the obstacles put in place by the state as shareholder and/or regulator (McLaughlin - Mehran [3]). The case in the United States brings out, for ezample that in the regulated enterprises, hostile bids are less likely to succeed [2].

---

[2] Purchases of more than 5% of PUs in more than one state are subject to SEC authorization.

TABLE 3

PUBLIC UTILITIES AND THE GOLDEN SHARE

Companies	Nation	Sector	Veto rights over large investors	Right to directors	Expiration date
British Telecom	United Kingdom	Telecommunication	yes	yes	at the government's discretion
Cable & Wireless	United Kingdom	Telecommunication	yes	yes	at the government's discretion
KPN	The Netherlands	Telecommunication	no	yes	at the government's discretion
Singapore Telecom	Singapore	Telecommunication	yes	yes	at the government's discretion
TCNZ	New Zealand	Telecommunication	yes	no	at the government's discretion
National Power	United Kingdom	Electric power	yes	no	at the government's discretion
PowerGen	United Kingdom	Electric power	yes	no	at the government's discretion
12 power distribution companies	United Kingdom	Electric power	yes	no	31/3/1995
Scottish Power	United Kingdom	Electric power	yes	no	at the government's discretion

TABLE 4

RECENT TAKEOVERS IN
THE ELECTRIC POWER DISTRIBUTION COMPANIES IN THE UNITED KINGDOM

Acquiring company	Target	Type of takeover	Date of bid	Type of acquiring company	Outcome
Trafalgar House	Northern Electric	hostile	19/12/94	conglomerate	pending
Southern Company	SWEB	hostile	10/07/95	integrated electric utility	accepted
Scottish Power	Man Web	hostile	24/07/95	integrated electric utility	accepted
Hanson	Eastern Group	friendly	31/07/95	producer of electrical energy	accepted
North West Wales	Norweb	friendly	8/09/95	distributor of electrical energy	pending
PowerGen	Midlands	friendly	18/09/95	distributor of electrical energy	pending

The increase in the value of the company does not however necessarily imply an increase in social welfare. The modification of regulation and more specifically, the expiry of the golden share can provoke, in non-competitive market conditions, discriminatory behavior toward consumers which would not otherwise be permitted.

So the answer to our question, if a modification in the ownership of a company following a modification in the regulation increases or decreases the social welfare, is empirical and it will depend, case by case, on the type of enterprise in question and the type of modification which is carried out.

BIBLIOGRAPHY

[1] BAUMOL W.J., «On the Perils of Privatization», *Eastern Economic Journal*, vol. 19, 1993, pp. 419-40.

[2] BECKER G.S., «Rule No. 1 in Switching to Capitalism: Move Fast», *Business Week*, 29 May 1995.

[3] BOARDMAN A.E. - ECHEL C. - VINING A.R., «The Advantages and Disadvantages of Mixed Enterprises», in NEGANDHI A.R. (ed.), *Research in International Business and International Relations*, vol. 1, London, Jai Press Inc., 1986.

[4] BOARDMAN A.E. - VINING A.R., «Ownership and Performance in Competitive Enviroments: a Comparison of the Performance of Private, Mixed and State-Owned Enterprises», *Journal of Law and Economics*, vol. 32, 1989, pp. 1-33.

[5] —— - ——, «The Behavior of Mixed Enterprises», *Research in Law and Economics*, vol. 14, 1991, pp. 223-50.

[6] BÖS D., *Privatization - A Theoretical Treatment*, Oxford, Clarendon Press, 1991.

[7] BÖS D. - PETERS W., «Privatization, Internal Control, and Internal Regulation», *Journal of Public Economics*, vol. 36, 1988, pp. 231-58.

[8] DEMSETZ II. - LEHN K., «The Structure of Corporate Owership: Causes and Consequences», *Journal of Political Economy*, vol. 93, 1985, pp. 1155-77.

[9] FAMA E. - JENSEN M.C., «Agency Problems and Residual Claims», *Journal of Law and Economics*, vol. 26, 1983, pp. 327-49.

[10] GROSSMAN S.J. - HART O.D., «Takeover Bids, the Free Rider Problem and the Theory of Corporation», *The Bell Journal of Economics*, vol. 11, 1980, pp. 42-64.

[11] JENSEN M.C. - MECKLING W.H., «Theory of the Firm: Managerial Behavior, Agency Costs and Ownership Structure», *Journal of Financial Economies*, vol. 3, 1976, pp. 305-60.

[12] LEVY B. - SPILLER P.T., «The Institutional Foundations of Regulatory Commitment: A Comparative Analysis of Telecommunications Regulation», *The Journal of Law Economics Organization*, vol. 10, 1994, pp. 201-46.

[13] MCLAUGHLIN R.M. - MEHRAN H., «Regulation and the Market for Corporate Control: Hostile Tender Offers for Electric and Gas Utilities», *Journal of Regulatory Economics*, vol. 8, 1995, pp. 181-204.

[14] MILGROM P. - ROBERTS J., *Economics, Organization and Management*, Englewood Cliffs, Prentice Hall International, 1992.

[15] SMITH M., «Bid Likely to Redraw the Lines of Power», *Financial Times*, 25 July 1995.

[16] STIGLITZ J.E., *Whither Socialism?*, Cambridge, The Mit Press, 1994.

[17] VINING A.R. - BOARDMAN A.E., «Ownership Versus Competition: Efficiency in Public Enterprise», *Public Choice*, vol. 73, 1992, pp. 205-39.

[18] YAFEH Y. - YOSHA O., «Large Shareholders, Banks, and Managerial Moral Hazard: An Empirical Investigation», *Competing Models of Capitalism*, Workshop, Brussels, CEPR, 1994.

II - INTERNATIONAL EXPERIENCE

The Privatisation of the British Public Sector: An Assessment of a Policy Innovation

Peter M. Jackson
University of Leicester

Introduction

The privatisation of public utilities is a universal phenomenon throughout the world. Started as a policy innovation in Britain during the early 1980s it has occupied a place on the policy agenda of the major industrialised countries, the newly developing countries and those of the former eastern European communist bloc. Not all countries have, of course, pursued privatisation with equal vigour. Amongst the countries of the OECD Britain has been one of the most strident advocates of privatisation policy.

After almost fifteen years of privatisation it is now appropriate to look back and examine what has been achieved. Has, for example, the change in the status of public utilities to private companies produced the efficiency gains which were envisaged? This, along with a number of other questions, will be explored in this paper.

1. - The Rationale of Privatisation

Privatisation has been pursued with many objectives in mind. Principally the aim of privatisation has been to improve the efficiency of those organisations which were initially classified as public utilities. There have, however, been other policy objectives of a more ideo-

---

N.B.: the numbers in square brackets refer to the Bibliography at the end of the paper.

logical nature including that of reducing public expenditures and rolling back the frontiers of the state. Libertarians and public choice theorists following in the footsteps of Mises and Hayek have long sought to redress the balance between public and private ownership especially since the emergence of the welfare state.

It would, however, be a mistake to conclude that the advocates of privatisation belong only to the right wing of the political spectrum. The left wing has also been suspicious of the degree of producer monopoly power held by those professional groups who make decisions about the level of public sector provision and its distribution (Miliband [34], O'Connor [41] and Gough [17]).

The primary objectives of privatisation can be summarised as follows (Vickers and Yarrow [46]): 1) to reduce government involvement in industry; 2) to improve efficiency; 3) to reduce public sector borrowing; 4) to promote wider share ownership in a property owning democracy; 5) to enhance employee share ownership; 6) to reduce public sector subsidies to private industry; 7) to weaken public sector trades unions.

Central to all privatisation programmes is the quest for improvements in efficiency and the general belief that public ownership is inherently less efficient than private ownership. The relative inefficiency of public enterprises is assumed to have its origins partly from the absence of competition in the product market and partly because of an inappropriate distribution of property rights. These combined circumstances do not generate an appropriate set of incentives for public enterprise managers to pursue efficient allocations of resources.

It has long been recognised (Coase [8]; Alchian and Demsetz [1]; Furubotn and Pejovich [16]; De Alessi [10]) that if incentives are clearly specified and if there is a clear link between an individual's actions and their rewards then the individual's performance will be better. Because the ownership of public enterprises is general and diffused, managers of these organisations do not necessarily face incentives which will ensure that their decisions produce efficient outcomes. Moreover, the asymmetrical distribution of information between those who manage the public enterprise and the politicians who control them gives to the managers a great deal of discretion

(Williamson [49] and [50]). This classic *principal-agent* problem is reinforced by the public choice theorists who argue that the discretion given to the managers of public enterprises and bureaucrats generally enables them to pursue their own professional self interests rather than the public interest as articulated through the ballot box. The separation of ownership from control usually ends up in gaming behaviour in which opportunistic managers seek to maximise their own utilities, (Downs [12]; Tullock [43]; Niskanen [40]).

This literature leads to the *hypothesis* that in the absence of a clear link between managerial action and profits (performance) then public sector organisations/agencies will seek to maximise the size of their budgets that will result in non optimal levels of employment in public enterprises. Not only might there be allocative inefficiency there will also be X-inefficiency (Leibenstein [31]).

The structure — conduct — performance paradigm suggests that highly competitive product markets are more likely to result in allocative efficiency and cost minimisation. Moreover, the discipline of the capital market, which is absent in the case of public enterprises, will help to ensure that managerial actions produce enhanced performance in the form of higher profits.

Whilst this line of theorising provides an intellectual foundation for privatisation policies it is not conclusive. Theory is ambiguous regarding the potential efficiency gains which privatisation might provide. First, public choice theorists ascribe to bureaucrats a particular set of values and motives. That is, they are assumed to be self interested. Set against this is the Weberian bureaucrat who is very much a "civil servant" and motivated to serve the public interest and would be prepared to sacrifice his/her own self interest. Thus whether or not bureaucrats as public enterprise managers are inherently inefficient crucially depends upon the dominant cultural/value system which is assumed (Fiorina and Nell [14]; and Posner [42]). Second, profit related pay or performance related pay has been introduced to many private and public sector organisations with very limited success. Third, the discipline of the capital market is much weaker than is normally thought (Grossman and Hart [19]; and Stiglitz [45]). Fourth, a number of arguments have been used to support the argument that monopoly power does not necessarily imply inefficiency when compared to atomistic competition. If there is free entry and if exit is costless then markets are contestable and the fear of potential competition will result in monopolists maximising their profits. Moreover, the market for corporate control will ensure that mangers of monopolistic firms will search for efficient solutions. To do otherwise can result in a threat of takeover. Large scale can also result in a reduction in transactions costs (Coase [8]; and Williamson [49] and [50]), whilst many firms grow in order to achieve efficiency gains (Demsetz [11]).

If economic theory is ambiguous about whether or not a change in the status of an organisation from public to private ownership will result in an improvement in efficiency then it should not be too surprising if the changes in efficiency, which are actually recorded post privatisation, are non existent or not as great as expected. This is explored in a later section.

What economic theory does, however, teach us is that whilst the change in ownership does not matter (or is at least necessary but not sufficient) for efficiency, nevertheless, the nature of competitive forces and regulating policies are important, especially the threats of actual or potential competition (Vickers and Yarrow [46]; Yarrow [51]; Kay and Silberston [29]).

It was indicated in the list of objectives of privatisation that improvements in efficiency was only one of a number of intended consequences of a privatisation policy. This is especially true of Britain's case. Privatisation was a policy which was stumbled upon. The incoming 1979 Thatcher Government did not have a well established privatisation policy. Instead, privatisation policy emerged or evolved. It was a policy which enabled politicians the means of achieving a number of policy objectives. The revenues raised from the sale of public enterprise assets enabled the various Thatcher administrations to reduce the public sector borrowing requirement without having to cut deep into public expenditure on the welfare services whilst at the same time reducing the basic marginal rate of income tax. Privatisations also helped to inject discipline into the public sector trades unions and to depolitise trades union actions. The political damage of the miners' strike of 1974 to the Heath conservative government had taught the Conservatives that any policy which moved powerful trades unions out of the public sector was to be welcomed.

2. - The Nature of Privatisation

Privatisation can and does, in Britain, take a variety of forms: *a*) denationalisation - selling the assets of public utilities and other public sector agencies; *b*) deregulation and liberalisation of markets; *c*) the introduction of competitive tendering to public sector departments; *d*) the establishment of agencies which perform functions on behalf of the public sector; *e*) the introduction of managed competition into public sector agencies through the establishment of internal or quasi markets.

The sale of public assets can be effected in a number of different ways. First, most privatisations in Britain have been through public flotations on the capital market. Shares in the newly privatised companies are sold to the general public and financial institutions at a fixed price. Rather than be left with a large number of unsold shares, and the embarrassment that would cause, the initial share price was heavily discounted. Because of the low price and hence the expectation of rapid capital gains share offers in privatised public utilities have been over subscribed. In some cases, eg Britoil and Enterprise Oil, tenders were invited from potential purchasers. Second, direct or trade sale, where the assets are purchased by another company eg British Rail Hotels; British Aerospace; the Royal Ordinance Factories and Sealink. Thirdly, management buyouts (and employee buyouts) eg the National Freight Corporation and buyouts in the bus transport industry.

These various forms of privatisation have changed the landscape of the British economy by changing the boundaries that exist between the public and the private sectors. Privatisations in Britain have been dominated by asset sales not only the sale of public utilities but also the sale of publicly owned (council) housing and the sale of unwanted land by local government; the National Health Service and public utilities such as British Rail.

Another significant form of privatisation has been the introduction of competitive tendering into the National Health Service and local government. As a result of the *Griffiths Report* [18] general managers were introduce to manage NHS facilities and the "hotel" support services of hospitals (ie catering, laundry and cleaning) were put out to competitive tendering, which was compulsory. Compulsory competitive tendering (CCT) had been introduced into local authorities in the 1980 *Local Government Planning* and *Land Act* which covered services such as highways and building maintenance work. The *Local Government Act* 1988 extended CCT to refuse collection; building cleaning; other cleaning; schools and welfare catering; grounds maintenance and vehicle maintenance.

Whilst the establishment of Next Steps Agencies is a form of contracting out they are worthwhile mentioning separately. The *Ibbs Report* 1988, *Improving Management in Government: The Next Steps* (Cm 524) recommended the decoupling of many of the functions and activities of central government departments by putting out, on an "agency basis", those departments which are involved in the delivery of services (ie executive functions). Those departments which advised Ministers and formulated policy (ie the legislative functions) were kept in. The "Next Steps Agencies" or "Executive Agencies" were given new freedoms including the freedom to negotiate local wages; employment levels; conditions of service, IT policies etc. Plans currently exist to set up 80 agencies which will employ 75% of the current civil service. Examples of agencies include, the Stationery Office, Passport Department; Vehicle Inspectorate; Companies Registration Office, etc.

Executive Agencies exist to carry out the executive functions of government within a policy framework set by a sponsoring department. Each agency obtains a contract or a "framework document" from a central government department which specifies the services to be provided; performance targets; and of course its budget. The Chief Executives of the agencies are accountable to Parliament for the delivery of their agency's services and for the general operation of the agency.

The incentive structure which faces public sector managers has also been "privatised" or "marketised" throughout the British public sector. Greater emphasis is now placed upon devolved budgeting following the Financial Management Initiative (FMI) in central government (see Metcalfe and Richards [38]; and Jackson [26]); a greater decentralisation of decision making and the use of performance measures (see Jackson [28]); and the introduction of quasi-markets (see Jackson [28]; and Le Grand [30]). Changes in the incentive structure is an obvious attempt at dealing with the principal agent problems of asymmetric information and moral hazard.

3. - British Privatisation

In the previous section the principal forms of privatisation in Britain were reviewed. This section looks at some of these in more detail.

Privatisation in Britain began as a radical experiment early in the first Thatcher administration. It proved to be both acceptable and successful (Moore [38]). In 1986 Moore [37], one of the political architects of privatisation, claimed it to be, «... one of the most extraordinary political and economic transformations that has taken place in the last 15 years ... Privatisation has not only proved possible but popular...».

The first major privatisation in Britain was the sale of British Telecom in 1984. Prior to that privatisation had been carried out on a modest scale and had mainly been confined to the sale of council houses and the deregulation of the buses. British Telecom shares were over-subscribed five times and 49% of the shares sold for £3.9 billion. This represented a significant impact on the stock market. The total amount of money raised during 1984 other than for British Telecom was £1.4 billion.

Between 1980 and 1991 accumulated privatisation proceeds for Britain amounted to £44.5 billion. Amongst other OECD countries only Japan and New Zealand engaged in privatisation programmes of similar scale. By 1990 over 30 organisations had been privatised by asset sales and about 800,000 employees had been transferred from the public to the private sector (see Cmnd 1021, 1990).

The principal privatisations, by means of asset sales, are shown in Table 1 and the proceeds from privatisation are shown in Table 2.

TABLE 1

MAJOR PRIVATISATIONS IN THE UK

Organisation	Date	Industry
British Petroleum	various 1979 to 1987	oil
National Enterprise Board	various 1980 to 1986	various
British Aerospace	1981 and 1984	aerospace
Cable and Wireless	1981, 1983 and 1988	telecommunications
Amersham International	1982	scientific products
National Freight Corp'n	1982	road transport
Britoil	1982 and 1986	oil
British Rail Hotels	1983	hotels
Associated British Ports	1983 and 1984	ports
British Leyland (Rover)	various 1984 to 1988	car manufacture
British Telecom (BT)	1984, 1991 and 1993	telecommunications
Enterprise Oil	1984	oil
Sealink	1984	sea transport
British Shipbuilders & Naval Dockyards	from 1985	shipbuilding
National Bus Company	from 1986	transport
British Gas..................	1986	gas
Rolls Royce	1987	aero engines
British Airports Authority	firm issue 1987	airports
British Airways	1987	airlines
Royal Ordinance Factories	1987	armaments
British Steel	1988 and 1989	steel
Water	1989 and 1990	water
Electricity Distribution	1990	electricity
Electricity Generation	1991	electricity
Trust Ports..................	1992	ports
British Rail	from 1994	railways
British Coal	1995	coal

Source, PARKER D., «Has Privatisation Improved Performance?» Causeway Press, *Developments in Economics*, vol. 11, 1993, pp. 19-46.

4. - Financial Consequences of Privatisation

One of the objectives of privatisation was to create a property owning democracy. Some measure of success can be claimed in this area. In 1981 7% of the adult population in Britain owned shares. By 1992 this figure had increased to 22%. The number of shareholders

TABLE 2

PRIVATISATION PROCEEDS
(£bn)

Year	Proceeds
1979-1980	0.4
1980-1981	0.2
1981-1982	0.5
1982-1983	0.5
1983-1984	1.1
1984-1985	2.0
1985-1986	2.7
1986-1987	4.5
1987-1988	6.1
1988-1989	7.1
1989-1990	4.2
1990-1991	5.3
1991-1992	7.9
1992-1993	8.2
1993-1994	5.4
1994-1995	6.3*
1995-1996	3.0*

* Planned. Figures rounded to one decimal place.

Source, HM TREASURY, *Autumn Statment*, London, HMSO, 1991, p. 27; *Financial Statement and Budget Reports 1992-93, 1993-94 and 1995-96*, London, HMSO.

who held onto their shares one year after they purchased them is about 60%. This figure has now fallen to 40%. Moreover, 70% of shareholders have a very small number of shares. Thus, whilst share ownership has undoubtedly increased significantly following privatisation it is most unlikely that this will have had an impact upon the efficiency of capital markets or indeed upon the efficient management of the newly privatised companies. The dilution of ownership weakens the effective power of any single shareholder whilst high transactions costs reduce the profitability of shareholders forming coalitions to promote their collective interest. The powerful players in capital markets still remain the institutional investors — the Insurance Companies; Banks and Pension Funds.

The revenues from privatisation played a major role in enabling the Government to reduce the public sector borrowing requirement. Between 1986 and 1990 the borrowing requirement was negative!

The market value of the newly privatised companies is greater than the revenues raised by government via the sale of assets. Is this due to enhanced efficiency since privatisation? To answer this question is not easy and a number of factors have to be taken into consideration before an improved P/E ratio can be unambiguously used as an indicator of enhanced performance. For example, prior to the privatisation of many public utilities their existing debt was written off. For example, £5 billion of debt was written off at the time of water privatisation. Efficient capital market theory suggests that this will influence the share price immediately after privatisation. Given that shares were heavily discounted when the companies were privatised then significant increases in the share price does not necessarily imply an improvement in efficiency. It simply reflects the new balance sheet of the company. Share prices should reflect the prospect of profits rather than the valuation of assets. After privatisation share price movements have reflected the policies of the regulators. For example, during 1995 the Electricity Industry Regulator announced a tougher policy which was immediately reflected in a massive fall in the share prices of the various electricity companies.

One argument which was frequently advocated prior to privatisation was that the public enterprises' capital investment programme was severely constrained because of lack of access to the capital market and the imposition of external financing limits. Since privatisation only British Gas and British Telecom have raised external finance on capital markets. The reason for this is that the prices of the products/services of the privatised companies have been set with a view to providing an adequate rate of return to shareholders and also to generate sufficient internal sources of finance. This implies that under the privatised regime capital expenditure is now financed by customers rather than as previously by taxpayers. There are distributional consequences of this change which are worthwhile noting. Because the prices charged for commodities such as water and electricity are regressive, when compared to capital financing from progressive taxation, then there will be a shift in the distribution of income against the least well off in society, following privatisation.

The National Audit Office [39] has noted the high transactions costs that have been associated with the sale of assets. These include the fees paid to merchant banks; accountants; lawyers; public relations firms, etc. involved in the sale. To 1991 the NAO estimated these accumulated costs to be £2.4 billion. This is about 5% of the total revenues raised.

Capital spending in public enterprises was constrained during the 1970s and early 1980s in order to hold down the public sector borrowing requirement and because it was generally argued that the marginal productivity of capital in that sector was below that of private sector firms. The fact that the sale of shares in these newly privatised firms has been so successful is a testimony to the suboptimisation of the earlier policies towards the nationalised industries. If it was worthwhile investing in capital projects immediately after privatisation then it must also have been worthwhile to do so before.

5. - Efficiency Effects

Whether or not privatisation resulted in significant improvements in efficiency is a moot point. It has already been pointed out that theory is not unambiguous about the size of the potential efficiency improvements — if indeed they exist at all. There are also a number of empirical problems which have to be confronted. If a single dimension of performance is chosen, such as profit, then what is happening to quality? Is like being compared with like; is the quality of the output of the nationalised industries the same as that of the newly privatised industries? A similar issue arises when comparing the objective functions of organisations pre and post privatisation. Public enterprises pursued multiple objectives which included political as well as economic aims. For example, the price (and hence profits) of nationalised industries were frequently used as part of government's income distribution policy — price rises were often constrained. Also, the nationalised industries were at times employer of last resort. After privatisation these socio-political objectives were lost rendering pre and post privatisation comparisons difficult.

Did the profits of the privatised industries rise because of reductions in costs or because of increases in prices? If it was the latter then capital gained at the expense of customers and this has distributional implications. Electricity prices rose by 13% in 1992 after privatisation but customers complained about the quality of the services that they received.

Early studies of the relative efficiency of public enterprises produced no conclusive picture against which privatisation efficiency studies might be compared. Millward [35]; Millward and Parker [36]; Bishop and Kay [2]; Estrin and Perotin [13] could not find conclusive evidence for the view that the private sector was superior. Borcherding *et* Al. [6] reviewed 50 studies from 5 countries and concluded that the consistent view was that public firms had higher unit cost structures — but were they comparing like with like?

A study by Hartley and Parker [20] examined the efficiency (performance) of the newly privatised companies from three perspectives, (*i*) total factor productivity (*ii*) employment and (*iii*) financial ratios. The authors were careful in their use of concepts and recognised the problems involved in employing these three sets of performance measures. They could find no significant improvements in efficiency for the Royal Mint; National Freight; British Airways or British Aerospace. Of the remaining organisations that they studied they could not find convincing improvements in efficiency. Hartley and Parker conclude that changes in ownership status are not the key to efficiency improvements. Rather the quality of management and the degree of product market competition are essential if efficiency is to increase after privatisation. This implies that there is a need to focus upon the contracts given to the managers of privatised companies to ensure that they will deliver efficiency improvements. The literature on the principal agent problem predicts the importance of designing appropriate contracts.

Hutchinson [25] in his study found mixed results with respect to the impact of changes in ownership upon performance. Public ownership corresponded to higher levels of growth in labour productivity whilst private ownership gave rise to higher levels of profit. The interpretation of these results is difficult for all of the reasons given previously.

Bishop and Kay's ([2], pp. 40-1) study of the profits, prices, outputs and productivity of the newly privatised firms between 1979 and 1988 revealed that improvements in performance were not related to privatisation: «The overall picture to emerge ... is one of substantial change. Output and profits have grown, margins have increased, employment has declined. But the relationship of these changes to the fact of privatisation is not immediately apparent from the data. The privatised industries have tended to be faster growing and more profitable, but it seems that the causation runs from growth and profitability to privatisation, rather than the other way round».

Other studies have produced a pot-pourri of results. Foreman-Peck and Manning [15] in their study of British Telecom's productivity changes since 1984 found that whilst it had increased since privatisation so too had the productivity of public enterprise telecoms in other countries. How much of British Telecom's improvement was, therefore, a result of privatisation and how much was simply a general industry wide improvement? Burns and Weyman-Jones [7] examination of electricity distribution companies could not establish a significant relationship between privatisation and productivity change. Bishop and Thompson [5] found that the productivity of both state owned enterprises and privatised companies grew faster in the 1980s than in the 1970s but that there was no significant difference between the two groups. Similar results were found by Haskel and Szymanski ([21], [22], [23] and [24]).

Finally Martin and Parker [32] examined 11 organisations which had been privatised during the 1980s. These organisations were studied in considerable depth and for a long period of time. Their results are summarised in Table 3. Prior to privatisation British Airways' labour productivity grew at 8.6% pa. This growth has, however, reduced since privatisation. Similar results are found for British Gas; Rolls-Royce and the British Airports Authority. In another study Parker and Martin [32] report similar results for total factor productivity.

Was privatisation, therefore, a waste of time? Bishop, Kay and Mayer ([3], p. 6) provide a powerful argument in favour of privatisation despite the weak empirical evidence of performance improvements: «Even in the absence of competition it allows more powerful incentives (market-value related incentives, takeovers and bankruptcy) to be introduced. It separates public and private good

TABLE 3

AVERAGE ANNUAL PERCENTAGE CHANGES IN LABOUR PRODUCTIVITY
('Date' refers to the period studied*)

Privatised	British Airways	British Airport Authority	Britoil	British Gas	British Steel	British Aerospace	Jaguar	Rolls Royce	National Freight	Associated British Ports	British Telecom (BT)
	Feb. 1987	July 1987	Nov. 1982	Dec. 1988	Dec. 1986	Feb. 1981	July 1984	May 1987	Feb. 1982	Feb. 1983	Nov. 1984
Nationalisation period	6.8 1977-1981	1.2 1979-1983	(1.2) 1978-1981	2.4 1979-1983	28.4 1981-1988	0.6 1978-1980	34.9 1981-1983	7.4 1980-1983	0.3 1973-1977	(3.4) 1977-1980	8.8 1977-1981
Pre-privatisation period	10.8 1981-1985	8.9 1983-1987	2.7 1980-1982	6.8 1983-1987	11.3 1985-1989	0.6 1978-1980	27.0 1983-1984	8.8 1983-1986	8.7 1977-1981	3.0 1978-1988	6.8 1981-1985
Post-annonce-ment period ..	8.6 1981-1987	8.1 1984-1987	9.3 1982	9.8 1985-1987	13.9 1987-1988	3.3 1979-1980	3.8 1984	1.0 1986	11.4 1979-1981	9.3 1981-1982	6.9 1983-1988
Post-privatisation period	2.9 1987-1991	2.3 1987-1991	6.3 1983-1986	3.7 1987-1991	(0.8) 1988-1992	8.3 1981-1984	3.7 1985-1988	1.6 1987-1990	4.1 1981-1986	16.4 1983-1988	7.3 1988-1990
Recession period	4.6 1988-1992	4.8 1988-1992	n.s.	1.8 1988-1992	(0.1) 1988-1992	14.1 1989-1992	(16.7) 1988-1991	1.2 1989-1992	0.4 1988-1992	24.1 1989-1992	8.3 1988-1992

* Dates refer to accounting years, e.g., 1977-1981 includes dates for accounting years beginning in 1977 to accounting year ending in 1981.
n/a = not applicable. Britoil was purchased by BP plc in 1988 and consequently no data on later economic and financial performance are available. No reliable data exist for Jaguar prior to the early 1980s.
( ) Negative.

Source, MARTIN S. - PARKER D. [32].

elements of supply, and provides more information on which to base the regulation of public elements».

The link between privatisation and performance does not guarantee performance improvements and is much more complex and problematic than is popularly supposed. When a public sector monopoly is transferred to the private sector and still remains a monopoly then it is difficult not to make higher profits and give the appearance of improving performance. The privatisation policies adopted by the British Government did not, however, pay sufficient attention to injecting competition into the system where it was possible to do so. In these cases where natural monopoly is prevalent, as in gas pipelines and the electricity grid it is difficult to introduce competition without also creating severe disruption through negative network externalities. Competition is, however, possible in areas such as the management of networks or public sector facilities and in the production and supply of commodities such as gas and electricity.

There is no doubting that privatisation has made organisations more transparent. Information is more tangible; costing systems were necessary to establish how much key activities cost and there is greater attention given to focusing upon what customers want.

Incentives have also probably become more transparent but not necessarily more binding.

The incentives from takeover or bankruptcy are still weak. Is it possible to imagine a water company or a gas company being allowed to go bankrupt? One credible threat, however, is that if the management of the organisation were to lead the company to that situation then they would be replaced. It is, therefore, in management's interest to deliver acceptable performance but that might simply be a suboptimised solution. Moreover, since privatised firms face little competition then they are unlikely to face financial distress.

6. - Regulation of Privatised Industries

An important feature of British privatisation policy has been the associated emergence of regulation policy and the establishment of regulatory agencies such as the Office of Telecommunications regulation (OFTEL); OFGAS (gas industry); OFWAT (water) and OFFER (electricity). The role played by the regulators in these industries is of strategic importance and is necessary to curb the monopoly power of the privatised industries.

Regulation can take a variety of forms (Weyman-Jones [47]). There are three principal categories:

1) limitations on entry to a market or exit from it, as in the case of licensing arrangements whereby a producer requires permission from the government to sell a product or service;

2) specifications relating to the quality of the products supplied - this is similar to the previous form but quality thresholds are specified in the contract;

3) price regulation - setting maximum or minimum prices for a product; setting price by formulae or setting a formula for the rate of return on capital. Price and rate of return regulation are related. Let Q be a firm's sales volume, P the price per unit of sales, OC its operating costs, K its stock or capital and R the rate of return on capital, then; $R = (PQ - OC)/K$.

The main form of regulation which has been used to constrain the newly privatised companies in Britain has been price caps. There is, however, a mixture of the different kinds of regulation. British Telecom, for example, has a 25 year operating license. This sets out the conditions under which it must supply its services and specifies quality of service including the provision of emergency 999 calls and services to rural areas. Changes in the license are negotiated with the regulator.

In all cases the generic form of the price cap formula is similar, though there are variations for each specific industry. The price change formula is $(RPI - X)$ ie the maximum price rise permitted each year is related to the retail price index (RPI) minus an efficiency factor X which is set by negotiation between the industry and its regulator. X is an indicator of cost increases. For example, if, as in the case of telecommunications, technical change is improving and is reducing costs then X will be negative. This ensures that some of the benefits of the productivity gains arising from technical change are passed on to the customer. On the other hand if there are special factors causing costs to rise as in the case of the water industry which has to invest in order to meet European water quality standards then that will be reflected in a K factor, which is positive. That is the formula becomes, $(RPI - X + K)$. A summary of British price regulation is shown in Table 4.

TABLE 4

UK PRICE REGULATION

Organisation	Main features of price regulation	Comment
British Telecom (BT)............	1984-1989 $RPI -3\%$ 1989-1991 $RPI -4.5\%$ 1991-1993 $RPI -6.25\%$ 1993 $RPI -7.5\%$ domestic rental increase limited to $RPI +2\%$	Now applies to switched inland calls, line rentals & international calls.
British Gas......	1987-1993 $RPI -2\%$ 1992-1994 $RP -5\%$ 1994 $RPI -4\%$ standing charge to rise by no more than the RPI	Excludes gas input costs, which can be passed on to the consumer less a 1% efficiency factor. Price regulation applies to domestic market only.
British Airport Authority	Now $RPI -4\%$	Applies to airport charges, e.g. aircraft landings, passenger usage.
Water companies	$RPI + X$	X varies for each company to reflect capital investment needs.
Regional electricity companies. England & Wales (separate regulation applies in Scotland)	$RPI - X + Y$	Applies to prices for transmission, distribution and supply to other than large users (now > 1 MW demand). X for distribution prices set at 0% to 2.5% until 1995, though after 1995 regulation to be tightened. For supply prices, X set at zero. Allowed to pass on certain generation costs (y).

There are a number of problems associated with industry regulation. One obvious problem is that of "regulatory capture" in which case the regulator becomes an advocate of the industry's interests rather than the interests of the customer (Stigler [44]). There is no evidence that this has happened in Britain. Indeed the opposite is the case. The frequent complaint of the privatised industries is that the regulator is too powerful a champion of customers interests.

Another problem with regulation is that it can end up destroying managerial incentives. If the rate of return target is set too low then there is little incentive to cut costs if it is set too high then it can be achieved through price increases (at the consumers' expense) rather than efficiency savings. The incorporation of the X factor in the price cap formula gives managers an incentive to search for efficiency gains but clearly if X is set too high then it can have the opposite effect.

The use of the K factors means that industries, especially gas, water, and electricity, can pass those costs which the regulator regards as outside of their control on to the customers. The identification of these costs is, therefore, of paramount importance.

Recent experience with price cap regulation in Britain suggests, however, that there is a subtle game which is played out between the regulator and the industry. If price caps under $(RPI-X)$ are set for all time then management might supply cut costs up to the efficiency factor X. Or any efficiency gains greater than X will not be passed onto the customer. Where then is the incentive to cut costs greater than X but at the same time allow the customer to share some of the benefit: if the regulator was to intervene and cut prices part way through the period before the cap expires then the industry would in the future not cut costs because they would assume that if they were successful in cost cutting then the regulator will simply tax away the efficiency gains through price cuts. Moreover, suddenly announced price cuts will be reflected in a fall in share prices as happened in March 1995 when the electricity industry regulator announced that he would be reviewing the price cap because the performance of the electricity companies was better than expected. Almost overnight share prices in the electricity companies fell by 20%.

Also, unless companies have a degree of confidence that the price cap is fixed then their investment plans will be affected. Either retained profits will be insufficient to provide internal finance for investment or the share price will be depressed which will make it more difficult to raise external finance.

The performance of the regulated privatised industries is, therefore, sensitive to the industries' expectations of the moves that the regulator will make within the framework of the regulatory game.

7. - Effectiveness of Other Privatisations

Privatisation in Britain is much wider in scope than simply selling the assets of public utilities. The introduction of performance incentives; the decentralisation of decision making; the use of competitive tendering and contracting out; the establishment of Executive Agencies and the promotion of internal markets are all features of the changing topography of Britain's public sector. What has been the impact of these reforms? Jackson [27] gives a comprehensive review.

The picture relating to competitive tendering is mixed. Many recorded efficiency gains derive from lower wages; poorer working conditions and reductions in the quality of service. Many contracts were successfully won and retained by local authorities and health authorities. There is evidence to suggest that the threats, and hence changes in incentives, that have accompanied competitive tendering have resulted in improvements in both the quality of management and, hence, internal efficiency.

The devolution of budgets to schools and individual doctor's practices (in the NHS) was an attempt to improve allocative efficiency. One result has been a tendency for budget holders to go for "cream skimming". This in the language of the principal agent literature is adverse selection. That is, schools will tend to admit high performance students who will enhance the schools' prospects of attaining a high ranking in the performance league tables. Students of low educational achievement are also more expensive to educate. Doctors have a tendency to engage in similar games and will prefer to choose young healthy patients rather than the old and sick. Clearly this reaction of budget holders has important distributional consequences which need to be traded off against any apparent efficiency gains.

It is too early to judge the effectiveness of the reforms which brought about the Executive Agencies. Indicators do, however, suggest that the cultural changes that have been promoted by the new incentives are working towards improved efficiency and effectiveness.

8. - The Future of Privatisation

Whilst politicians have heralded the privatisation policy initiative as a major success there are clear signals that the general public do not necessarily share that view. There has been public opposition to privatisation and this is indicated in various national opinion polls conducted by Harris and Gallup (see Crewe [9] and Meredith, 1992). Opposition was particularly strong in the case of water privatisation and the prospects of rail privatisation are currently viewed with suspicion. Recently the *Economist* gave the view «... to say that privatisation is unpopular in Britain is an understatement. Every week brings fresh outrage at tales of bosses of privatised firms picking up huge pay rises while over-charging customers». Indeed, it was as a result of the massive rewards given to the senior managers of the privatised industries, especially the cashing in of their share options, that the Prime Minister, John Major, set up the Greenbury Committee to enquire into executive pay for Britain as a whole.

In the future privatisation might achieve more than it has in the past. There has been a tendency for the results of privatisation to fall below their potential. This is summarised well by Williams ([48], p. 123): «The Thatcher Government has had an impoverished concept of management as revealed by telltale signs: a mechanistic view of control; a disregard for civil servants' morale; and a costs mentality. For this government the most basic elements management — people, dynamic organisation, motivation, leadership — often have been left out, replaced by costs and an archaic command and control mystique of leaders and docile followers, coupled uneasily with the belief that recalcitrant civil servants must be brought to heal».

A more sensitive and professional approach to change management could have motivated public employees and resulted in greater efficiency and effectiveness. It is to be hoped that by reassessing the value of the public sector along with the values that drive a privatised market economy then future privatisations will be more successful.

Privatisation is here to stay in Britain. Whilst the process is undoubtedly reversible this is most unlikely. However, the processes through which further privatisation might be implemented are a matter of choice.

9. - Conclusion

The scale of privatisation in Britain has been immense. By 1990 over 30 organisations had been privatised and 800,000 public employees had been moved to the private sector.

It would be wrong to judge the success, or otherwise, of Britain's privatisation programme purely in terms of efficiency. Society has other goals and many of these were reflected in the objectives of the public enterprises. Transferring public enterprises into the private domain means that the trade off between the efficiency objective and other objectives, such as distributive justice and macro-economic stabilization, becomes heavily skewed in favour of efficiency. In a post privatised world more thought will have to be given to how these policy objectives are to be achieved.

An element of the folklore of economic thought is that increased competition will yield welfare gains by reducing internal slack in organisations. These are regarded to be the dynamic effects of markets. The efficiency gains from some of the privatisations seems to bear this out, however, the improvements in efficiency have not been as large as many of the proponents of privatisation had supposed. The mechanisms through which welfare gains are achieved remain vague.

Privatisation is not a panacea. It creates new problems while solving old ones or recreates the difficulties which nationalisation and increased public activity sought to solve. It provides an attractive solution to governments which wish to reduce (or stabilise) fiscal deficits. But this is a one shot solution. The family silver can only be sold once.

The privatisation policy initiative which was started in Britain in the 1980s is not yet complete. There remain industries such as British Rail which will be privatised in the future. The establishment of new Executive Agencies will continue and more internal markets are likely to be created. The longer the policy exists the clearer will become its effects. One clear effect is that attitudes towards public sector provision and the balance between the public and the private sectors has changed significantly. Other countries seeking to pursue a policy of privatisation can learn from the British experience.

BIBLIOGRAPHY

[1] ALCHIAN A. - DEMSETZ H., «Production, Information and Economic Organisations», *American Economic*, vol. 62, 1972, pp. 777-95.

[2] BISHOP M. - KAY J., *Does Privatisation Work? Lesson from the UK*, London, London Business School, 1988.

[3] BISHOP M. - KAY J. - MAYER C., *Privatisation and Economic Performance*, Oxford, Oxford University Press, 1994.

[4] —— · —— · ——, «Introduction: Privatisation in Performance», in BISHOP M. - KAY K. - MAYER C. (eds.), *Privatisation and Economic Performance*, Oxford, Oxford University Press, 1994.

[5] BISHOP M. - THOMPSON D., «Regulatory Reform and Productivity Growth in the UK's Public Utilities», *Applied Economics*, vol. 24, 1992.

[6] BORCHERDING T.E. - POMMEREHNE W.W. - SCHNEIDER W.W., «Comparing the Efficiency of Private and Public Production: Evidence from Five Countries», *Zeitschrift fur Nationalokonomie*, Supplementum, 1982, pp. 127-56.

[7] BURNS P. - WEYMAN-JONES T., *The Performance of the Electricity Distribution Business - England and Wales 1971-1993*, Centre for the Study of the Regulated Industries, CIPFA, *Discussion Paper*, n. 8, 1994.

[8] COASE R.H., «The Nature of the Firm», *Economica*, vol. 4, Nov. 1937, pp. 386-405.

[9] CREWE I., «Has the Electorate Become More Thatcherite?», in DEBLEY R., *Thatcherism*, London, Chatts and Windus, 1988.

[10] DE ALESSI L., «The Economics of Property Rights: A Review of the Evidence», *Research in Law Economics*, vol. 2, 1980, pp. 1-47.

[11] DEMSETZ H., «Industry Structure, Market Rivalry and Public Policy», *Journal of Law and Economics*, vol. 16, 1973, pp. 1-9.

[12] DOWNS A., *Inside Bureaucracy*, Boston, Little Brown, 1967.

[13] ESTRIN S. - PEROTIN V., «The Regulation of British and French Nationalised Industries», *European Economic Review*, vol. 28, 1987, pp. 361-7.

[14] FIORINA M.P. - NOLL R.G., «Voters, Bureaucrats, and Legislators: A Rational Choice Perspective on the Growth of Bureaucracy», *Journal of Public Economics*, vol. 9, 1978, pp. 239-54.

[15] FOREMAN-PECK J. - MANNING D., «How Well is BT Performing? An International Comparison of Telecommunications Total Factor Productivity», *Fiscal Studies*, vol. 9, n. 3, 1988, pp. 54-67.

[16] FURUBOTN E.G. - PEJOVICH S., *Economics of Property Rights*, Cambridge (Mass), Ballinger, 1974.

[17] GOUGH I., *The Political Economy of the Welfare State*, London, Macmillan, 1979.

[18] GRIFFITHS REPORT, *NHS Management Inquiry*, Department of Health and Social Security, London, HMSO, 1983.

[19] GROSSMAN S.J. - HART O.D., «Takeover-Birds, the Free Rider Problem, and the theory of Corporations», *Bell Journal of Economics*, vol. 11, 1980, pp. 42-64.

[20] HARTLEY K. - PARKER D., «Privatisation: a Conceptual Framework», in OTT A. - HARTLEY K. (eds.), *Privatisation and Economic Efficiency: A Comparative Analysis of Developed and Developing Countries*, Aldershot, Edward Elgar, 1991.

[21] ASKEL J. - SZYMANSKI S., «Privatisation Jobs and Wages», in *Employment Institute Report*, vol. 6, n. 7, 1991.

[22] —— · ——, «A Bargaining Theory of Privatisation», *Annals of Public and Comparative Economy*, vol. 63, 1992.

[23] —— · ——, «Privatisation, Liberalisation, Wages and Employment: Theory and Evidence from the UK», *Economica*, vol. 60, 1993.

[24] —— · ——, «The Effects of Privatisation, Restructuring and Competition on Productivity Growth in UK Public Corporations», London, Department of Economics, Queen Mary and Westfield College, University of London, *Working Paper*, n. 286, 1993.

[25] HUTCHINSON G., «Efficiency Gains Through Privatisation of UK Industries», in OTT A. - HARTLEY K. (eds.), *Privatisation and Economic Efficiency: A Comparative Analysis of Development and Developing Countries*, Aldershot, Edward Elgar, 1991.

[26] JACKSON P.M., «Management Techniques in the UK Public Sector», *International Review of Administrative Sciences*, vol. 54, 1988, pp. 247-66.

[27] ——, «The New Public Sector Management: Surrogate Competition and Contracting Out», in JACKSON P.M. - PRICE C.M. (eds.), *Privatisation and Regulation*, London, Longman, 1994.

[28] ——, «Reflections on Performance Measurement in Public Service Organisations», in JACKSON P.M. (ed.), *Measures for Success in the Public Sector*, London, CIPFA, Public Finance Foundation, 1995.

[29] KAY J.A. - SILBERSTON Z.A., «The New Industrial Policy - Privatisation and Competition», *Midland Bank Review*, Summer 1984, pp. 8-16.

[30] LE GRAND J., «Quasi Markets and Social Policy», *Economic Journal*, Sep. 1991, pp. 1256-67.

[31] LEIBENSTEIN H., «Allocative Efficiency vs X-Efficiency», *American Economic Review*, vol. 56, 1966, pp. 392-415.

[32] MARTIN S. - PARKER D., «Privatisation and Economic Performance Throughout the UK Business Cycle», *Managerial and Decision Economics*, vol. 16, 1995, pp. 225-37.

[33] METCALFE L. - RICHARDS S., *Improving Public Management*, London, Sage, 1990.

[34] MILIBAND R., *The State in Capitalist Society*, London, Quartet Books, 1969.

[35] MILLWARD R., «The Comparative Performance of Public and Private Ownership», in ROLL E. (ed.), *The Mixed Economy*, London, Macmillan, 1982.

[36] MILLWARD R. - PARKER D., «Public and Private Enterprise: Comparative Behaviour and Relative Efficiency», in MILLWARD R. (ed.), *Public Sector Economics*, London, Longman, 1983.

[37] MOORE J., *Privatisation in the UK*, London, Aims of Industry, 1986.

[38] ——, «British Privatisation: Taking Capitalism to the People», *Harvard Business Review*, Jan.-Feb. 1992, pp. 115-24.

[39] NATIONAL AUDIT OFFICE, *Department of the Environment: Sale of Water Authorities in England and Wales*, London, HMSO, 1992.

[40] NISKANEN W.A., *Bureaucracy and Representative Government*, New York, Aldine Atherton 1971, Aldershot, Edward Elgar, 1995.

[41] O'CONNOR J., *The Fiscal Crisis of the State*, Helsinki, St Martins Press, 1973.

[42] POSNER M., «Privatisation: the Frontier Between Public and Private», *Policy Studies*, vol. 5, 1984, pp. 22-32.

[43] TULLOCK G., *The Politics of Bureaucracy*, Washington (DC), Public Affairs Press, 1967.

[44] STIGLER G., «The Theory of Economic Regulation», *Bell Journal of Economics and Management Science*, vol. 1, 1971.

[45] STIGLITZ J.E., «Credit Markets and the Control of Capital», *Journal of Money, Credit and Banking*, n. 17, 1985, pp. 133-52.

[46] VICKERS J. - YARROW G., *Privatisation an Economic Analysis*, Cambridge (Mass), MIT Press, 1988.

[47] WEYMAN-JONES T., «Deregulation», in JACKSON P.M. - PRICE C.M. (eds.), *Privatisation and Regulation*, London, Longman, 1994.

[48] WILLIAMS W., *Washington, Westminster and Whitehall*, Cambridge, Cambridge University Press, 1988.

[49] WILLIAMSON O.E., *The Economics of Discretionary Behaviour*, Engelwood Cliffs (NJ), Prentice Hall, 1964.

[50] — —, *Markets and Hierarchies*, London, Free Press, 1975.

[51] YARROW G., «Privatisation in Theory and Practice», *Economic Policy*, vol. 2, Apr. 1986.

An Attempt to End Monopoly: the Privatisation of the UK Electricity Industry

Franco A. Grassini
LUISS «Guido Carli», Roma

1. - Introduction

Together with Judge Greenen's famous ruling of 1984 which led to the dismemberment of ATT, the privatisation of the UK electricity industry is perhaps one of the most important attempts to radically modify a sector which had hitherto enjoyed a monopoly regime. The attempt therefore merits study, even though the period which has passed since the decisions (the *White Paper Privatising Electicity* was published in 1988 and the implementation provisions, the *Energy Act*, came out in 1989) is too short to allow conclusions to be drawn about a process — that of introducing competition — which was conceived of as gradual from the very outset. The problems to be examined beside being numerous and very complex should be treated in a variety of approaches so much so that they require a certain amount of caution. They range from the standard problem of the theory of the firm which considers the advantages and disadvantages of the market versus a hierarchal system, to oligopolistic behaviour, the main issue of industrial economics, and financial, regulatory policy and ecological questions.

Undaunted, LUISS's GRIF set out to analyse the problem (Grassini - Paniccia - Martoccia [5]). The present paper, which is based largely, though not solely, on this analysis, seeks to highlight the

---

N.B.: the numbers in square brackets refer to the Bibliography at the end of the paper.

fundamental aspects of the privatisation. The second section will attempt to illustrate the structural changes which have taken place. The third section will summarise the regulatory problems that arose in the electricity industry although the question of prices will be dealt with in the fourth section which is dedicated to this issue and competition. The fifth section will examine the recent *White Paper* on the privatisation of the nuclear power industry to draw some considerations on the UK government's policies. Finally, the sixth section will seek to draw some tentative conclusions which will be headed as general considerations and allow us to touch upon some aspects not examined in the other sections.

2. - The New Structure

From a structural viewpoint, the UK electricity industry has undergone considerable change. Before privatisation the Central Electricity Generating Board (CEGB) was responsible for electricity production and transmission in the UK and 12 Area Boards were responsible for distribution in their respective areas. There were two independent electricity bodies for Scotland, the North of Scotland Hydro-electric Board (NSHEB) and the South of Scotland Electricity Board (SSEB), and one in Northern Ireland. There was also a governmental body, the Electricity Council, which was responsible for coordination, strategic planning and decisions regarding many prices, including, importantly, those charged by CEGB to the Area Boards. In addition, the CEGB enjoyed a dominant position, even though the 1983 *Energy Act* had deprived it of its legal monopoly on electricity generation. The new provisions had, in fact, been rendered inoperative via the dual expedient of not specifying the economic terms under which any new private producers would have access to the high-voltage transmission network (the so-called «grid») and by modifying the charges practised by the CEGB to the Area Boards, increasing the fixed quota and reducing the variable quota (the «avoidable costs» which any potential new suppliers would have had to take into account). Under the 1989 *Energy Act*, the CEGB was divided into four separate companies: National Power, which took charge of some

2/3rds of CEGB's non-nuclear power stations, Power Generation which took charge of the remaining 1/3rd of non-nuclear power stations, Nuclear Power which took charge of all nuclear power stations, and the National Grid Company (NGC) which took over the national high-voltage transmission network.

The traditional power stations were unequally shared between Power Generation and National Power because the latter was to have taken over all the nuclear power stations with their unknown decommissioning, waste disposal and ecological costs and hence it was considered that they could be privatised only within the ambit of a big company. The financial markets however, made clear their perplexity concerning the assumption of such risks and thus it was decided to transfer the nuclear plants to an ad hoc company which, as we shall see, was scheduled for privatisation in 1996, leaving the traditional power stations shared between the two players as envisioned by the original design.

As regards NGC, its demerger from CEGB derived from the assumption that all forms of vertical integration had to be broken to end the monopoly. NGC's shares were assigned to the former Area Boards, which were transformed into Regional Electricity Companies (RECs). The new RECs were obliged to satisfy all «reasonable» requests for electricity in their areas and at the same time they were granted a temporary monopoly on clients who used less than 100 Kw until 1998 while until 1994 the monopoly also included clients who consumed up to 1 MW. The RECs are particularly active in the electricity supply market, i.e., the purchasing of electricity and its retail outside their own areas to big users. They can take — and they have made abundant use of this right — stakes in independent electricity producers from whom they cannot acquire more than 15% of their supply needs. Finally, the household electrical appliance retail businesses «inherited» from the Area Boards account for an important proportion of turnover for some RECs. Some analysts believe that NGC was assigned to the RECs because, being a new company it was not easy to sell (Armstrong - Cowan - Vickers [1]).This belief would appear to be borne out by the circumstance, which we will also deal with later, that in 1995 the privatisation of NGC appears imminent, now that it has a few years of operations to its credit.

The NGC has been entrusted with some very important tasks, namely acting as a central dispatcher, i.e., deciding from which power plants to obtain the electricity for the national grid, to manage — via its subsidiaries — the Pool, the spot market for electricity, and to ensure the reliability and security of the high-voltage transmission network.

To complete our overview of the new structure of the UK electricity industry, we would point out that an integral part of the industry is the Office of Electricity Regulation (Offer) which furnishes technical support to the Director General of Electricity Supply (DGES), Professor Stephen Littlechild, who has held the post since its institution in 1989, being reconfirmed in 1993. Professor Stephen Littlechild has played a fundamental theoretical and practical role in introducing the $P = RPI - X$ price cap formula to the UK. The issue of regulation will be dealt with in greater detail in Section 3.

It should be noted that the decision to create a narrow oligopoly with, in addition, a clear leader as regards production, has engendered much perplexity. Some economists, even with all the caveats necessary for these types of calculations, have estimated that adopting a model similar to the UK's, a symmetric duopoly would have given rise to an equilibrium price some 80% higher than that which would have been obtained with prices equal to marginal costs, while under a five-producer oligopoly equilibrium prices would have approached marginal costs (Green R.I. - Newbury D.M. [6]). The reality is somewhat more complicated as there were three producers, they grew in post-privatisation period and there is also Electricité de France and the two Scottish companies which account for some 10% of supply to UK.

As the ownership arrangements are an integral part of the structure, it should be noted that the 12 RECs were privatised in December 1990, raising some £8 million for the UK Treasury, 60% of National Power and Power Generation were privatised in March 1991 raising £2.2 billion. The Treasury sold its remaining 40% in both companies in March 1995 for £4 billion.

Since privatisation, most of the RECs have diversified into related sectors such as gas distribution, stakes in independent producers and in some cases also financial activities (Caroli [3]).

3. - Regulation

We noted above that Offer and DGES are an integral part of the UK electricity industry's structure and we shall now examine some of their specific characteristics.

First of all, unlike most other countries in the world, the Regulator in the UK is a single person and not a commission which has to mediate between its components. This circumstance is particularly important because the terms of the legislation are somewhat broad and the Regulator thus has considerable freedom of interpretation and implementation. As noted by Martoccia ([8]): «The factors which have led to the discretionary nature of the *modus operandi* of these regulatory bodies lie in an almost inexistent supervisory structure and in the low level of impact of any legal reviews of the working of the bodies by the administrative judicial authorities». In fact, the Regulator has the power to negotiate with the companies he regulates with the threat, if no agreement is reached, of referral to the Monopolies and Mergers Commission (MMC). The regulated companies also have the right to turn to the MMC should they not be satisfied with the Regulator's decisions. To date, there has been only one case, in 1995, when a producer, Scottish Hydroelectric, availed itself of this right and it was a net beneficiary as the MMC's recommendations will lead to an improvement in revenues (Monopoly and Mergers Commission [11]).

The only power proper of the Regulator is the determination of the price cap. Nonetheless, perhaps by virtue of the weight that individual persons can have, and perhaps because an investigation by the MMC could lead to substantial structural measures, negotiations have a quite significant impact. This was seen in 1994 when National Power and Power Generation agreed to the Regulator's invitation to negotiate the sale or disposal of respectively 4000 and 2000 MW of generating capacity (equal to six power stations in proportion to the companies' respective capacity) within two years to allow the doubling of the share of production of independent producers and hence facilitate the attainment of near-competitive prices.

On this occasion, the Regulator obtained also the agreement and hence the commitment of the two big generating companies to introduce in the following two years supply prices for the Pool which led to a reduction of 7% vis-à-vis the prices recorded in the previous two-year period.

As can be seen, even though applied by agreement, the Regulator's powers can have a significant impact.

In March 1995, the DGES's announcement that he intended to carry out a new review of the RECs' prices, a mere six months after he had decided prices which were to have remained in force for three years, caused an outcry and was the subject of much discussion. It is debatable whether the timing of the announcement was appropriate coinciding as it did with the closing of the sale of the 40% of Power Generation and National Power still held by the Treasury, a sale which raised a further £4 billion for the Treasury. Even though the announcement concerned the RECs and not the two generating companies, the latters' shares immediately fell by 17% although they subsequently rose to above the issue price. Nonetheless, debate continues in the UK as to whether the governement was guilty of insider trading (an offence which is normally applied to persons and for which the Crown cannot be accused under English law) as it had withheld information from the public. Professor Stephen Littlechild stated he had notified the Treasury of his intention to carry out a price review at the end of February 1995.

It is particularly significant that the announcement and the subsequent decision of July 1995, which we shall deal with below, were brought about because one of the RECs, Northern Electric, had fought off a takeover bid from a conglomerate with no electricity interests by offering its shareholders buy-backs and other sweeteners which indicated that its financial health was considerably better than generally thought. This decision underscores on the one hand the independence of Professor Stephen Littlechild (who would appear to have made his announcement when the Treasury decided to proceed with the offer despite having being informed of the situation by the DGES) and on the other that the information asymmetry between the regulated body and the Regulator is one of the most critical problems which await solution, if such is ever possible. It should also be emphasised that on more than one occasion when exercising his power, Professor Littlechild had demonstrated his unwillingness to create turbulence on the financial markets. As the DGES himself has stated: «if the Regulator continuously intervenes in the activities of a company, there will be an adverse effect on the incentives for that company to improve efficiency and reduce costs. But, above all, the company in question may be perceived as being subject to an excessive level of regulatory risk and as a result investors may require higher returns — i.e., in the cost of the company's capital — and hence users may in the long term pay higher prices» (quoted by Paniccia in [13]).

A final observation regarding regulation is called for. There is considerable literature (Stigler [16]; Posner [15]; Pelzman [14]) which maintains that the Regulator is a hostage of the regulated body as a result of information asymmetry, the more charitable interpretation, or specific interests, the less charitable interpretation. In the case of the UK electricity industry it would not appear that this has come about to date. The author is unable to state whether this is a result of the relatively short period of time that has passed, of the personality of Professor Littlechild, of the Anglo-Saxon tradition or of the fact that, albeit with considerable discretionary powers, there is always the MMC which could intervene.

4. - Prices and Competition

The most conspicuous and bold innovation of the reform of the UK electricity industry was the creation of the Pool, a market in which prices are formed on the basis of supply and demand meeting, albeit while taking into account the technical characteristics of electrical energy, which is a good that cannot be conserved and for which interruptions in supply engender serious damage.

Most electrical energy is traded on the basis of long-term contracts which contain at least a clause which allows for adjustment to the prices of the primary energy source and only part via the Pool. In the pool, producers each day offer the prices for each half-hour the following day and the NGC lays down a merit order and also the purchase price for each half-hour based on the estimate of the demand which is called the system marginal price (*SMP*). Nevertheless, as the forecasts cannot take into account possible demand peaks or power breakdowns, the pool purchase price takes account of the loss of load probability (*LOLP*) and its cost to the user, the value of lost load (*VOLL*). Hence the pool purchase price (*PPP*) is:

$$PPP = SMP + LOLP(VOLL - SMP)$$

The Pool obviously adds to *PPP* a margin, called uplift, which takes into account its own costs and also the fact that vis-à-vis the merit order on which the *SMP* is based there are plants which are called upon to supply energy even if the offer price is above the chosen *SMP* and furthermore, some plants may be excluded from the supply as a result of grid load and their location.

While *VOLL* is determined administratively, all the other prices are free but subject to a limit, the price cap laid down by the Regulator using the formula $P = RPI - X$ which allows the companies not to transfer all the efficiency gains, spurs them to achieve specific targets and avoids the inconveniences of rate of return regulation even though, as has been perceptively pointed out in theoretical literature «If the price cap reviews are carried out as those in a rate return regulation system, the distinction between the two systems becomes blurred» (Train [17]).

With regard to the price cap, it should be pointed out that while for the generating companies it is applied to the average price of KWh weighted in relation to both the amount sold and the prices practised for the various half-hour periods (obviously the two weighting criteria give rise to two different results and hence there is a dual ceiling), for the RECs the average price is weighted on the basis of four different classes of users and also contains an element which introduces an allowed dispersion standard and one which rewards, but only for a limited period, improvements achieved over time. In addition, the formula adopted for the RECs allows them to transfer costs which lie beyond their control and in particular the amount borne by the user for the purchase, to which the generating companies are obliged in the initial post-privatisation period, of specific quantities of UK coal at prices above international prices and for other renewable sources of which nuclear energy is the most important. All these expedients and adaptations of the pure formula allow to attenuate, but not completely eliminate, one of the major limits of price caps based on average prices. These limits, in order to permit, as considered normally opportune, a certain amount of flexibility allow price discrimination and also a certain amount of cross-subsidies. On this issue, it should be recalled that in the UK the principle of equal electricity prices for the same power and consumption on a national base has never existed. In the year preceding privatisation, prices for a standard domestic user varied by up to 14% between the more and less favoured areas, after privatisation this spread rose to 18% in the period 1993-1994.

The prices for the transmission of electrical energy by NGC are also subject to price cap formulas. There are, moreover, considerable doubts concerning the economic rationality of a system of prices proposed by NGC and approved with some modifications by the Regulator in 1992 based on additional investments and the relative maintenance costs needed to cope with demand peaks and grid safety and maintenance costs without taking into account the electricity losses and the constraints which the capacity of the network imposes on the use of some power plants which would not otherwise have been selected by the merit orders (Armstrong - Cowan - Vickers [1]). Furthermore, a private company obviously seeks to maximise its profit and does not aim, or if it does only to a secondary extent, to maximise social welfare even though its position at the heart of the electricity system is fundamental from this viewpoint. In particular, it would not appear that NGC's tariffs provide an incentive for the location of new power stations in those areas of the UK which have none or few as generating capacity is concentrated in the North and consumption in the South. It should also be pointed out that one of the main costs of a network, namely energy losses, are the result of physical laws which can lead to situations which are, for an economist, paradoxical: increases in the amount introduced into the grid at specific points can reduce the losses, so that the marginal cost is negative. In such a situation, the quest for economically rational prices is rather arduous.

Without embarking on a detailed analysis, also because the various sources do not always coincide, one can state that after the considerable increases in the period immediately preceding privatisation and in the first few years after privatisation electricity prices in the UK have fallen in real terms for almost all categories of users, with the exception of big users (who however enjoyed a privileged regime), in 1993-1994, precisely when the first period of the application of the price cap formula laid down by the Regulator was approaching expiry. The price reductions the RECs will have to introduce following the Regulator's July 1995 decisions mentioned above are quite big. In fact, unless any of the companies appeal to the MMC, which the specialised press appears to think highly unlikely, Professor Littlechild laid down that X in the formula $P = RPI - X$ should be set at 3% starting from the tax year 1997-1998 until 1999-2000 for all RECs. This on top of the reductions which differed from company to company for the tax years 1995-1996 and 1996-1997. Overall, the reductions in real terms for the entire period in question should range from a minimum of 27% for two RECs to a maximum of 34% for one REC (by coincidence Northern Electricity, whose sweeteners aimed at rebutting a takeover bid engendered the price review). The *Financial Times* (on 7 July 1995) estimated that the losses for the RECs (or perhaps more correctly the benefits for the users) would amount to £1.25 billion.

It should be emphasised that the price reductions are not the result of increased competition but rather of the existence of a regulatory system. In any case the Pool has not functioned as a perfect market in which prices equal marginal costs. On the contrary, the two big generating companies, National Power and Power Generation, as Offer itself recognised in its analysis published at end-1992, «have a substantial market power which they have exercised in a significant manner» (Offer [12]). In reality, this market power has been wielded in various ways. One of these is to declare that some power stations are not available on the supply day and thus obtain an increase in the production capacity factor, only to declare the stations available the following day. Another is to eliminate production capacity. The Regulator has even called on generating companies not to close certain power stations but to put them up for sale in the hope (which had still to materialise when GRIF carried out its study) that another player may be interested in acquiring them.

Yet another, which is very probable though yet to be proved, is that electricity future contracts have been strategically deployed to reduce the Pool's spot prices, which are those most visible for third parties, and hence act as a deterrent to the entry of new producers (Martoccia [9]). It should be recalled that Offer has recognised that the average avoidable costs (understood as the outlay costs for obtaining a specific level of production) of National Power and Power Generation in the first period of the Pool were in excess of those practised on average and this could be interpreted not as a contradiction, as some (Armstrong - Cowan - Vickers [1]) have already done, but rather as proof of strategic behaviour. Strategic behaviour which was facilitated by the fact that in reality the Pool prices are applied only to a small part of the electricity sold for two reasons: firstly because within the Pool most of the transactions are covered by «difference contracts» and secondly because, as noted above, the big users — those with a capacity in excess of 1 MW up to April 1994 and in excess of 100 KW after that date — do not pass through the Pool.

Two observations should be made as regards new generating capacity. Firstly, almost all the investments in this ambit have been for combined-cycle gas-fired power plants which have a relatively short construction time (circa 3 years), require less capital investment than other types of power plants with a similar capacity, have considerable operational flexibility, are ecologically clean and — at least while North Sea gas is still available — have low fuel costs.

Secondly, it is by no means certain that the new capacity will be efficient from the viewpoint of social welfare. It may have been induced by the existence of oligopolistic prices which were insufficiently controlled by the Regulator, or by moves on the part of the RECs toward vertical integration. Furthermore, it could be included among private capital's expectations of premiums as a result of the risk deriving from excessive regulation. Some authoritative economists have even mooted that «the prices of factors — fuel and capital costs — may not accurately reflect the true costs of the resources (in other words the price signals may be wrong)». (Armstrong - Cowan - Vickers [1]).

The situation is however fluid: in the first place the dominant position of National Power and Power Generation will diminish in relative terms as a result of the starting up of production in February 1995 of a new nuclear power plant (Sizewell B) which will lift nuclear energy's share of the market to 18% of installed capacity. In the second place the afore-mentioned closure of numerous plants, the upcoming sale of plants with a capacity of 6000 MW (equal to just over 10% of their total capacity) will reduce the market share of the two leading producers. In the third place the entry of new independent producers, which at end-1994 accounted for circa 6% of generating installed capacity, is destined to increase in view of the number of power plants under construction. Finally the futures market could be made more transparent, with a greater number of players, and have an influence on competition.

The upshot of all this is that it is extremely difficult to say whether the situation that has *de facto* existed to date, substantially that of a duopoly, will continue in the future or whether the degree of concentration of the oligopoly will give rise to strategic behaviour and/or forms of implicit collusion.

The supply market, where electricity is purchased from the producers and resold to big users, is, on the other hand, by and large competitive. Many RECs operate in this market, often outside their geographical «home» base. In terms of turnover, this type of operation accounts for the main part of RECs' business, but its contribution to operating profits is low, as should be the case with a very competitive market (Caroli [3]).

However, it is justified to question whether effective competition can exist in what will be, until 1998, a legal monopoly of the RECs. It is true that the meter market has been liberalised so that the user can own a meter and this leads one to assume that RECs will have to transport electricity for third parties, but the prices have still to be decided and one can only conclude that the attention to financial equilibrium of the companies that has prevailed to date will continue, even though — as noted above — with his latest price review, the Regulator has all but overturned the previous approach and has not hesitated to make announcements concerning the price review to the dismay of the financial markets that sent the very signals that induced the Regulator to launch the review.

On the issue of signals from companies, it is undoubtedly significant that in the situation of uncertainty between the afore-mentioned announcement by Professor Littlechild and his decision, one of the RECs, Seeboard, on 6 June 1995 announced unbudgeted savings of £30 million (equal to circa 3.5% of revenues) and the allocation of 2/3rds of this amount to reduce prices starting October 1995 and 1/3rd to increase dividends. The amount in question increases dividends by more than 30%, while, for domestic users, Seeboard calculates that the impact is equivalent to the Regulator having reduced X in the price cap formula from 2% to 5% (as noted above in the end X was set at 3%). Such an initiative testifies that the previous formula adopted by the Regulator had left space for lower prices, and hence confirms the opportuneness of Professor Littlechild's initiative, and also demonstrates autonomous behaviour on the part of the individual RECs. It is true that the RECs compete only in the supply market, nevertheless, their small number does not in theory exclude collusive behaviour as regards common interests and hence the confirmation of independent choices is not without importance, even though the behaviour of only one of the companies can be explained away as that of a maverick.

5. - Privatisation of the Nuclear Power Industry

We have already touched on the fact that the state transferred the twelve nuclear power stations in England to Nuclear Electricity and the three nuclear power stations in Scotland to Scottish Nuclear in view of the City's disinclination to acquire shares in generating companies with nuclear-fired stations.

In May 1995, the government laid before Parliament a *White Paper* (Department of Trade and Industry [4]) which outlined its policy and announced its intention to privatise in 1996 part of the two nuclear power companies grouping them under a single holding while leaving the older, Magnox, power stations to another state company, British Nuclear Fuels.

There were several reasons why the privatisation of the main nuclear power stations is considered possible in 1995 when this was not the case only a few years before. First and foremost, the consistent improvement in their operating costs. Operating costs at Nuclear Electric, which owns the older Magnox stations, fell from 5.2p per KWh in 1989-1990 to 2.7p per KWh in 1995-1996. The percentage improvements achieved by Scottish Nuclear, which closed its only Magnox station, were lower but in 1994-1995 its operating costs per KWh were 2.2p. Significantly, for the financial year 1994-1995 ending 31 March, Nuclear Electric posted a profit after tax (but gross of the nuclear energy surcharge due to terminate in 1996) of £1.2 billion (without the surcharge the company would have posted a loss of £33 million), a 24% reduction in operating costs and a 12% increase in productivity against the previous financial year.

We do not intend to examine these problems here, merely to highlight two aspects of this proposed privatisation.

The first is that it would not appear that significant economies of scale can be achieved by placing the two companies to be privatised under the control of a single holding. Neither would it appear that the risks the companies to be privatised are likely to face (which are, according to the government's advisers, changes in the electricity prices, the technical risks of lower-than-expected production and technical or normative risks which increase the decommissioning costs for nuclear power stations) can be more easily covered by a company with more power stations. In reality, economies of scale could be achieved, as the French experience teaches, only by building a series of power stations of the same type. As the UK government's *White Paper* states that the UK would not need new nuclear power stations in the near future, the doubt expressed in the *Financial Times* editorial of 10 May 1995, namely that the two companies may be worth more individually than together thanks to «their capacity to obtain higher prices from users by virtue of their market power», appears founded. In other terms, as it appears likely that the revenues from the privatisation of the nuclear power stations may be used to reduce taxes ahead of a general election, there is the suspicion that political reasons may prevail over reasons of competition.

The second aspect to be highlighted is the intent of the UK government to eliminate in 1996 the subsidies from which the UK coal industry, until 1993, and the nuclear power industry have benefited. Subsidies which, as a result of privatisation, are no longer borne by the Treasury but by the users. However, the subsidies for alternative energy will remain.

This intent is fully in line with the desire to leave any decisions regarding energy supplies to the market. On this issue, it is worth drawing attention to the profound difference between this position, upheld in the UK government's *White Paper*, and the opposing position of the French government, which in a report dedicated to the reform of the electricity and gas industry, stated that public powers had the duty to ensure «the satisfaction of certain general interests considered priority» which include «continuity, that is to say security, of supply» which «implies a continuous policy of investment» (*Rapport du Groupe de Travail* [10]). The other two obligations that arise, according to the document just cited, from the safeguarding of the general interest are the universal service provision (i.e., the obligation to supply whomsoever makes a such a request anywhere in France), and equality of treatment regardless of geographical location. The stance of the UK government on nuclear power is quite different, it poses the question whether the country's energy sources are sufficiently diversified and secure and also asks what ecological impact and consequences for UK industry the building of new nuclear power stations in the UK would have and whether they should be financed by private capital. Only after having replied to these questions and proved to its satisfaction (this is not the place to deal with the merit of the arguments, some aspects of which the author of this paper considers dubious) that the situation should not engender concern, the UK government affirms its faith in the market and in the latter's capacity to also ensure its future electricity needs from different sources. In other words, while, as we noted above, political considerations have been of crucial importance in many decisions, as regards energy policy which has been criticised by several observers, there is an attention to the *de facto* situations which would probably allow appropriate measures to be taken should it be concluded that the UK's energy supply was being threatened by new facts. It cannot be ignored, for example, that new power stations require long building times and that the capacities envisioned by the markets can be influenced by risk considerations which do not always coincide with the general interest.

6. - General Considerations

As pointed out in the *Introduction*, both the short period of time which has passed since privatisation and the complexity of the problems it has engendered make it impossible to draw specific and final conclusions. Moreover, while (1995 summer) the present paper is being printed, the mentioned bid for Northern Electric has elapsed. There are bids to acquire RECs by outsiders. Probably the most important one, from our point of view, is that by one of the two vertically integrated Scottish electric companies. It is still unknown what the reaction of the Regulator, the Monopolies and Mergers Commission, the Government and the shareholder will be. If the proposed acquisitions or mergers are fulfilled, the entire structure of the English electricity industry shall be a few vertically integrated enterprises shall survive. Nonetheless, the exploration above enables us to formulate some observations of a general nature concerning what has happened up to now.

The first is that, contrary to common assumptions, the transition from an institutional monopoly (and we use this term to emphasise that the monopoly of the electricity industry in the UK was guaranteed not only by some characteristics of natural monopoly but also by the law) to a competitive market has yet to take place in the English electricity industry. This is in part the result of the structure of concentrated oligopoly with which the generating companies were endowed, perhaps to facilitate their sale. In part probably because such wide-ranging changes require rather long periods of time, even in situations such as that existing in the UK where there were numerous players (the Area Boards and the Scottish companies) which could be sold as they had a history and a management with a proven track record. It is significant that the management of the Area Boards pushed for privatisation while the management of the Central Electricity Generating Board was opposed. More recently, Nuclear Electric and Scottish Nuclear have come out in favour of privatisation. The management's pro-privatisation stance should perhaps be linked to a criticism which was made when it took complete responsibility for management, namely that it excessively boosted remuneration. It is significant that the Major government, after having stated that the question of the remuneration of top management of private companies is not its concern, sponsored the Greenbury committee to investigate this issue and the committee's final report criticises some elements of the remuneration structure of directors of the electricity companies (*Financial Times*, 18 July 1995).

A second general observation concerns the importance of political or ideological choices in the privatisation process of the UK electricity industry (and perhaps also in other sectors). The example cited above of the planned privatisation of the nuclear power industry is only one of the many encountered by those who study this problem. It is obvious that it is not the economist's job to give value judgements, but one cannot avoid underscoring that many choices have been influenced by them.

On this matter, it is probable that if one did analyse the results achieved to date, one would conclude that the main beneficiaries have been those who bought shares when the industry was privatised. As regards the other categories of stakeholders, the electricity users have had, with the afore-mentioned exception of the big users, cheaper prices in real terms when comparison is made with the pre-privatisation years and the more recent past, mainly as a result of the reduction of primary fuel costs and intervention by the Regulator.

The gains for shareholders are demonstrated by the fact that the 12 RECs were sold for £8 billion when they were privatised in 1990 while in early-July 1995 they had a stock market capitalisation of £13.7 billion and still increasing later. On 12 July 1995, after Professor Littlechild's review, their stock market capitalisation stood at £15.2 billion. Two facts should be emphasised in this regard. In addition to the Regulator's decision as mentioned above a number of bids for RECs have been advanced and others are expected. The acquisitions are facilitated by the upcoming expiry of the government's golden share. Acquisitions and mergers could, in theory, drastically restructure the UK electricity industry. The second circumstance to which attention should be drawn is that the shares of the RECs, at least since 1993, outperformed the stock market in general and the shares of those thought possible targets for predators outperformed their peers, albeit with considerable oscillations. The stability of cash flow produced by a natural monopoly and capital returns in the order of 7%

permitted by the controlling authorities (Monopoli and Mergers Commission [11]) only enhance the RECs' attraction for the financial markets.

Equally important, for an overall evaluation of the privatisation, is the RECs' planned sale of the NGC scheduled for autumn-1995. When privatised, the RECs had NGC on their balance sheets for a book value of £1.2 billion, while the proposed offer price is much higher (the UK press gives figures of between £3-4 billion). The Major government is pressuring the RECs to allocate part of the surplus to customers as a bonus or similar, while in a letter to a Labour MP, the Comptroller and Auditor General did not rule out an investigation into the issue. It is interesting to note that both the government and the Comptroller are deploying the leverage acquired from the golden share still in public hands. For privatised companies, as far as is known, this is the first time this has occurred. Nonetheless, the impression is that this tool is used as a means of pressure rather than being deployed formally.

A third general observation concerns the functioning of the regulatory arrangement: the information asymmetries between the managers and the regulator are uneliminable. Hence, whenever an element of natural monopoly persists, as in the specific case of electricity transmission and distribution, it is impossible to obtain that optimal situation to which economists aspire. And from this viewpoint, it is significant that at least in this initial period the hope expressed by Beesley and Littlechild [2] prior to privatisation, namely that «a stricter competition policy is preferable to a rate of return regulation, efficiency controls and related forms of wet-nursing by the state», has not been realised.

As an authority such as Khan [7] suggests, empirical solutions rather than rules should be aimed at, but this is anything but easy in democratic societies which demand both transparency and perfection. All this leads to the existence of regulatory risks which the financial markets may evaluate differently and may lead to considerable uncertainty in the offer prices of the companies to be privatised. This, coupled with the fact that the financial intermediaries who manage the placement have a natural tendency to undervalue the shares to be placed, makes it difficult to attribute to public utility companies to be privatised a price that proves congruous over time. Perhaps in the case of the UK electricity industry there was a bias in one direction because the momentum for the privatisation of the electricity industry derived not only from the desire to put an end to a monopoly but because there was also a political interest to create a large number of shareholders. However, it should be borne in mind that whenever one wishes to privatise a public monopoly one has no choice but to accept a selling price that is less than that which would be attributed abstractly.

This leads us to our final consideration. As has been repeatedly stated, five years is too short a period to permit an accurate and valid judgement. This is even more true in the electricity industry, where investment has realisation times that in some cases (such as non gas-fired plants) are somewhat long and should be calculated over a much longer time horizon. Nonetheless, I believe that with all the limits the paper describes, the attempt to end the natural and legal monopoly that existed in the UK electricity industry has led to elements of dynamism in the management of the companies and dialectics between the companies and the Regulator which tend towards more efficiency and improved satisfaction for the users. It is therefore an attempt which should be carefully considered so as to adapt its lessons to other situations, in particular that in Italy.

BIBLIOGRAPHY

[1] ARMSTRONG M. - COWAN S. - VICKERS, *Regulatory Reform: Economic Analysis and British Experience*, Cambridge (Mass.), MIT Press, 1994.

[2] BEESLEY M.E. - LITTLECHILD S.C., «Privatisation, Principles, Problems and Priorities», *Lloyds Bank Review*, July 1983, reprinted in BEESLEY M.E., *Privatisation, Regulation and Deregulation*, London, Istitute of Economic Affairs or Routledge, 1992.

[3] CAROLI M., *I bilanci delle società elettriche privatizzate*, in GRASSINI, F.A. *et* AL. [5], 1995.

[4] DEPARTMENT OF TRADE AND INDUSTRY, *The Prospect for Nuclear Industry in the UK*, London, HMSO, 1995.

[5] GRASSINI F.A. - PANICCIA I. - MARTOCCIA M. - CAROLI M., *La privatizzazione dell'industria elettrica inglese*, Bologna, Il Mulino, 1995.

[6] GREEN R.I. - NEWBURY D.M., «Competition in the British Spot Market», *Journal of Political Economy*, n. 100, 1992.

[7] KAHN A.E., «Regolamentazioni e concorrenza nelle imprese di pubblica utilità: un inquadramento teorico», *L'industria*, n. 2, 1992.

[8] MARTOCCIA M., *La regolamentazione nel Regno Unito*, in GRASSINI F.A. *et* AL. [5], 1995.

[9] — —, *Il mercato a termine dell'energia elettrica*, in GRASSINI F.A. *et* AL. [5], 1995.

[10] MINISTÈRE DE L'INDUSTRIE, DES POSTES ET TELECOMMUNICATIONS ET DU COMMERCE EXTÉRIEUR. DIRECTION GÉNÉRAL DE L'ENERGIE ET DES MATÉRIES PRIMIERES, *Rapport du Groupe de Travail sur la Reforme de l'Organisation Electrique et Gazière Française*.

[11] MONOPOLY AND MERGERS COMMISSION, *Scottish Hydro-Electric PLC*, London, HMSO, 1995.

[12] OFFER *Review of Pool Price*, Offer, Birmingham, 1992.

[13] PANICCIA I., *Concorrenza e regolamentazione nell'industria elettrica inglese*, in GRASSINI F.A. *et* AL. [5], 1995.

[14] PELZMANN S., «Towards a More General Theory of Regulation», *Journal of Law and Economics*, n. 14, 1976.

[15] POSNER R., «Theories of Economic Regulation», *Bell Journal of Economics*, n. 5, 1974.

[16] STIGLER G.J., «The Theory of Economic Regulation», *Bell Journal of Economics*, vol. 2, 1971.

[17] TRAIN K.E., «Optimal Regulation - The Economic Theory of Natural Monopoly», Cambridge (Mass.) and London, MIT Press, 1991.

The European Union's Policy on the Electricity and Natural Gas Industries

Guido Cervigni *

Università Bocconi, Milano and
European University Institute, Florence

Introduction

The European Union's policy regarding the establishment of the internal market in the electricity and natural gas industries is analysed. Two strands of policies are discussed: the first directly focused on competition; the second on the development of trans-European network infrastructures, insofar as such development is regarded as a necessary condition for competition to be effective in these sectors.

The first strand is dealt with in Section 1. The objectives of the Union, as interpreted by the Commission, and the programme for the implementation of the single market in these industries are considered. The directives on the procurement procedures of public utilities, on the transparency of electricity and gas prices, on the transit of natural gas and electricity through the major systems, and the recent proposals of directives on common rules for the internal market in electricity and natural gas are analysed and discussed. The

* This paper is partially based on the work done by the authour within the project «Ricerca di Base: Regole del Mercato, Difesa della Concorrenza e Razionalità delle Politiche Industriali nel Quadro Internazionale», at the Bocconi University, Milan. The author thanks L. De Paoli, F. Amman for comments on an earlier draft. Final version submitted in July 1995.

N.B.: the numbers in square brackets refer to the Bibliography at the end of the paper.

strand of the Union's policies relating to the development of trans-European energy networks is examined in Section 2. Section 3 concludes.

1 - The Single Market of Energy

1.1 *Objectives and Constraints*

According to the Art. 7 A of the *Treaty* (former Art. 8A) the Single Market is defined as «an area without internal borders in which free movement of goods, of persons, of services, and of capital is ensured». Energy, in any form, is comprised by that definition[1].

In the Commission's working document on «the internal energy market» (EEC [11]), the integration of the Member States' energy markets is aimed at: 1) reducing the costs to provide residential and industrial customers with energy; 2) strengthening the competitiveness of the Union's energy industry; 3) increasing the security of energy supply through greater interconnection of the Member States' systems.

These results are expected to derive from greater competition and larger inter-state exchanges of energy, as far as greater co-ordination in the use of existing capacity and in the supply of new capacity are induced.

The constraints to be kept into account in establishing the internal market of energy are identified in: *a)* the «strategic» nature of the energy industries; *b)* the need to take preliminary action to eliminate the existing technical and fiscal barriers — the latter caused in particular by the heterogeneous nature of the indirect taxation regimes of these sectors amongst Member States — and to open up to competition the market of public utilities procurement; *c)* increasing social and economic cohesion as a fundamental political objective of the Union; in particular it is feared that the completion of the single

---

[1] That means, in particular, that the provisions of the European Union Treaty on free movement of goods and services (Arts. 30-36), on national monopolies of a commercial nature (Art. 37), on the abuse of dominant position competition (Art. 86), and on national exclusive rights to public interest firms (Art. 90), apply to the energy sectors. On this point see EHLERMANN C.D. [6].

market of energy could widen the differences in wealth and living standards among citizens of the Union.

The scope of the subsidiarity principle, as interpreted by the Commission, in the establishment of the single market of energy, is also explicit: the external dimension — the policies regarding the supply of energy sources from countries outside the Union and the provision of energy infrastructures by non-Union firms — is to be managed at the Union level. The powers of the national authorities are limited to safety and environmental protection, the «public service» components of the provision of energy, and the social and regional implications associated with the supply of energy.

1.2 *Price, Transparency, Procurement by Public Utilities, Transit Through Major Systems, Import and Export Freedom*

The recommendation of the Council on «the tariff structures of electricity in the European Communities» (EEC [9]) lays down principles to be followed in setting the tariffs of electricity: 1) each class of customers should be made liable for the costs to which it gives rise; 2) the adoption of two-part tariffs, one part fixed and one consumption-dependent, should be widespread; 3) promotional tariffs should not be used; 4) multi-time tariffs and interruptible clauses should be introduced; 5) the tariffs should not be used to pursue goals, such as social or industrial or macroeconomic objectives, different from that of allocative efficiency; 6) clauses providing for the update of the tariffs at regular intervals should be introduced into supply contracts.

However, the recommendation is not part of a broader project for the establishment of a single market of electricity within the Union. In particular, even though the principles laid down reflect the marginal approach, when dealing with costs any reference to a static or dynamic notion of efficiency is missing. The implementation of this recommendation by the national authorities has anyway led to very heterogeneous tariff systems among the Member States, the main common aspect being some cross-subsidisation amongst different classes of customers.

The directive on «a Community procedure to improve the transparency of gas and electricity prices charged to industrial end-users» (EEC [13]) promotes transparent pricing as a necessary condition to avoid discrimination among users and, in a more general perspective, to introduce competition within the Single Market of energy. Electricity and natural gas suppliers shall periodically communicate to the Statistical Institute of the European Communities: *a)* prices and terms of the electricity and natural gas supplies to industrial end-users, gross and net of every fiscal and para-fiscal component and «special factors» (such as those relating to interruptibility of supply); *b)* the price systems in use; *c)* the distribution of customers by consumption level.

Based on these data the Institute publishes the prices of electricity and natural gas for industrial users in the Member States and the criteria for their determination.

A first step in opening up the electricity and natural gas markets to competition is to be seen in the area of supply of generation and transmission plants, with the directive on «the procurement procedures of utilities operating in the energy, telecommunications, water and transport sector» (EEC [14])[2].

The rationale of the directive is that the lack of competition in the downstream phases of the industry induces a lack of competition in the upstream. Regarding the electricity and natural gas industries, purchases of energy sources as well as of electricity do not fall within the scope of the directive. Thus, the directive disciplines the purchases relating to the supply of transmission and distribution networks, electricity generation plants, gas storage facilities and liquefied natural gas terminals[3] — areas in which most of the purchasing has traditionally been characterised by some form of «reserve» in favour of the national firms. For the contracts falling within its scope, the directive requires and regulates a series of activities, including the publicity of tender invitations and results, the eligibility and selection rules for

---

[2] This directive has been replaced by that «co-ordinating the procurement procedures of utilities operating in the water, energy, transport, and telecommunications sectors» (EC [20]), whose contents, as regards this paper, do not differ from those of the earlier directive.

[3] The directive does not apply to some categories of independent suppliers, those whose main business in not the supply of natural gas or electricity.

candidates in the case of restricted or negotiated procedures, and the awarding criteria, in order to avoid discrimination among potential suppliers.

The directives on «the transit of electricity (EEC [15]) and gas (EEC [16]) through major systems» introduce the right of access to transmission networks by third parties, as far as it is necessary to carry out transactions involving movements of electricity or natural gas across the borders of Member States. It is made compulsory — provided it is technically feasible, economically convenient, and it does not put at risk the security of supply — to carry third parties' electricity and natural gas at fair and non-discriminatory terms. Such terms shall be negotiated by the involved transmission systems' operators, and the obligation to provide access, which is implicit, results from the possibility of recourse to the Commission in its adjudicatory capacity, a remedy being available if «the reasons of the inability to reach an agreement are insufficient or unjustified» (Art. 4).

However the impact of these directives is extremely limited, for they do not deal with the crucial issue of the direct relationships between customers and generators. In fact only the transmission systems' opertors are granted the right to negotiate the access to each others' networks; further, this takes place in a context in which the dominant organisational model, at the State level, is characterised, especially for the electricity industry, by a vertically integrated or quasi-integrated structure, and, with the exception of the United Kingdom, by a nation-wide monopoly on supply. As a consequence most of the international exchanges take place between operators who are not in competition with each other, rather it is in their common interest to maintain a system of relationships oriented to co-operation. For these reasons the implicit obligation to carry third parties' gas and electricity has probably not led to greater exchanges compared to those which would have taken place on a voluntary basis.

Finally, as far as the liberalisation of the import and export of electricity and natural gas is concerned, in 1991 the Commission opened infringement procedures against several Member States, granting legal reserves over the import and export of electricity and natural gas. Six actions against Member States for failure to fulfil an obligation in these infringement procedures were referred by the Commission to the Court of Justice in 1994. The import-export liberalisation is strictly linked to the right of access to transmission and distribution systems by third parties; since the access to the networks is essential to exercise the right to import or export electricity and natural gas, networks must by necessity be opened up once import and export are liberalised.

1.3 *Liberalisation, Network Access, Unbundling*

The directives on the transit of electricity and gas through major transmission systems, and transparent pricing, form, in the Commission's programme, the first of three stages in which the Single Market of electricity and natural gas is to be established. The second stage is the object of the Commission's proposals for directives on «common rules for the internal market in electricity and natural gas» (EEC [17]; [21] which are the amended version after the negative opinion by the Council of Ministers and a counter-project by the Parliament)[4]. The second stage would consist of: 1) the liberalisation of electricity generation; 2) the liberalisation of electricity and natural gas supply (sale and delivery), to large customers; to be attained through either a non-discriminatory licence regime, or a 'call for tender' system, to make available additional capacity (for extension and replacement); 3) the introduction, on a limited scale, of third party access (TPA) to the transmission and distribution networks; 4) the unbundling of the vertically integrated firms' activities.

Below the main provisions for the electricity sector are discussed; the last part of the section deals with the provisions for the gas sector.

Generation

Building new generation plants shall be licensed by the state on whose land the plant is to be built, using objective and non-discrimina-

---

[4] The determination of the contents of the third stage is postponed until the effects of the liberalisation introduced in the second stage are assessed.

tory criteria. Such criteria can deal also with the kind of primary sources feeding the plants. As an alternative to the licence system the Member States can opt for a «call for tender» procedure for the provision of the new capacity.

Supply and Access to the System

Only large industrial customers (those whose consumption exceed 100 GWh per year, or a lower limit set by the national authorities) and distributors can negotiate their supplies directly with the generators. In that case, in addition to the situation in which the supplier had been awarded a contract through a tender procedure, access to the transmission system shall be provided by the transmission system operator on terms resulting from a «voluntary commercial agreement» between the operator and the supplier.

Transmission System

Each Member State designates a transmission system operator, whose attributes have quasi-regulatory connotations. In particular the transmission system operator is responsible for: 1) maintaining and developing a secure, reliable and efficient transmission system; 2) dispatching the generating installations localised in its area, and managing the flows to and from the interconnected systems. The dispatch shall, as long as the contractual obligations between the transmission system operator and the independent suppliers are fulfilled, follow rules which take into account the economic merit order of the available plants (that is, minimising the total generation cost). Such rules, which are set by the national authorities, shall be non-discriminatory and shall not disturb the functioning of the internal market; 3) providing ancillary services[5].

---

[5] As far as the distribution system is concerned, provisions *mutatis mutandis* analogous to those of the transmission system apply (in particular, the distribution system operator has, in the area covered by its system, responsibilities equivalent to those of the transmission system operator, excluding those relating to dispatching; also, the distributor cannot refuse to negotiate interconnection and use of the system agreements with suppliers at non-discriminatory terms).

Customers not Supplied Through Direct Contract

Small and medium customers, who are not allowed to purchase electricity on the market, have to supply themselves from the respective local distributors, who thus enjoy a monopoly position over their «obliged» clients. However, the national authorities can impose on the local distributors universal service obligations and can regulate the tariffs charged to those final customers who are not eligible for access to the direct supply market, to protect these customers from monopoly exploitation by the distributors and to pursue social objectives, such as equalising the tariffs over given geographical areas.

Unbundling

Vertically integrated electricity firms are required to keep separated accounts for each of their businesses (accounting unbundling). In particular, if the transmission system operator is a branch of a vertically integrated firm it shall be organised as an independent, at least administratively, unit.

By comparing the initial with the amended version of the proposals of directives the compromise nature of the latter emerges. The main differences relate to:

a) the form of exercising the right of access to the transmission and distribution networks. While in the former version TPA is a sort of «pre-defined» right, whose contents are determined by the regulator, under the system envisaged in the latter version such contents are to be negotiated by the supplier and the network operator on a time by time basis. This provision, even without questioning the right of access to the networks by third parties, seems to reduce considerably the impact of TPA in terms of inducing more competition in electricity supply. When the conditions of access are regulated, as in the original version of the directive proposal, as many aspects of the transactions as possible are set *ex-ante*, by or with the approval of the regulator; such predetermination will typically lead to some form of standard contract, to which all the agreements have to conform. Instead, when access is negotiated by the interested parties, as under the provisions of the amended version of the proposal, the only bounds to the outcome of the negotiation are those implicitly deriving from the control activity by the authority in charge of overseeing the industry, and from the available recourse procedures.

b) supply of generation plants and network lines. In the first proposal the licence system only is provided for. The «call for tender» system, as an alternative, is introduced in the amended version.

c) unbundling. In the former proposal it is requested that both the accounts and the organisation are kept separate in vertically integrated firms, while in the amended proposal only the weaker form of unbundling, the account separation, is requested.

As a result the general orientation of the proposal is changed. While a definite idea of the organisation of the electricity industry, basically modelled on that recently introduced in the United Kingdom[6], underlies the first version of the proposal, this is no longer the case in the next version. In the amended proposal the focus is moved from the objective of inducing competition in supply to that of inducing competition in generation. The range of the institutional arrangements amongst which the national authorities can choose is widened, while the directive is silent regarding a greater area of issues.

As far as the general organisation of the national electricity industries is concerned, each of the alternatives provided for in the directive proposal, licensing and tender procedure, implies specific forms of co-ordination which are not immediately compatible with each other. On the one hand, a system in which the right to supply is granted by a tender procedure[7], leads to an organisation centred on one operator which organises the tender procedure for supplying the customers. The evolution of the system is determined by the planning activity of the authority who promotes the invitations to tender, and the incentive to invest in new plants is given by the fact that the sale of the electricity which is the object of the awarded tender is guaranteed. There are two main implications. First, since it is the planner which sets the «required» additional capacity, the existing generation plans

---

[6] See VICKERS J. - YARROW G. [29], ARMSTRONG *et* AL. [1].

[7] As will be emphasised below, a «pure» tender system is not compatible with the provisions of the directive proposal; here the reference to such model is made for simplicity.

are not exposed to competition until the planner decides they have to be replaced. Competition is thus limited to a narrow subset of the generation capacity. Second, since the tender procedure presupposes that the winner of the tender is guaranteed to sell, developing competition in generation through a tender system requires that competition be inhibited in supply. In a tender system the market risk is entirely borne by the counter-party to the tenderer awarded the generation contract, namely the tender promoter which, in order to translate that risk onto the customers, must serve a captive market. On the other hand, in an authorisation regime generators and non-generator suppliers can supply directly the customers. The very logic underlying this organisational model is radically different from that underlying a tender system in two major respects. First, competition in generation is driven, instead of being hampered, by competition in supply, further, generation competition in generation is induced among all existing and newey connected plants. Second, in an authorisation regime the adjustment to the demand of the generation set — as number, type, and localisation of the plants — is entrusted to the signalling function of the market price. Within a pool sysem like that of the United Kingdom, for example, an uplift is applied, in setting the price on the wholesale spot market, to the system marginal cost[8] whenever the demand brings the generation capacity close to its full utilisation level. When that takes place for sufficiently long periods a rent accrues to the available plants, which makes the investment in additional generation capacity convenient[9]. Even though the relationship between the value of the uplift and the degree of capacity utilisation is a matter for regulatory decision, the process is essentially driven by a market mechanism[10]. The market risk is borne by the generators, who share it with customers through the use of long-term supply contracts. Further problems arise from the fact that, if a model

---

[8] The system marginal cost is meant to be the marginal cost evaluated with respect to all available generating facilities.

[9] In this model technical progress and changes of the relative price of the primary sources stimulate investment in new capacity by creating a gap between the system marginal cost and the marginal cost of the new plants.

[10] Further, the value of the uplift can be determined on strong theoretical grounds, since the uplift is directly related to the notion of curtailment premium in the theory of peak-load princing.

where supply is liberalised and the authorisation system is applied to all the generation plans is compatible with the provisions of the directive, this does not hold for a system where winning a tender is the only way to enter the generation market[11], so that a single operator intermediates all the electricity exchanges from, to, and within a certain area, being a monopolist to the customers and a monopsonist to the generators[12]. So, if a Member State chooses the tender regime, which is likely for those States whose present electricity industry organisation is monopolistic, some sort of mixed system will have to result, in which part of of the supplies, namely those to the customers not willing or not entitled to negotiate directly with the suppliers, would be awarded to tenderers, while the remaining supplies would be directly negotiated in an organised market. It is not clear what kind of organisational solution, if any, can effectively guarantee the coexistence of the two regimes. For example, introducing a tender promoter within a system such as the British, could be done by considering this «tender-buyer», acting as a delegate of the regional distributors[13], as the subscriber of long-term contracts (the so-called *Contracts for Differences*) with the suppliers awarded the tender; in this way the market risk would be entirely translated onto distributor-obliged customers. However, in this set-

---

[11] Art. 21.(l.i) of the amended proposal states: «Member States shall take the necessary measures for: *(i)* electricity producers and transmitters either inside or outside the territory covered by the system to be able to negotiate access to the system so as to conclude supply contracts with final customers who are large industrial consumers and with distributors on the basis of voluntary commercial agreements».

[12] The French proposal of a «single buyer» system is on these lines. The regime envisaged by the proposal is characterised by a single buyer monopsony over the generators and monopoly in supplyng the customers who cannot negotiate their supplies. A tender regime (only) in used to supply the capacity necessary to supply the domestic demand. Entry in generation via authorisation is allowed only to generators which will export their production. Domestic generators cannot directly supply domestic consumers, even though they can directly supply foreign customers. Exports by generators and imports by large industrial customers are realised through (pairs of) bilateral exchanges in which one of the parties is the single buyer. For a discussion of the single buyer proposal see ENER [7]. In is worth noting that on several occasions Commission members have stated that the French proposal is not compatible with the Commission provisions on the Common Market of electricity.

[13] For the reasons mentioned above such delegation can only regard the purchase of the capacity necessary to supply the segment of the demand which is distributor-obliged.

ting, since the authority which activates the tender procedure would
be responsible for the adequancy of the generation and transmission
capacity, that component of the spot market price which has to signal
the scarcity of capacity by creating rents would be meaningless.
Furthermore, if the tender promoter is allowed to operate also as a
competitive supplier of non-obliged customers, and also, say, as the
transmission system operator, it is very likely that a proactive
behaviour on the side of the provision of new capacity, together with
the selective development of the trasmission system and with some
anti-competitive use of the tariffs of access to the network, will give
rise to a situation of *de facto* monopoly in supply and monopsony in
generation by the tender promoter.

The possibility of horizontal and vertical integration in the electricity industry, which is not ruled out by the directive proposal,
seems problematic, especially with respect to the trasmission system
operator, which, if integrated in generation or supply, would be
placed in a dominant position. A dominance which, as the United
Kingdom experience of the 1983 Electricity Act demonstrates, would
be extremely difficult, if not hopeless, to countervail through regulation. First, the transmitter-generator would have the incentive to
subsidise his generation business at his trasmission business' expense
and to negatively discriminate against the competing suppliers' plants
in providing his transmission service, in a situation in which an
effective regulation of the transmission charges is extremely complex,
both to define and enforce, since it relies on very detailed information
about the transmitter-generator costs. Second, the transmitter-
generator could bias anticompetitively the development of the trasmission system; conditions of regional monopoly for the transmitter's
generating plants can be established by creating bottle-necks in the
transmission system. The same argument holds when applied to
trans-border interconnections; competition between neighbouring
transmitters which compete as suppliers can perpetuate the closure
which characterised the past development of the national transmission systems. A thorough analysis of the possibilities to cross-subsidise
and to bias competiton which are open to the generators integrated in
the supply business and to the distributors integrated in supply and/or
generation, as well as of the links between such possibilities and the

specific way the wholesale electricity market works and the non-competitive businesses are regulated, is beyond the scope of this paper[14]. However, it is important to note that one of the key elements of the liberalisation process recently undergone by the British electricity supply industry has been the horizontal and vertical de-integration and, as far as regulation is concerned, the introduction of limits to the generators' market share in the supply market and to the distributors' quota of self-generated electricity. This fact reflects the objective limitation, recognised even by Britain, one of the countries with the longest-lasting regulatory tradition, of the traditional regulatory tools, among them access price regulation and account unbundling, in inhibiting abuses by firms placed in a dominant position. To conclude, it seems that a highly de-integrated structure is a necessary condition for an effective competion to be induced in supply.

As far as network third party access is concerned, the difference between the regulated and negotiated TPA regimes is not merely formal. In comparison with the regulated access system, the negotiated system is likely to shift the balance of bargaining power in favour of the network operators, with foreseeable negative effects on supply competition. This is especially true considering the diversity of the Member States' regulatory traditions and expertise and of their propensity toward introducing competition in the energy sectors.

The proposed directive delegates to the State authorities the organisation of dispatching. Minimising the aggregate short term generation cost requires that the available plants be dispatched following the economic merit order; thus the efficient dispatch will generally not coincide continuously with that determined by the straightforward implementation of the long term direct contracts between suppliers and large customers or between the winners of the tenders and the tender promoter. The problem is that of finding a device to share the surplus between the generator who is supposed to generate because of a contractual obligation, and the one dispatched in his place because he is able to produce at lower costs. Making short run total cost minimisation compatible with the opening up to competition of the Union's electricy supply market requires a sophis-

---

[14] See VICKERS J. - YARROW B. [29]

ticated solution of institutional engineering which must guarantee equivalent terms to all the generators of the Union[15]. It is unlikely that this can be achieved without any Union-level law-making.

As regards the «general interest» or public service objectives associated with the supply of electricity, their definition and the policy to pursue them are delegated by the directive to the State authorities. Yet the tools used until now to achieve such objectives in most European countries — namely the award of a legal monopoly status to an integrated firm in exchange for the imposition of public service obligations — is clearly incompatible with the free-trade approach of the directive. The way of funding the public service requirements, either out of the general taxation system or through cross-subsidisation among classes of customers, should be transparent and neutral toward competition. However, the series of clearing-houses necessary to fund, say, uniform tariffs for all the residential customers throughout a country, could hide rents taking the form of productive inefficiency or anti-competitive subsidies in favour of the large customer supply business.

Regarding harmonisation measures, the directive proposals, both on gas and electricity, commit the Commission to present a programme by the end of 1995; no reference is made to issues such as the assumption at the Union level of the responsibility for the security of supply of energy sources and the harmonisation of the national fiscal and environmental legislation. At present the policies of the Member States on these matters are very diverse. Further, even though — according to the Commission — the advocation at the Union level of every aspect of the energy policy is not a necessary condition for the introduction of some level of competion in the energy industries, such a condition seems to be constituted by a radical revision, aimed a controlling their distortive impact on competition, of the tools with which the Member States implement their energy policies[16].

---

[15] ENER [7] considers the issue of reciprocity between two countries' electricity systems, of which one is characterised by a single-buyer organisation, the other by a British-style competitive supply system.

[16] Think, for example, of the national coal industry support burden on the electricity industry in the United Kingdom and Germany.

The same logic underlying the directive proposal on the electricity industry is the basic for the proposal on the natural gas industry. The main differences concern the discipline of capacity provision, where the tender regime is not provided for, and the transmission system management, which is entrusted to each gas firm for the owned part of the transmission system rather than to a single transmission system operator. Compared to the electricity industry, technical constraints are less critical in the gas industry than strategic constraints. Indeed, the European natural gas industry is characterised by:

1) a heavy dependence on suppliers outside the Union (who supply 40% of the present levels of consumption and will meet virtually all future increase in demand);

2) a highly concentrated supply, which, when the external suppliers are considered (the state-owned firms of Algeria, Norway, and the former Soviet Union are practically the only external suppliers), adds a relevant political dimension to the risk of supply unreliability;

3) a high average load factor of the transmission system, which is also characterised by a very limited duplication, that is, by the rarity of alternative routes to move gas between two points of the system;

4) a steadily and rapidly increasing demand[17].

In this context the beneficial effects arising from the liberalisation of the supply to large customers, to be implemented through a negotiated TPA regime, seem uncertain. As an immediate consequence of the liberalisation of supply, the demand for bulk natural gas, until now represented by the national gas companies, would be split among a greater number of smaller buyers. This is unlikely to happen to the producers, whose main problem is not access to the market, but that of being able to share the risk of the investment required to develop new productive capacity Thus. greater market power of the producers, rather than stronger competition among them, is the foreseeable outcome of liberalisation.

Serious problems could arise in the period of transition to the regime introduced by the directive because of the long term take-or-

---

[17] It is worth noting that the liberalisation of the US gas industry in the Eighties took place in a context characterised by demand and supply conditions radically different from, and in many respects opposite to, those presently existing in Europe (WOOD-COLLINS J. - LEE W. [30]).

pay obligations already assumed by the gas companies on the basis of estimates of their future sales which could turn out to be much greater than the actual fugures, as a result of the liberalisation of supply. In the new regime the gas companies will have to compete with the producers, to which they are bound by take-or-pay obligations assumed under the former regime, to supply customers who, in the pre-directive system, would have been supplied by the gas companies as monopolists[18].

Perhaps the crucial aspect is that, if direct contracting between producers and users became the dominant supply arrangement, the system through which the security of supply — both in terms of development of the productive capacity and of geo-political diversification of the suppliers — has traditionally been guaranteed could be compromised, unless the relevant responsibilities are assumed at a higher institutional level. The development of new fields, in countries with limited capacity to bear financial and commercial risks, has indeed been made possible by the subscription by the gas companies of very long term take-or-pay agreements (typically with lengths of some decades), through which the market risk has been transferred to consumers. Such capacity for long term commitment, which is presumably not enjoyed by the independent suppliers, would be reduced to that sustainable by the gas companies' captive businesses, chiefly residential and commercial customers. As a consequence it would become more difficult to finance expensive long term projects, such as the import of liquefied natural gas from Nigeria, which would allow some geographical diversification of the suppliers, while the market share of the existing suppliers would increase, since they can expand their productive capacity with the lowest costs.

To conclude, it is worth underlining that the practical relevance of the above sketched scenario crucially depends on how effective the

---

[18] The situation of a gas company finding itself in major economic difficulties because its sales have fallen below the level of the minimum off-take obligation contracted under the previous regime is regarded in the directive as justifying some support measures by the national authorities, nevertheless, what type of measures is allowed is not specified. In the liberalisation of the US gas industry, this problem was solved by annulling, under law, a large share of the existing take-or-pay obligations; which is clearly not realistic in the European context.

Union level energy policy will be, especially regarding the relationships between the Union and the external suppliers[19].

2. - Trans-European Energy Networks

While the above discussed measures are centred on the monopoly status of the electricity and natural gas industries, with the purpose of redefining its scope, the programme on the development of trans-European networks focuses on the infrastructure character of the public utilities. As a consequence the objectives of Union action are different: competition, disaggregation, transparency in the former case, co-operation, co-ordination and standardisation in the latter (McGowan [27]

The origins of the Commission's policy on the development of the Union's infrastructures are to be found within the ambit of regional policy. In that context, the policy on infrastructures typically took the form of the Community financing the provision of infrastructures, most often road links, in the poorest regions. Priority was given to the development of depressed zones rather than to cross-border network interconnection. A much wider role for the Union's action, in terms of both scope and type of intervention, is envisaged by the proposal for a Council resolution on «trans-European networks» (EEC [12]). The attention is moved from financing to co-ordinating the strategies of the Member States' utilities and national authorities; the network paradigm is extended to — besides transportation, telecommunication and the energy sectors — areas like education, research and environment protection.

In the proposal for a European Parliament and Council decision on «a series of guidelines on trans-European energy networks» (EEC [23]), strengthening trans-border interconnection among European energy networks is regarded as necessary in order to: 1) activate the Single Market of energy, to which network interconnection is a

---

[19] The assumption at the Community level of the responsibilities relating to the supply of primary sources has been among the Commission's objectives since the 1990 Rome Conference. The first step in this direction is the proposal of a «European Charter of Energy» (EEC [18]), aimed at setting up a framework for the relationships in the energy sectors between Europe and the former URSS.

prerequisite; 2) reduce regional inequalities; 3) increase the security of supply of primary sources, also from outside the Union.

The role of the Union is seen as consisting of: *a)* the identification of projects of common interest[20]; *b)* the creation of a technical, administrative, and financial environment favourable to the realisation of such projects[21].

From a general perspective the trans-European energy network policy allows of two different interpretations. On the one hand, because of its emphasis on co-operation and co-ordination, it can be regarded as an alternative to the branch of policy discussed in the previous section, explicitly aimed at introducing competition in the electricity and gas industries. That seems to be the position of the national utilities, who support the former policy while firmly opposing the latter. On the other hand, as the Commission has recently started to claim more vigorously, the two policy streams can be considered as strictly complementary, since the interconnection of the transmission systems is a necessary condition for effective competition to develop in the sectors under examination. However, if the Commission's view is to be accepted, a general lack of connection between the two streams has to be recognised; since in the provisions on trans-European networks a co-operative approach to interconnection strengthening and transmission system operating is developed independently from the issues raised by supply liberalisation. Nevertheless the Commission's policy on trans-European networks has been politically successful, as the introduction into the Treaty of a section on trans-European networks (Art. 129 B and C) shows.

3. - Conclusion.

The policy to establish a single market of energy in Europe has to cope with very different electricity and gas industries among Member

---

[20] A non-exhaustive list of common interest projects is included in the document.

[21] EEC [24] provides a series of measures with that purpose. As to financing, EEC [19] proposes a «European Interest Declaration» to be granted to the projects of common interest in order to facilitate financing by the private sector EEC [25] sets general rules on the financial support by the Union of Trans-European network projects.

States; such heterogeneity concerns both the degree of integration and the ownership regime, as well as the regulatory system. Further, the objectives historically ascribed by each contry's authorities to the energy industries are widely differing: firstly, there are those objectives relating to the utilities' public service function, such as, typically, universal access and uniform tariffs; secondly, those referable to the «strategic» role of these sectors, such as the protection of domestic suppliers of primary sources as a way of maintaining some politically valuable independence from foreign suppliers, or the protection of national plant suppliers as a way to support the development of the national high-tech industries; and thirdly those relating to macro-economic stabilisation, such as the setting of anti-inflation tariffs not reflecting actual costs, or the forcing of some level of over-employment to control the unemployment rate.

Th Union's programme for the energy sector has two facets. On the one hand the scope of the notion of natural monopoly is reassessed in industries which have historically been regarded as natural monopolies in their entireties. On the other hand strict limits are placed on the strategic and public service roles of these sectors and, above all, on the form in which such roles are fulfilled.

As to liberalisation, the actual effects of the Commission's proposals, if accepted, will heavily depend upon whether or not an in depth revision of the electricity and natural gas industries' organisation at the national level results. It is submitted that the provisions of the amended directive proposals discussed in Section 1.3, especially under some of the emerging interpretations, might not be able to induce such a revision. In particular, even though some competition is likely to result in generation, so long as the monolithic, highly integrated structures characterising most Member States' energy sectors are maintained, competition in supply will not develop. However, in sectors like those under examination, in which natural monopoly conditions prevail in certain stages of the supply process, and a large share of the demand, namely that from residential and small business customers, has no acces to competitive supplies, regulation is crucial for effective competion to develop and be maintained. Implementing the more competition-oriented provisions of the directive proposals will require, in most Members States, greater and more sophisticated regulation than ever before. In some cases the regulatory system will literally have to be built from scratch. In this regard, the Commission's free-trade ambitions will have to face the challenge of national administrations with quite different traditions, attitudes and expertise.

Regarding the policy tools available at the State level in the regime envisaged by the proposed directives, applyng the free market paradigm in the energy sectors will subvert the devices — mainly cross-subsidisation and command-and-control — through which social and energy policy aims have been pursued by the national authorities until now. As far the social objectives are concerned, uniform tariffs and universal access under a competitive supply regime, require a complex and transparent system of clearing houses. With respect to energy policy, the establishment of the Single Market was originally expected to coincide with the end of the national authorities' autonomy, and with the assumption at the Union level of the corresponding responsibilities. The timing of this transition is, at present, highly indeterminate.

BIBLIOGRAPHY

[1] ARMSTRONG M.A. - COWAN S. - VICKERS J., *Regulatory Reform: Economic Analysis and British Experience*, MIT Press, Cambridge (Mass.), 1994.

[2] CERVIGNI G., «La privatizzazione dell'industria elettrica nel Regno Unito, un'analisi critica», *Economia delle Fonti d'Energia e dell'Ambiente*, n. 1, 1993.

[3] DE PAOLI L., *Il mercato interno dell'elettricità tra ATR e acquirente unico*, mimeo, IEFE, Milano, Università Bocconi, 1995.

[4] DE PAOLI L. - FINON D., «Implication of Community Policy for the Electricity Industries», *Utilities Policy*, July 1993.

[5] DE VANY A. - WALLS D.W., «Open Access and the Emergence of a Competitive Natural Gas Market», *Contemporary Economic Policy*, vol. XII, apr. 1994.

[6] EHLERMANN C.D., «Role of the European Commission as regards National Energy Policies», *Journal of Energy and Natural Resources Law*, vol. 12, n. 3, 1994.

[7] ENERGIEWIRTSCHAFTLICHES INSTITUTE (ENER), *TPA and Single Buyer Systems. Producers and Parallel Authorizations. Small and Very Small Systems*, University of Köln, mimeo, 1995.

[8] EUROGAS, «*Eurogas Views on Third Party Access*», *Addendum to PCCG Report*, Apr. 1991.

[9] EUROPEAN COMMISSION (EC), «Electricity Tariff Structures in the European Community. Recommendation of the Council of the European Community», *Official Journal of the European Communities*, L 337, 1981.

[10] —— , «Council Resolution on New Community Energy Policy Objectives for 1995», *Official Journal of European Communities*, C 241, 1986.

[11] —— , «The Internal Energy Market», Commission of the European Communities, *Working Document, COM* (88) 238, 1988.

[12] —— , «Trans-European Networks Project for a Council Resolution», Brussels, *COM*, (89) 643, 1989.

[13] —— , «The Introduction of a Common Procedure to Guarantee Industrial Users the Publicity of Prices for Natural Gas and Electricity, Council Directive», Brussels, *Official Journal of the European Communities*, L 185, 1990.

[14] —— , «Procurement Procedures of Utilities Operating in the Water, Energy, Transport, and Telecommunications Sectors, Council Decision», Brussels, *Official Journal of the European Communities*, L 297, 1990.

[15] —— , «Transit of Electricity on the Major Systems, Council Directive», Brussels, *Official Journal of the European Communities*, L 313, 1990.

[16] —— , «Transit of Natural Gas on the Major Systems, Council Directive», Brussels, *Official Journal of the European Communities*, L 147, 1991.

[17] —— , «Common Rules for the Internal Market in Electricity and Natural Gas, Proposal for a Council Directive», Brussels, *Official Journal of the European Communities*, C 65, 1991.

[18] —— , «A Common European Energy Charter, Communication from the Commission», Brussels, *COM*, (91) 36, 1991.

[19] —— , «Introducing a Declaration of European Interest to Facilitate the Establishment of Trans European networks, Proposal for a Council Regulation», Brussels, *Official Journal of the European Communities*, C 71, 1992.

[20] ——, «Coordinating the Procurement Procedures of Utilities Operating in the Water, Energy, Transport, and Telecommunications Sectors, Council Directive», Brussels, *Official Journal of the European Communities*, L 199, 1993.

[21] ——, «Common Rules for the Internal Market in Electricity and Natural Gas, Amended Proposal for a Council and Parliament Directive», Brussels, *Official Journal of the European Communities*, L 123, 1993.

[22] ——, «Marché Interiéur de l'Electricité-Conclusions du Conseil», Brussels, *Energy Council*, 20 Nov. 1994.

[23] ——, «Proposal for a European Parliament and Council Decision Laying Down a Series of Guidelines on Trans-European Energy Networks», *Official Journal of European Community*, C 72, 1994.

[24] ——, «Proposal for a Council Decision Laying Down a Series of Measures Aiming at Creating a More Favourable Context for the Development of Trans-European Networks in the Energy Sector», *Official Journal of European Community*, C 72, 1994.

[25] ——, «Proposal for a Council Decision Laying Down General Rules for the Granting of Community Financial Aid in the Field of Trans-European Networks», *Official Journal of European Community*, C 89, 1994.

[26] HAMMON E.M. - HELM D.M. - THOMPSON D.J., «Competition in Electricity Supply: Has the Energy Act Failed?» in HELM D.R. - KAY J.A. - THOMPSON D.J., *The Market for Energy*, Oxford, Oxford University Press, 1989.

[27] McGOWEN, «Trans-european Networks: Utilities as Infrastructure», *Utilities Policy*, July 1993.

[28] PRIOR M., «The Supply of Gas to Europe», *Energy Policy*, vol. 22, n. 1, 1994.

[29] VICKERS J. - YARROW B., «The British Electricity Experiment», *Economy Policy*, n. 12, 1991.

[30] WOOD COLLINS J. - LEE W., «The Relevance of US Experience to the Completion of the European Internal Energy Market for Natural Gas», *Journal of Energy and Natural Resources Law*, vol. 8, n. 1, 1990.

III - SECTORIAL ASPECTS: ELECTRICITY, NATURAL GAS, RAILWAYS, TELECOMMUNICATIONS, THE POSTAL SERVICE

The Italian Electricity Sector Between Privatization and the Fear of Competition*

Michele Polo - **Carlo Scarpa**
Università Bocconi, Milano   Università di Bologna

1. - Introduction

Italy's state electricity company ENEL came into being in December 1962 when more than 1,200 electricity companies were nationalised and merged in a single entity, to which the law reserved the monopoly (with only a few exceptions) of the production, distribution and sale of electricity in Italy. ENEL had the status of an economic public body and characteristics (direct operativeness, monosectoriality, clear identification of objectives) which left very limited room for any real entrepreneurial autonomy from the Ministerial Committee charged with laying down the appropriate directives[1]. In fact, underscoring the strategic role of electricity in Italy's development, Parliament entrusted ENEL with the role of an economic-policy tool, particularly at a macro-economic level.

Only in the 1980s was there any serious discussion of re-organising ENEL and separating its tasks from those of the State. In

---

* The authors are Associate Professors of Economics at the Istituto d'economia politica and the Dipartimento di scienze economiche respectively.

N.B.: the numbers in square brackets refer to the Bibliography at the end of the paper.

[1] Although the real degree of autonomy of economic public bodies in general is also subject of legal debate, the fact remains that *ex-lege* it was the political power which drew up ENEL's annual and long-term programmes, decided the construction of new plants, their location, and the financing for the development programmes, etc. Even ENEL's internal structure was subject to norms (for example, D.P.R. n. 342 of 1965, which disciplined its territorial and central structure).

August 1992, a law transformed ENEL into a joint-stock company, converting the legal monopoly, which moreover ENEL had *de facto* lost some considerable time back, into a licence for electricity services. The subsequent step — which shall be discussed in this paper — should be the sale of ENEL to the public, an operation whose impact on the economy as a whole will be such as to necessitate attentive reflection on the future structure of the electricity sector in Italy.

This paper seeks to offer a series of elements useful for this purpose, and to put forward some essential quidelines for an overall reform proposal. This would appear to be particularly important given also the serious dearth of information regarding the privatisation process, which is reflected in both the scarcity of «official» data and in the difficulty of finding clear and well-argued public statements (for example, a «white paper») by the governments which have dealt with the question.

ENEL's importance emerges only too clearly if we consider that it is a company with about 95,000 employees which has for many years accounted for some 10% of Italian industry's total investment; it is one of the world's three leading electricity groups as regards users served, installed capacity and energy sold (by 1993 data). Moreover, its balance sheets were in the red for more than twenty years and only since 1985 have they shown a profit.

The present discussion on the privatisation of ENEL is taking place some thirty years after the electricity sector's nationalisation, an event which marked the end of a long debate in Italy[2] on whether so crucial a service for the country's development should be provided under state guidance. There were many reasons for the nationalisation of 1962 and considerations of space do not allow us to properly illustrate the complex debate of that period[3]. However, it is interesting to recall that, in addition to the reasons of planning — put forward by the nascent centre-left which saw nationalisation as a driving element for the economy as a whole — Italy's electricity system then suffered from at least two big problems. The first was the persistent

---

[2] Mori G. [16] notes that the debate commenced as far back as 1989, with a speech by the then young Luigi Einaudi.

[3] Forte F. [9] and Mori G. [16] do justice to at least the political aspects of the debate of that period.

lack of agreement between the electricity groups which had prevented the construction of a national electricity network (Zamagni [24]), the second was that the by-now intolerable weight of the electricity oligopoly on politics and its industrial users which generated a reaction from both the left and the big electricity users (Mori [16]).

In other words, the economic objectives nationalisation was supposed to achieve were coordination of big investment and the safeguarding of users[4]; it is interesting to note that, albeit in a different form and within a somewhat different economic context, these are still the crucial nodes of the reform of the electricity sector. In fact, as we shall see on the basis of the latest theoretical analyses and in the light of a careful analysis of Italy's present-day electricity sector, some of the «historical» issues continue to surface and remain centre-stage.

This paper is organised as follows. The next section briefly illustrates some technical elements which are essential for an understanding of the sector's functioning. Section 3 is dedicated to an overview of the present situation in the sector, with reference to both structural demand and supply data and to ENEL's position vis-à-vis the other players in the market and the public policies in question. Section 4 summarises some of the main theoretical arguments which can serve to evaluate the situation and the various hypotheses for reform. These alternative hypotheses, together with the indications from the EU are then illustrated and assessed in Section 5 which also proposes some possible reform guide-lines. Section 6 contains some concluding considerations.

2. - Technical Characteristics of the Sector

The electricity sector can be divided into (at least) five logically distinct stages: generation, dispatch, «wholesale» transmission, local (low and medium voltage) distribution, retail (connections and general management of customer relations). Without claiming to exhaust

---

[4] It should be borne in mind that prices were then determined by the Interministerial Price Committee (CIP) of whose capacity for control, moreover, there were very serious doubts which, as MORI G. [16] points out, were expressed by economists such as Lombardini and De Maria.

the question from the technical point of view or to treat it with «engineer-like» rigour, we believe it important to preliminarily point out some technical features which are of particular importance from the economic viewpoint.

The generation phase makes use of natural energy sources such as water or sunlight or else transforms inputs such as fuel oil into high-voltage electric energy. The optimal scale of production varies according to the energy source, but is generally somewhat small compared with the size of the market. It should be borne in mind that there are significant fluctuations in demand on both a daily and seasonal basis. Hence, a constant feature of generating systems is that they should have a significant excess of generating capacity justified by the extreme indesirability of having to ration demand (black out).

Dispatch, which links generation and transmission and is therefore an element of coordination rather than of production in the narrow sense, involves guaranteeing a continuous balance between demand from the network and supply: it should be noted that electricity — in all phases of the production process — is practically non-storable and this is why (also in view of the variability of demand) dispatch plays a crucial role for the functioning of the system. Normally, the agent which manages dispatch also has the authority to decide who effectively should be called upon to satisfy the demand at each moment; in other words, this is the level at which it is possible to select the generation plants to be brought into action, usually on the basis of efficiency or minimum cost criteria[5].

Transmission is the service which transports electricity from the generator to peripheral nodes in proximity to the consumer via a network of high-voltage cables which cover the entire country. This is probably the segment where one can most realistically speak of a natural monopoly at national level. The first technical aspect to be borne in mind is that, once in the network, energy distributes itself in accordance with laws of physics which are difficult to control; hence the relation between the generator and the final user is totally

---

[5] It should be noted that the concept of minimum cost requires one to specify whether such cost is only the pure cost of generation or else the sum of this cost and that of transmission: only if dispatch took this cost also into account would it be able to minimise the costs of the entire system.

«anonymous» in the sense that it is impossible to determine the origin of electricity obtained from the network.

A second important point is that some energy is lost in the network[6], the electricity introduced into the network is partially dispersed as a result of imperfections in cables, and these losses are higher the lower the voltage and the greater the distance between the generator and final consumer. This means, for example, that if one introduces new electricity at a node near to the final user, the average distance the electricity travels decreases and this leads to savings in terms of lower losses. In other words, introducing electricity to the network can entail a (marginal) cost which may be negative, if the location of the generator vis-à-vis demand is such as to reduce the average distance travelled by the electricity.

Distribution is somewhat similar to the previous phase, as it entails transporting electricity from the high-voltage network to the final user. This normally requires lowering the voltage (transformation), an operation which is also expensive. Distribution therefore has the same natural monopoly elements as transmission, but the territorial ambit is different, as the national territory could be divided without relevant shortcomings of a purely technical nature.

It should be noted that the sale of electric energy, i.e., the relations with the final user as regards connections, invoicing, etc., is logically distinct from the distribution phase; indeed, producers and consumers can use the transmission and distribution network to carry out direct exchanges and furthermore, the sale operations can be entrusted to a specialised broker company. This production phase is not characterised by a significant minimum scale of production vis-à-vis the extension of the national market.

3. - Italy's Electricity Market: Starting Data

Having briefly illustrated some important technical characteristics, we shall now turn our attention to the institutional and market data which comprise the *status quo*.

---

[6] This loss — in the case of Italy — amounts to 8% of consumption.

3.1 *Production Plants and Demand*

An important aspect of demand is the low level of per-capita consumption, which is about 5/6 that of the UK, 2/3 that of France and only 1/3 that of the USA. On the one hand, this could indicate a potential increase in demand in coming years should consumer habits change as they have done in these countries[7], and on the other serve to explain some difficulties which ENEL is encountering as regards efficiency. In fact, as average consumption is quite low, distribution finds it impossible to exploit economies of scale which are enjoyed by, for example, the French group EDF, which has higher productivity in terms of electricity sold per employee. Furthermore, the average user in North Italy consumes much more than his counterpart in the Mezzogiorno, and this is reflected in the distribution costs which are obviously much higher (per KWh) in southern Italy.

Another important feature is the imbalance between the location of demand and that of the generating plants. There are very high regional deficits, particularly in central and southern Italy, which increase the average distance electricity travels and entail higher electricity losses and costs; the main direction of the electricity flow is therefore from North to South[8]. This has two implications which are worth mentioning. Firstly, the quality of the transmission network in central and southern Italy is particularly important, for both the overall cost of the national system and for guaranteeing an essential service to regions in southern Italy. Furthermore, although the construction of alternative North-South energy routes is essential to ensure supply to the southern regions in the event of failures, Italy's geography makes this quite a problem. Apart from the main link, the situation as regards this connection remains unsatisfactory; the unreliability of alternative routes[9] increases the risk of interruption to

---

[7] This should therefore be borne in mind when determining prices.

[8] Circa one third of the electricity sold in southern Italy comes from other areas; the Campania region has the biggest deficit, 77% of electricity sold in Campania is «imported» from other regions. North-west Italy also has a considerable deficit, in part because there is less incentive to produce as low-cost energy can be imported from neighbouring France.

[9] The main problem is the lack of transversal connections between the two main lines which carry energy from northern to southern Italy.

services in southern Italy. These observations only serve to emphasise that the question of investment in the high-voltage network is still important and far from resolved[10].

As regards production, one serious concern is Italy's heavy dependence on imports of energy inputs. It should be noted that this dependence has significantly increased in the last two decades, also because Italy's nuclear power programme was brought to a halt by the 1987 referendum which thus made futile a programme of heavy investment which had already been largely implemented. At present, thermoelectric plants account for the lion's share, some 80%, of electricity generated in Italy. As we shall see below, starting from 1991, incentives were introduced for the construction of plants which used renewable inputs but so far these measures have had a limited effect.

3.2 *ENEL on the Threshold of Privatization*

At present, ENEL is a monopolist as regards management of the network (and dispatch) and co-exists with other public and private players in generation and distribution (which is for the moment totally integrated with retail). ENEL is therefore a vertically integrated company, an aspect which, as we shall see, is centre-stage of the present debate on its privatisation. The final cost of electricity for ENEL is attributable for (circa) 60% to generation, for 5% to transmission and for the remaining 35% to distribution and retail sale. In particular, 32% of the total is attributable to the purchase of fuels or electricity from third parties.

As noted, ENEL came into being following the nationalisation of most of Italy's electricity companies in the early 1960s. Two characteristics of this nationalisation have weighed and continue to weigh on the company's situation. The first is related to the state of the transmission network, which required massive investment and above all lacked the interconnection which was one of the most important

---

[10] It should be noted that the question of territorial re-equilibrium has still to be properly resolved for distribution as there is a strong imbalance between the quality of service and level of costs.

and onerous tasks undertaken by ENEL. We have already pointed out that this problem has still to be fully resolved.

The second is that ENEL was forced to start out from a somewhat difficult economic situation, which was subsequently further compounded by a tariff policy (as we shall see below, not attributable to ENEL) which was for many years incompatible with a balanced financial management of the group: we have already noted that profitability has been possible only since 1985. The most important consequence is the difficult financial situation recorded in the 1994 balance sheet which shows debt of 51,000 billion lira (about 32 billion U.S. dollars) equal to 40% of assets and 105% of total revenues[11].

Any evaluation of ENEL's economic efficiency — in itself objectively difficult — is made even more arduous by the limited availability of data, and also by the difficulty of finding firms with which it can be compared. In any case, it should be clear that the constraints imposed on ENEL by the political system are such to make any judgement on the firm's management difficult as its autonomy has been severely limited by its semi-public role.

The dynamics of labour productivity from 1963 to the present (measured in users per employee) would appear to be in line with that of other big European groups although it is hampered by the structural features of demand mentioned above which place objective limits on the possibility to compare different firms and to improve productivity. The question of the efficient use of the workforce is however somewhat delicate, also because there is a widespread suspicion (which is difficult to confirm given the problems in obtaining relevant data) that there is a surplus of personnel. However, such a situation would be in line with that in many Italian state companies, which have often had to provide a response to the unemployment problem, especially in the less-developed zones of Italy.

The persistence of labour hoarding is indirectly proven by the present process of reduction of the workforce. In recent years, also under the 'threat' of privatisation, the group's personnel turnover has been blocked, thus reducing personnel by 9.4% from 1990 to 1994

---

[11] And also to 212% of revenue that ENEL obtained from sales of electricity. Most of ENEL's financial debt is long-term and has been a constant feature of its balance sheet since its institution: the long-term debt-equity ratio is 3.63.

and by a further 5,000 units in the first half of 1995 alone[12]. These inefficiences are further compounded by the question of labour costs; labour costs are in fact very high, the result of wage levels which are the highest in Italy[13] and a working week which is one of the least onerous in the country[14].

As regards capital accumulation and productivity, it should be acknowledged that while the situation is far from satisfactory, this has been decisively assisted by causes external to ENEL. In particular, the energy policy choices and the opposition of local authorities to massive generation facilities in their areas have placed obvious limits on ENEL's activities[15]. Furthermore, ENEL is bound to acquire energy produced by private players, who can therefore fully expoloit their productive capacity; hence fluctuations in demand are absorbed either by imports or else by varying the degree of utilisation of ENEL's plants which are often underutilised. This obviously ends up affecting ENEL's productivity which shows an (indispensable) excess of productive capacity.

Here also, the consequences of the (announced) privatisation have been felt in a reduction in investment. For example, ENEL's 1991 investment programme envisaged 74,000 billion lire of investments over five years; this plan was subsequently revised in 1993, with investment falling to circa 55,000 billion lire, a reduction which touched not only generation, but also distribution and transport; lower demand for electricity in a period of economic stagnation would not appear sufficient to justify such a reduction, which concerns long-term investments. At least for a while, a (not surprising) concern for short-term objectives would appear to have prevailed so as to render the balance sheet more attractive to potential investors.

---

[12] This trend is also the consequence of the computerisation of many internal services, which makes it necessary to «reconvert» a larger number of employees.

[13] The average real wage for the electricity sector is one of the highest of all production sectors, even including some services such as credit (ISRIL [11]). A similar conclusion is obtained when one breaks down the average data so as to compare homogeneous professional figures.

[14] In 1993, ENEL's contract envisaged 1,682 working hours per year versus an average 1,734 for the industrial sector (ISTAT [13]). Overtime working hours amount to circa 6% of total working hours.

[15] Take for example the freezing of the nuclear power programme imposed by the 1987 referendum which meant that thousands of billions lire of investment remained totally unproductive and that it has even been necessary to leave a certain (albeit limited) number of employees to keep watch on plants which generate only concern.

This picture, already far from satisfactory, is further compounded by a problem which, in the long term, is even more worrying; we refer to the need to upgrade existing generation facilities to the environmental standards which have been laid down by the European Community and already implemented in Italian legislation. This is also related to the age of the plants, which were constructed in accordance with criteria considerably different from those prevailing today[16]. The amount of investment needed has not been officially estimated with precision, but undoubtedly is high enough to cast a long shadow over the future profitability (of a certain part) of ENEL[17].

A final observation concerns ENEL's territorial structure. The cost per kWh of the distribution service is higher in southern Italy where the average user is smaller. It should also be pointed out that a superficial analysis of the data for the different areas of Italy does not bring to light any significant differences in the employee-user ratios, a productivity index which «neutralises» the differences in user size. However significant differences exist in the quality of service (service interruption rates and the duration of such interruptions) in which the performance of southern Italy and in particular of Sicily and Sardinia is well below that of northern Italy[18].

3.3 *ENEL and the Public-Private Relation*

Generation and distribution are market segments where ENEL and the other players are simultaneously present, but basically without any real competition.

---

[16] It should he borne in mind, for example, that circa half of ENEL's thermoelectric power comes from plants which were built before 1975 and the average energy efficiency index of ENEL's power plants is 38% against the 51% which the government's planning committee (CIP) indicated in its provision no. 6 of 1992 as the minimum threshold for the granting of subsidies (on which see Section 3.4) or 60% which is the average of the same index for projects presented by private agents in recent years (GATTI G. [10]).

[17] One should also bear in mind that the impact on the landscape of pylon lines and the possibility of laying them underground has yet to be raised in Italy, as happened in France.

[18] Data for 1992 indicates that the duration of accidental service interruptions for users in the Palermo area was 7 times that of Milan and twice the average for Italy as a whole.

As regards generation, ENEL undoubtedly holds a dominant position; its production accounts for 65% of Italy's national demand against the 19% of private players and municipal utilities (1993 data). The remaining 16% is imported by ENEL — which retains the legal monopoly of electricity imports and exports — primarily in view of the low cost of imported energy. In the present situation, any talk of «competition» is entirely misplaced as ENEL has to buy whatever amount of electricity is produced by other players, moreover, at prices laid down by government bodies[19].

The installation of generation plants is subject to public authorisation, which is awarded on the basis of the merit order of the project presented, drawn up considering primarily the efficiency of the use of energy and the energy source used. There is therefore some form of competition «for the market» between private players, as the projects presented are evaluated against each other, bearing in mind the overall amount to be produced, which is laid down by Italy's National Energy Plan.

The distribution (and retail) in the several areas of Italy (mainly parts of urban areas) is instead the responsibility of the utilities which local public bodies either wholly control or in which they hold a majority stake[20]. Here again, ENEL clearly dominates the market: ENEL supplies some 93% of energy needs, above all to big users, while the municipal utilities account for 7%, mainly to households and small firms.

The contractual relations between these utilities and ENEL have always been the subject of contention: in particular, once the thirty-year concessions introduced shortly after nationalisation had expired, the debate on the right of local utilities to offer this service, and on the limits and conditions of such service still continues. We shall return to this problematic issue in the concluding section. However, once again competition is basically absent as there are local monopolists with

---

[19] The determination of these prices is the subject of a fierce debate which will be dealt with below.

[20] Law n. 142 of 1990 laid down that municipal utilities should become more autonomous, eventually with private players holding the majority. To date, there have been projects for transforming the municipal utilities into public companies in the short term, but no cases in which private agents have actually acquired the firm's control.

zones of very limited (eventual) competition only between the areas served by the municipal utilities and those served by ENEL.

3.4 *The Price Structure*

In all segments of Italy's electricity sector, at least formally, the tariffs are determined by CIP and hence it is impossibile to evaluate ENEL's price policies. However one should point out that *de facto*, as least starting in the 1980s, ENEL's power of proposal turned into a power to determine tariffs which were then ratified by the public bodies[21]. We shall focus in particular on final prices and generation prices, which are the most controversial aspects.

The prices ENEL pays to third parties for electricity introduced into the national network are regulated by law no. 11 of 1991 and subsequent measures of CIP which, for the purpose of promoting environmental protection, established a series of incentives for those who produce electricity using either renewable sources (which are in principle non-polluting) or those with a particularly high thermal efficiency. In fact — considering the actual destination of the funds in question — this law served to introduce a series of very important subsidies to producers who used non-renewable sources (gas) with combined-cycle plants which guarantee particular efficiency in energy use[22].

The price paid by ENEL is therefore given by the sum of the «avoided cost» (calculated in a manner which the relevant legislation, with its usual lack of transparency, leaves totally implicit) and an incentive component, which is paid for the first eight years and can in cases of particularly low pollution production, be as high as 200% of the avoided costs. The value of these incentives is quite high and following these provisions there was a considerable increase in the

---

[21] On this issue, see CASSESE S. [3], in particular Chapter 7. CIP's powers were transferred to the Ministry of Industry in 1994.

[22] The greater efficiency of these plants is such that even without these subsidies their diffusion would probably have been «natural» in view of their lower costs. In fact, it would appear that these subsidies served to further encourage the entry of private players into the electricity generation market rather than foster the adoption of «cleaner» technologies.

weight of private producers, so much so that now these incentives — so expensive for final consumer — face increasing resistence.

The final price, on the other hand, consists of three components, the tariff true and proper, taxes (about which there is little to say) and the «thermal surcharge».

As regards tariffs, the fundamental principle is that of the single national tariff: there are no regional differentiations. However, differentiation of prices is the norm, but refers either to the type of purchaser or use (residential or non-residential; distributor (i.e., municipal utility); public lighting, etc.), to the time or else to the levels of consumption and installed power[23]. The result is a somewhat complex structure with a peculiarity which distinguishes Italy from the other major European countries. The marginal price (per kWh) increases with the installed power for residential uses and decreases for all other uses. Unlike France, the United Kingdom and Germany, where the tariffs are lower for big users whatever their type, in Italy the price of electricity for residential use is always set to favour energy savings (and perhaps also with redistributive aims).

Hence, there is a *de facto* cross-subsidy which the big residential users (and probably the small firms) pay to the benefit of «ordinary» households (the so-called social band — in fact, 95% of users — which enjoys prices which are decidely below the European average) and larger firms. In some cases, the average price paid by the latter is lower that that at which ENEL acquires the electricity from private producers (above all considering the incentive components laid down by CIP).

Another undoubtedly privileged category is that of the local public companies (the municipal utilities) which buy electricity from ENEL at prices which are generally lower than production cost. The present legislation guarantees these companies a position of protected rent[24], which as we shall see below is one of the cruxes of the overall reform of the electricity sector.

---

[23] The recent trend, also in line with the EC's recommendations, is to extend the possibility of multi-time tariffs, thus increasing the general efficiency of the tariff system.

[24] This is even truer if one considers — as noted above — that big users are served mainly by ENEL while local public companies are concentrated in the market segments where unit prices are higher.

The thermal surcharge was introduced after the oil shock to countervail variations in the price of fuel oil, i.e., the revenue raised by the surcharge is then distributed among the producers concerned compensating them for the increased costs incurred. In reality, however, this item, which is far from transparent, now conceals a series of *ad hoc* contributions, to compensate ENEL and other companies for abandoning their nuclear programmes or to pay production incentives.

4. - What Does Economic Theory Suggest?

There are therefore several questions to which one should seek to respond in dealing with the question of ENEL's privatisation and the future set-up of the entire electricity sector. Firstly, it should be ascertained whether and to what extent privatisation may actually represent a desirable alternative. Secondly, one should determine at each phase, what is the optimal market structure and how one can move towards it given the initial situation. This is related to the problem of understanding to what extent the market (in the hands of private players) allows the attainment of results sufficiently close to the social optimum, and which public regulatory measures may instead be appropriate. Finally, last but not least, there is the question of the desirability of preserving a vertically integrated firm. We shall proceed by analysing these theoretical problems separately, at least within the limits allowed by the complexity of the question[25].

4.1 *Public or Private?*

The theoretical reasons for privatisation are in reality very weak, and it can be stated that in general there is no reason to assume that private companies are superior to public enterprises as regards (tech-

---

[25] POLO M. - SCARPA C. [19] provide a more detailed discussion and bibliography. See also ARMSTRONG *et* AL. [2] and YARROW G. [23].

nological in addition to — obviously — allocative) efficiency[26]. In short, we can summarise that the efficiency of companies which operate in non-competitive regimes is normally entrusted to two types of incentives. On the one hand, those of the market for corporate control (the risk of a takeover) and on the other those laid down contractually in the relation between the principal-owner and the agent-manager.

As to the former, it should be pointed out that, while true that a state owned company does not risk a takeover, and hence this stimulus to management efficiency is absent, it is equally true that the efficacy of such a mechanism would also appear to be extremely limited in the case of private companies, especially large ones. Contractual incentives are instead more effective in a state owned company when the contracts are complete[27], while the comparison is even more ambiguous when one considers incomplete contracts. In general, the comparison is in any case between second best alternatives and it cannot be stated with any certainty that one opinion is more valid than another.

It should be noted that the economic literature considers as public objective the total surplus created in the market in question and not the public finance requirements which all too often inspire privatisation measures. From this perspective, it should be borne in mind that the sale of a public firm entails renouncing the flows of profits which the company could generate and again, if the sale can provide a one-off revenue, it is obvious that it can have negative effects on future financial flows[28].

---

[26] One speaks of efficiency in the technical sense with reference to the capacity to produce at lower costs, while one speaks of allocative efficiency with regard to companies' price choices, i.e., the relation between the prices chosen by the company and its (given) costs.

[27] DE FRAJA G. [6] SHAPIRO C. - WILLIG R. [21] emphasise however that the reverse may be true if the policy maker pursues objectives which are primarily «private» instead of focusing on social welfare.

[28] On this point, it can be argued that the profitability of many state owned companies is in any case low. The counter-argument is firstly that such companies have rarely pursued profit, and hence that their performance should be evaluated with regard to the objectives with which they are charged. Secondly, the sale of loss-making companies is considered at best very difficult, and as a rule prior to the sale such companies are restructured to re-establish their capacity to produce profit; at which point the trade-off between stock and flows again comes to the fore.

4.2 *What Market Structures?*

All segments of this market (possibly apart from retail) have significant elements which limit the possibility of developing competition as would probably be desirable. In transmission and distribution there are natural monopolies, while in generation the situation is only apparently more promising; we shall analyse this case in more detail.

Although the minimum efficient scale is rather limited, the generation sector is characterised by numerous elements which considerably blunt the effectiveness of competition. Entry to the market is subject to public authorisation, and in any case is a process which may require even several years just for the construction of a power plant; we can therefore exclude that the market is contestable. Moreover, return on investments is always deferred over time and any financial constraints could therefore prove determinant.

Furthermore, in the medium run, each plant has a known productive capacity, and as is known this renders price competition less forceful[29]. Finally, the market should continuously be in equilibrium and hence we have frequent repetitions of the market game; for this reason the interaction among the producers can be modelled not as a one-shot game, but rather as a supergame in which firms typically have a considerable incentive to collude to avoid future price wars. Furthermore, as these are public transactions, it should be possible to observe prices and amounts traded, which would facilitate any intervention on the part of the antitrust commission.

As mentioned above, Italy currently has a sort of competition for the market, i.e., to win the right to build generating plants, and it should therefore be asked whether and to what extent this «indirect» competition can really take the place of market competition. It should be borne in mind that the above remarks also apply to those segments where there is a natural monopoly, where competition à la Demsetz could perhaps appear feasible.

In reality, we believe the answer should be negative, at least as

---

[29] The «classical» reference in this sense is the work of KREPS D. - SCHEINKMAN J. [14] who show that a two-stage game in which price competition is preceded by capacity competition eliminates Bertrand's paradox in the sense that equilibrium price will be higher that marginal cost.

regards the determination of prices, above all for two reasons. Firstly, competition for the market effectively selects the best company and can force it to operate in a socially efficient manner when the tender award criteria are unequivocally laid down and subject to an objective check; this is unfortunately not true of tenders where the evaluation has to take account of a complex series of indicators. Secondly, given the necessary length of the production licences, it is unclear how one can expect to define a price profile for the entire duration of the time period. If, on the other hand, one were to shorten the duration of the licences, there would arise the problem of how to remunerate the necessary long-term investments, which as we have already noted are amortised over many decades.

Hence in this market, there are situations in which competition has a somewhat limited role, or in which the probability of collusive behaviour is so high as to require at least heightened vigilance on the part of the antitrust authorities.

4.3 *What Space for Public Intervention?*

Faced with such limitations of the competitive processes in these markets, it is only natural that one should ask whether regulatory interventions aimed at controlling natural monopoly situations are desirable.

Existing models offer two main alternatives: rate of return regulation and price regulation (usually indicated as price cap). The former, traditionally applied in the USA, has been to some extent shelved as it provides an inadequate solution to the question of efficiency: on the one hand controlling a company's profittability is too rough an approximation for an effective control of the relation between prices and marginal costs, and on the other there is no incentive to reduce costs[30].

The price cap mechanisms studied in theory are generally based on the assumption that there is an informational asymmetry between the firm and the regulatory authorities: it is therefore assumed that

---

[30] Theory has emphasised a tendency towards overcapitalisation, known as the «Averch Johnson effect». From the empirical point of view, it is however far from certain that this distorsion has actually taken place

the firm is wholly aware of its own costs, while the authority can only rely on imperfect information which is an obvious impediment to determining the optimal price. Finally, the public authority has a host of potentially alternative objectives such as: 1) allocative efficiency; 2) technological efficiency, which is a problem above all in a dynamic sense, i.e., considering the incentive for long-term investment; 3) objectives related to the distribution of income (in other words, the need to limit subsidies, which are expensive for the state).

When it is possible to carry out transfers to a company, the rule which would appear to emerge from literature[31] is that the price, which should be set as close as possible to marginal cost, is the tool for achieving technological efficiency while transfer to the company should be such to balance other needs. The question of investment incentives remains however substantially open, and multiperiod models — even though developed in a relatively simplified context — normally show that the results of «optimal» regulation are extensively inefficient from this point of view[32].

The situation is even worse if one takes into account that many institutional systems forbid public authorities from carrying out transfers to companies; an example of this is the EC's provisions which also mirror constraints to be found in many US states. In this case, public authorities have only one tool (price) with which to achieve three objectives, and this complicates the problem considerably. To give the firm an incentive to invest, it should be allowed to recoup at least part of this investment by a increase in prices, the so-called pass-through[33]. The mechanism however cannot allow a complete pass-through, because in this case the firm would have no incentive to invest in the most efficient manner. Whatever the case, it is obviously an imperfect tool which does not even permit second best results.

---

[31] See LAFFONT J.J. - TIROLE J. [15] and ARMSTRONG M. - COWAN S. - VICKERS J. [2].

[32] The main problem is the non-credibility of the commitment by the public authorities *(i)* not to exploit in the future the information acquired today and *(ii)* not to «expropriate» from the company the return on an investment which lasts for several periods. In particular, given the risk that the public authorities will in the future exploit their position to the disadvantage of the future exploit their position to the disadvantage of the company, the latter lacks incentives to carry out irreversible investments which the public authorities may appropriate.

[33] See SCHMALENSEE R. [20].

In the United Kingdom, the translation of these principles into practice led to the introduction of the *RPI-x* rule which is currently the reference point for the debate.

The first limitation to this rule is related to the credibility of the public authorities' commitment not to intervene on the price before the review deadline, should cost reductions be larger than those anticipated. In fact, if after setting the price it turns out that the value of x is too low, and thus the company is reaping substantial profits without any benefits for the consumers there would probably be strong political pressure to intervene ahead of the review, and this fear could therefore induce the firm not to improve its productivity as much as it could.

Moreover, this rule does not solve the problem of long-term investment, which requires that the classic *RPI-x* is flanked by a series of pass-through coefficients which transfer onto price some of the long-term investment made by the company, or else compensate the company for cost variations which it cannot control[34]. The need to allow a partial transfer of investment costs to prices is a negative element; in fact, on the one hand it diminishes the simplicity of the price rule, and on the other it introduces elements which could allow the company to offload part of its costs onto consumers, thus reducing the incentive to improve efficiency[35].

In conclusion, although economic theory offers a series of important elements which have also found significant applications, it also suggests that the delicate question of long-term investments may not receive wholly satisfactory solutions from regulatory interventions. The low level of credibility of public authorities and the lack of instruments available result in inefficiencies which can at times be quite significant.

---

[34] For example, in England and Wales, the price rule introduced for distribution companies can be written as $RPI - x + y$, where y indicates the pass-through and is in turn the sum of four elements which take account of transmission price changes, electricity purchase costs and a sort of thermal surcharge. In the case of the British Airport Authority, it concerns investments in safety, and in that of water distribution companies upgrading to meet environmental and quality standards; see ARMSTRONG M. - COWAN S. - VICKERS J. [2] for a more detailed analysis.

[35] In practice, it may not be easy to measure exactly what is the investment cost and what instead is a normal operating cost; the complexity of accounting norms cannot always offer absolute guarantees here.

4.4 *The Crucial Problem of Vertical Integration*

A problem which intertwines with those above and is perhaps one of the main topics of discussion in the present political debate is that of the opportunity to allow the same company to operate in all market segments: given the monopolistic nature of network management, the question is really whether it is desirable that a monopolist who operates the grid should compete with other companies in the other production phases. To some extent, the answer to this question depends on the structure that will be developed in the other segments of the market. For example, if one planned to maintain the present position of quasi-monopoly in distribution and generation, the traditional argument in favour of vertical integration would appear to suffice: a chain of monopolists in vertically connected markets is undoubtedly a worse alternative than the integrated monopoly as it adds the duplication of the mark-ups.

However, a series of factors clearly points against such a arrangement, firstly the Community directives which have repeatedly emphasised the recommendation to foster competition wherever possible. Another rather convincing argument is that the presence of an integrated company which dominates the sector would considerably reduce the power to extract information from firms, while it would aggravate the risk of regulatory capture. If therefore, as would appear not only desirable but also likely, one intends to promote more competition, at least in the generation market, then other theoretical considerations increase in importance.

First of all, the so-called hold-up problem which can be illustrated as follows. If the return on investment (for example) in generation depends on the future behaviour of the network operator, and if it is not possible to write a complete contract then there is the risk that the separation of generation and network management could lead to a reduction of investment in generation. This risk could be limited by regulating the network to offer adeguate guarantees for those who invest in related production phases.

The second important problem is related to the possibility that the behaviour of the monopolist who manages the network could be such as to limit the capacity of other players to compete in other phases. In particular, if the network manager had the capacity to increase the costs of his rivals or in any case to reduce their profits, manipulating the network access conditions to favour his plants, then vertical integration would appear undesirable, as it would become a means of foiling competition in generation, or at least of reducing its effectiveness[36]. It should be noted that if the network manager succeeded in discriminating against his competitors in the generation phase, the problem of hold-up would come preponderantly to the fore as regards the other companies.

The conclusion can therefore only be that the desirability of vertical integration depends to a large extent on the relative weight attributed to each of the aforementioned problems in the specific case at stake. If one believed that regulation of the network was wholly capable of observing and evaluating the behaviours of the various players, and hence of offering a satisfactory response to both questions, then vertical integration becomes a false problem. If instead one recognises that the possibilities of regulation are limited with reference (at least) to one of the two questions, then one should conclude that the response as to the desirability of an integrated structure should depend on which of the problems indicated above may remain. The answer to these questions will be found in the next section.

5. - Reform of the Sector: Which Paths to Take?

The evolution of the European provisions on competition in the public utilities market, and in particular in the energy market, for which these provisions have always been more cautious, have endowed the reform proposals with considerable momentum. However given the EC's nature as a seat of compromises between national situations and positions which are somewhat diverging, it should be

---

[36] For example, if there was no obligation to buy from private producers at predetermined prices, there would be the risk that the network manager would seek to favour his own plants, relegating rivals to the role of buffer between demand and supply currently played by ENEL. Similarly, electricity delivered to distributors can be decided by the network manager. If he was interested in limiting the capacity of a «rival» distributor, he would have the possibility to do so. It is obvious that there is a potential conflict between the interest of a vertically integrated company and the quest for the overall efficiency of the system.

no surprise that the proposal from the EC appears, in some aspects, contradictory.

The first fundamental document is Directive 90/547/EEC on the transit of electric energy on high-voltage networks which enshrines third-parties' right of access to the networks without however dealing with the question of the relation between generation companies and final users; this «oversight» considerably reduces the significance of the principle upheld. Further steps in the direction of liberalisation or at least of definition of the ownership arrangements have led only to a draft Directive, which was issued in February 1992, subsequently revised in December 1993 and has since been the subject of heated debate.

The current draft of the Directive appears to lack incisiveness and to be the result of above all fears and compromises. A particularly important aspect is that this draft envisages that access to networks be negotiated and not regulated; in other words, the conditions of access could be *de facto* dictated by the network operator, who could manipulate such access so as to favour associated companies present in other phases of the production process.

This norm therefore makes the vertical separation of the system crucial and the fact that the proposal on this issue recommends only unbundling the accounting of the various production phases, which can however still refer to a single management and single owner, is therefore entirely negative. The debate is still in progress and the struggle between the interests of the big groups which currently dominate the continental market and the advocates of competition is still quite open and evident.

Alongside these developments, in Italy there continued the debate which commenced when ENEL became a joint-stock company (SpA) in 1992. The Amato governement proposal, which was later adopted by the Ciampi government, was to privatise ENEL as a public company, but leaving the government with a golden share of powers which still await definition. The primary objective was to maximise the revenues from the disposal to reduce Italy's huge public deficit as much as possible[37].

---

[37] One can only agree with the analysis by AMMAN M. ([1], p. 35) which emphasises that the documents issued by the Amato government during the rearrangement of the

Debate true and proper on the overall reform of the electricity sector was commenced during the Berlusconi government (in 1994) by the Minister of Industry Gnutti who — although in a minority in the government — succeeded in passing the principles of the unbundling of ENEL and of opening the market to competition. The brief protocol signed in November 1994 by ministers Dini, Gnutti and Pagliarini envisaged (albeit somewhat nebulously) the division, at least as regards accounting, of ENEL into three arms, with the gradual disposal to private agents of the generation arm, after it in turn had been split into several separate units.

This agreement remained a dead letter, and the Dini government would appear inclined to dust off the original project to privatise ENEL as it is[38]. The approval of Law no. 481 of 1995 which institutes an authority for the electricity sector, sets up the structures needed to supervise the activities of any privatised public utilites and perhaps opens the path to a new phase of discussion.

This paper will be printed before the conclusion of the debate and hence it is particularly appropriate to attempt to outline the proposal which emerges from the theory and which we believe worthy of support. The proposal is articulated as follows:

1) elimination of the present vertical integration in the sector, with the separation of generation, transmission and distribution, and a ban on simultaneously operating in more than one of these sectors;

2) the introduction of the broadest possible competitive regime in generation, with the sale of ENEL's present plant stock to a host of (private) players;

3) the maintenance of public ownership of the transmission network and its integration with the dispatch side;

4) the awarding of numerous licences for distribution, to regulated local monopolies, ownership of which can be gradually transferred to private agents;

---

state's interests was characterised by a «disarming poverty of arguments vis-à-vis the issue at stake».

[38] Caution is obligatory in view of some apparent divergences between the ministers and the opaqueness of some public pronouncements, which are often entrusted only to verbal declarations to the press. The audition of the Ministry of Industry at the Senate — unfortunately too laconic to provide sufficiently argued motivations — provides one such indication (CLÒ A. [5]).

5) progressive liberalisation of retail, starting from the big users to eventually embrace all consumers.

It is appropriate to analyse each of these aspects separately.

5.1 *Generation: Exploit the Opportunities of Competition*

One argument that is often put forward to defend the continuing existence of a single player in generation is that such player enjoys a greater bargaining power on the input market, in particular for fuels. This argument has however never been backed up by data, which gives rise to some perplexity. Moreover, once a generator operates with an efficient scale of production he is in any case a sufficiently «big» purchaser on the factors market and can therefore enjoy many of the ensuing advantages.

We can thus conclude that the set-up in the generation market can only be one which maximises the efficiency gain vis-à-vis the present situation[39], and hence one should aim at a competitive set-up. One of the main reasons for preferring competition is the recognised greater effectiveness of antitrust policies relative to regulatory interventions and it is no coincidence that the idea of introducing «some» competition in the sector is now shared by almost all those concerned.

Furthermore, since the nature of competition in this field makes it quite easy to achieve collusive results, it is important to have a large number of companies so as to minimise the risks of collusion. Finally, one will have to avoid the presence of a dominant company which can act as a leader; drawing on the UK's experience in this field would be extremely useful[40].

How are these results to be achieved? Only two paths would appear to be open. The first, preferred in particular by ENEL and — it would appear — the Dini government, is that of freezing ENEL's plant stock, and allowing only competitors to build new plants. The second

---

[39] It should be borne in mind that more than 60% of the total costs of the service come from generation and hence reductions in these costs could have an extremely significant impact on the system as a whole.

[40] ARMSTRONG M. - COWAN S. - VICKERS I. [2] and GREEN R. - NEWBERY R. [11] clearly indicate that insufficient competition has been created in the UK electricity generation sector.

is that of dividing ENEL's power plants between a certain number of companies which would then be sold separately. In our view, this second path is by far preferable above all because it would prevent those asymmetries between competitors which make competition less efficient[41].

Finally, it should be acknowledged that Law no. 9 of 1991 and subsequent measures by the government's interministerial price committee CIP have failed in their primary objective, namely that of ensuring the development of production which uses renewable sources. As the incentives introduced only attract private agents to the market by virtue of their surcharges (vis-à-vis avoided costs) which are borne by the community as a whole the arrangement would appear totally inadequate and hence should be reviewed. The entry of private producers should be encouraged solely by the sale of plants which currently belong to ENEL and by a proper working of the competitive mechanism.

5.2. *Transmission and Dispatch*

As already noted when discussing the technical aspects of the market, there are good reasons for bundling the management of dispatch with that of transmission. In particular, it is important that the player who manages dispatch, and hence who has to choose which generation plants to use, does so by minimising the sum of the electricity purchase and transmission costs and not just the purchase costs. In other words, the dispatcher should take account of the costs of the system as a whole, and for this to take place, this service should be integrated with the transmission network[42].

As regards the ownership structure, we have seen that transmission is a natural monopoly, and that even the most sophisticated regulatory arrangements find it extremely difficult to give the regulated company suitable incentives to invest; in the case where investments (in particular long-term investments) are therefore crucial for

---

[41] In particular, the growth of Italy's generation needs is rather slow, and as a result the growth process for private agents would require a very long period of time.

[42] On this issue, see the considerations of EINHORN M. [7] on the UK case.

the development of the production process, indirect public intervention may turn out to lack bite. The reasons for public ownership are to be found prescisely in these considerations, namely in the convinction that the present set-up of the high-voltage networks is still not fully satisfactory and in particular is a potential crucial problem for the development of the Mezzogiorno. It would therefore appear appropriate that the networks remain in public hands[43].

5.3 *Distribution Between Local Monopolies and Competition*

Distribution is also a monopoly element even though — as already pointed out — it can easily be split into local monopolies[44]. There are two crucial questions here.

The first is that of the ownership structure. here, we believe that in some zones of Italy the considerations advanced above with reference to transmission hold, namely, those concerning regulation's limited ability to give the «right» incentives to investment. In some areas of Italy, this is still a serious problem; we have seen how the quality and the efficiency of the service differ significantly in different zones and how this risks weighing not only on a balanced development of the various areas but also on the overall performance of Italy's productive system. While in some areas privatisation would appear wholly plausible, in others the maintenance of a public presence could, at least for an interim, be the preferable option.

In zones where privatisation could proceed, there arises the second question, namely the regulatory regime to which the distribution companies should be subject. The possibility of subdividing Italy would allow the introduction of some yardstick competition in which the price changes allowed for each company should be based (above all) on the costs of the other companies; this should force each distributor to follow companies with lower costs on the efficiency

---

[43] A similar position — albeit with different motivations — is to be found in RAMPA L. [18] who points out that the development of the network has a pro-competitive effect on the generation market.

[44] For convincing arguments on the opportunity of svoiding excessive horizontal integration, see AMMAN F. [1].

plane. The difficulty of this model is that only a limited comparison can be made between the areas which differ in size, morphology and type of users.

We have no intention of minimising this problem, but we consider it important to underline two aspects. Firstly, it may be possible to develop cost adjustment or «normalisation» parameters, thus compensating those companies which operate in more difficult conditions, and hence compare the «normalised» costs instead of those recorded in the accounting. Secondly, this form of competition on the cost side would provide an incentive for companies to make their costs more transparent, with obvious advantages for the public authorities also in the future; we have repeatedly emphasised the lack of information on many aspects of the sector and this may be one way of remedying this significant obstacle.

Finally, we should also deal with the question of the future of local utilities. On the one hand, the present subdivision of Italy appears extremely irrational, in the sense that several towns are divided between ENEL and the local utility without reference to any economic logic. Furthermore, this division does not allow local utilities to exploit the economies of scale[45], and thus increases the costs of the system. Finally, ENEL's transfer prices for sales to the local utilities do not actually cover the production costs, again this is the result of a «political» decision with a dubious economic justification. The most important aspect here is to succeed in rationalising distribution areas so as to put an end to the present excessive fragmentation.

5.4. *How Much Vertical Integration?*

From the view point above all of ENEL, this is undoubtedly one of the most important questions and both the theory examined above and a survey of previous experiences clearly indicate that vertical integration can almost wholly eliminate any advantages one hopes to obtain by introducing competition wherever possible. As for the

---

[45] On this issue, see the study by FILIPPINI F. [8].

problem of hold-up by the (non-integrated) generators it may be considered somewhat limited, as their future profitability depends above all on prices whose dynamics are relatively predictable.

However, the main problem is the distorsion of competitive processes triggered by vertical integration. Control of the network gives a considerable *de facto* control on the up- and downstream production processes and unbundling (not merely of accounting or management but of ownership) is the only way to safeguard the competitive process in other phases. The UK experience, above all after the Electricity Act of 1983, clearly proves that the regulator's capacity to prevent a network operator discriminating against other competitors as regards network access is rather limited: the present set-up in England and Wales derives precisely from dissatisfaction with the results achieved without the separation of ownership between the network operator and other market players[46].

It is perhaps appropriate to recall at this point that one of the arguments which above all ENEL's present management has advanced to support the proposal to maintain an integrated structure is that such an arrangement would assist ENEL in international contracts (above all in the less industrialised countries) which would tend to favour groups able to supply services in all the production phases. On this point, ENEL's argument would not appear to be borne out by facts, as indicated for example by Vaccà S. [22], who instead emphasises that what is crucial is not integration but rather the capacity to forge alliances with groups with different specialisations[47].

5.5 *Sale, Prices and Tariffs*

The present price structure in Italy is undoubtedly complex (but this is not necessarily a bad thing) and has some distinctive char-

---

[46] The case of the UK telecommunications market and the limited competition between BT and Mercury probably leads to similar conclusions, although the technological context is obviously different.

[47] On this issue, see also AMMAN F. [1], who points out that the supposed advantages of an integrated structure in terms of greater coordination capacity are probably of little importance as technological development has increased the possibilities for intervention regardless of the group's degree of vertical integration.

acteristics vis-à-vis other European countries. The first aspect worthy of consideration is that of a single national tariff, confirmed by the law which institutes the Authority, which is an obvious obstacle to the achievement of allocative efficiency (marginal costs are not homogeneous throughout Italy) and in part to yardstick competition among distributors. Anyway, the trade-off between efficiency and «equity» in the distribution of income is known, as is probably known — at least in principle — the cost implicit in having a single national tariff.

Furthermore, it should be borne in mind that as regards sale, the application of the Community principles of network access entails a progressive liberalisation. If the principle of free access to the distribution network is accepted, contracts can be stipulated directly between consumers and producers[48], leaving distributors to manage only the (local) network service. The future liberalisation of this relationship will necessarily lead to some margin of freedom as regards prices which can be left to free negotiation between the parties, at least as regards big users, who have better ability to establish contacts with a sufficient number of retailers to derive a benefit from competition.

Another aspect to be considered, again in the wake of the numerous indications in this sense from the European Community, is what justification there is for tariff facilitations granted according not to the quantities acquired or other parameters relevant for the firm's management, but rather to the use of the electricity and the user's activity. The facilitations granted to electricity distributors and aluminium producers (to take just two examples which are rather known and significant) are merely a transfer of revenue borne by ENEL's balance sheet and can probably also be likened to cross-subsidies.

Finally, the problem of the transparency of norms. To date prices have been laid down on the basis of ENEL's reports to the competent bodies and the criteria followed have never been officially made public in a precise manner[49]. The innovation here is the recent law which institutes the sector Authority which has been given responsibility for

---

[48] In view of the impersonal nature of the relationship between generator and final user, already mentioned in Section 2, these contracts are primarily financial in nature.

[49] The widespread suspicion of abuses has recently stimulated the attention of a court, which has initiated proceedings against ENEL CEOs and some former Ministers.

prices. As this body exists for the moment only on paper, we can only hope that the practices of the past remain such. More specifically, the thermal surcharge should not continue to act as a more or less official cover for an endless series of subsidies distributed for a wide variety of reasons.

Finally, notice that the law in question, however valid it may be overall, contains some dangerous loopholes. On the one hand, it introduces a price adjustment rule of the RPI-x type. On the other, however, it introduces a pass-through principle which is not based on parameters fixed *ex-ante*: each year, the regulated firm has the right to propose that tariffs are adjusted to cover exogenous cost variations, qualitative improvements and other costs defined to date in too general a manner. The risk that the ground has been prepared for a system of «footing the bills» is all too evident. Moreover, the actual weight of the «general objectives of a social nature», mentioned in the law, which the government has to specify and which will be financed via prices have still to be defined. Although the Community principles of transparency may have been formally accepted their practical application has still to pass the test.

6 - Conclusions

We believe that a process of privatisation which limites itself to transforming a public (quasi-)monopoly into a private (quasi-)monopoly is not only a squandered opportunity but also a step in the wrong direction. The apparent superficiality with which the solution of the problem is entrusted to the virtues of the regulation of a private company[50] risks forcing the overall needs of Italy's electricity sector into the background. We hope that the institution of a regulatory Authority does not induce some to believe that bodies endowed with miraculous powers have suddenly been created: the size and importance ENEL enjoys as a result of its present structure raise consider-

---

[50] Above all if we are talking of an integrated — and hence less transparent — company whose size endows it with considerable bargaining power vis-à-vis the public authorities.

able doubts as to the real effectiveness of external control which an Authority can exercise.

The desirability of competition as a means for achieving an efficient allocation of resources should not be neglected. Italy's political debate oscillates in a worrying manner between the most aprioristic criticisms of state intervention and the reaffirmation of the traditional Italian mistrust of the market and competition; in the case of electricity, the combination of these two elements would appear to be leading along the path to the creation of a enormous private monopoly compared to which the state's presence (via the regulatory authorities) risk remaining a mere ornament, necessary to save the form (but not the substance) and justify the absence of competition. It is difficult not to believe that this type of public intervention is merely a useful «fig leaf» for continuing to protect the market.

Hazarding previsions on the actual outcome of ENEL's privatisation is far from easy: the final destiny of Italy's electricity sector is as unclear now as ever. One mistake that today appears quite probable is that the Treasury's cash needs will force an acceleration in the privatisation process and hence a *sine die* postponement of the restructuring phase. If one really believes in the opportunities to introduce competition, at least to bring Italy into line with the indications of the European Community, and hence to split up ENEL's present structure, such a postponement would be a serious mistake.

Furthermore, acquiring a company which may subsequently be subject to a drastic restructuring represents a high risk for potential buyers and it is easy to imagine that this could lead to a substantial underpricing which will cost the Treasury revenue. This could all have negative repercussions on the Italian government's reputation as a manager of privatisation, and thus compromise the success of future disposals. The privatisation process can be satisfactorily managed only by a government which can express a clear policy-line on the future of ENEL (namely a government prepared to define immediately and unambiguously the group's future structure) and offer sufficient guarantees that this policy will be carried through. Will privatisation ever take place?

BIBLIOGRAPHY

[1] AMMAN F., «La privatizzazione del sistema elettrico italiano: struttura-regolazione-proprietà», *Economia delle fonti di energia e dell'ambiente*, vol. 37, n. 3, 1994, pp. 29-66.

[2] ARMSTRONG M. - COWAN S. - VICKERS J., *Regulatory Reform: Economic Analysis and British Experience*, Cambridge, (Mass), MIT Press, 1994.

[3] CASSESE S. (ed.), *La determinazione autoritativa dei prezzi nel settore energetico*, Rimini, Maggioli, 1989.

[4] CERVIGNI G., «La politica dell'Unione Europea per il settore elettrico», Milano, Università Commerciale «Luigi Bocconi», *Working Paper*, n. 15, 1994.

[5] CLÔ A., «Politica industriale e privatizzazioni. Audizione del Ministro dell'Industria al Senato», *Economia delle Fonti di Energia e dell'Ambiente*, vol. 38, n. 1, 1995, pp. 59-64.

[6] DE FRAJA G., «Productive Efficiency in Public and Private Firms», *Journal of Public Economics*, vol. 50, 1993, pp. 15-30.

[7] EINHORN M. (ed.), *From Regulation to Competition: New Frontiers in Electricity Markets*, London, Kluwer Academic Publishers, 1994.

[8] FILIPPINI F., «Are Municipal Electricity Distribution Utilities Natural Monopolies?», Milano, Università Cattolica, *Quaderno CIFREL*, n. 11, 1994.

[9] FORTE F., *La congiuntura in Italia 1961-1965*, Torino, Einaudi, 1966.

[10] GATTI G., «Privatizzazione dell'ENEL e riforma del sistema elettrico. Alcune considerazioni preliminari», *Economia delle Fonti di Energia e dell'Ambiente*, vol. 37, n. 4, 1994, pp. 9-26.

[11] GREEN R. - NEWBERY R., «Competition in the British Electricity Spot Market», *Journal of Political Economy*, vol. 94, 1992, pp. 691-719.

[12] ISRIL, *Livello e struttura delle retribuzioni per settore e inquadramento professionale*, Roma, 1994, Istituto di Studi sulle Relazioni Industriali e di Lavoro.

[13] ISTAT, *Annuario di Statistiche del lavoro*, Roma, Istituto Centrale di Statistica, 1994.

[14] KREPS D. - SCHEINKMAN L., «Quantity Precommitments and Bertrand Competition Yield Cournot Outcome», *Bell Journal of Economics*, vol. 14, 1983, pp. 326-37.

[15] LAFFONT J.J. - TIROLE J., *A Theory of Incentives in Procurement and Regulation*, Cambridge (Mass.), MIT Press, 1994.

[16] MORI G., *La nazionalizzazione in Italia: il dibattito politico-economico*, in ZANETTI G. [25], 1994, pp. 147-73.

[17] POLO M. - SCARPA C., «La riforma del settore elettrico in Italia: una privatizzazione al buio?», in PENATI A. - TABELLINI G. (eds.) *Le nuove frontiere della politica economica*, Milano, Il Sole 24 Ore, 1995.

[18] RAMPA L., «Privatizzare con scarsi principi. L'orientamento del Governo a proposito dell'ENEL», *Economia delle Fonti di Energia e dell'Ambiente*, vol. 38, n. 1, 1995 pp. 7-20.

[19] RANCI P., «Concorrenza nella produzione e tariffa unica al consumo», *Energia*, vol. 15, n. 4, 1994, pp. 16-9.

[20] SCHMALENSEE R., «Good Regulatory Regimes», *Rand Journal of Economics*, vol. 20, 1989, pp. 417-36.

[21] SHAPIRO C. - WILLIG R., «Economic Rationales for the Scope of Privatization» in SULEIMAN E. - WATERBURY J. (eds.), *The Political Economy of Public Sector Reform*, Summertown (Oxford), Westview Press, Boulder, Co., 1990.

[22] VACCÀ S., «La privatizzazione dell'ENEL: tra mito e realtà», *Economia delle Fonti di Energia e dell'Ambiente*, vol. 37, n. 3, 1994, pp. 15-27.

[23] YARROW G., «Privatization, Restructuring and Regulatory Reform in Electricity Supply», in BISHOP M. - KAY J. - MAYER C. (eds.), *Privatization and Economic Performance*, Oxford, Oxford University Press, 1994.

[24] ZAMAGNI V., *Dalla periferia al centro*, Bologna, 1990, Il Mulino.

[25] ZANETTI G. (ed.), *Storia dell'industria elettrica in Italia. Gli sviluppi dell'ENEL 1963-90*, Roma, Laterza, 1994.

Deregulation and Privatization of the Natural Gas Market in Italy

M. Gabriella Briotti · **Elena Notarangelo** *

Confindustria, Rome   Istao, Ancona

1. - Summary

In recent years consensus seems to have been reached on the necessity to introduce market elements and greater competition into the natural gas sector and to proceed with more significant deregulation. In countries such as the United Kingdom and Germany the drive towards market deregulation has been accompanied by reasonably extensive privatization of state enterprises. The European Union has formulated numerous proposals with regard to the deregulation of the services of public utility networks, and in particular those operating in the natural gas market which, if approved in their entirety, are destined to significantly modify the current structure of the sector, and in particular the transport and distribution phases. These guidelines entail norms aimed at guaranteeing cost transparency in the distribution of gas, encouraging the transportation of natural gas by means of large networks, assuring conditions of transparency and non-discrimination in the issuing of exploration permits to locate and extract hydrocarbons. The steps proposed by the European Union are aimed at the creation of an integrated internal

---

* The authors, respectively research economist at the Centro Studi Confindustria and post-graduate scolar at ISTAO, wish to thank Ms. Anna Maria Tibuzzi of the ENI library for the documentation made available, and Mr. Carlo Briotti for the useful comments received. The opinions expressed by the authors are not necessarily shared by their respective employers, and the authors accept responsibility for eventual errors and omissions.

N.B.: the numbers in square brackets refer to the Bibliography at the end of the paper.

natural gas market governed by common rules which will guarantee a stable gas supply and promote competition and efficiency in the sector. More precisely the goals of these proposals are 1) to separate, at least on an administrative and management level, the production and distribution processes in order to guarantee cost transparency in the various phases of gas supply; 2) to permit access by third parties to large pipeline networks; 3) to fix service requirements with regard to quality and prices; 4) to establish transparent and non-discriminatory authorization for the construction of pipelines and the management of transport and distribution; and 5) to create a Trans-European Network (TEN). In general, while the accent is being placed on the necessity to implement policies of deregulation, no specific mention is made of plans to abolish public utilities.

The objective of the introduction of free-market elements into the sector is to increase the Union member states' efficiency in managing energy resources, thereby making them more competitive on the world market. The guidelines approved thus far and the proposals currently under discussion cover an extremely broad spectrum and entail significant changes to the structure of the sector which inevitably have given rise to cautious reactions on the part of the interested parties. Even though the EU member states are aware of the importance of these policies, they have opted for a rather conservative position. In fact, the immediate and total commercialization of the sector would lead to dramatic changes of the supply system, with considerable effects on the security of supply and the profitability of the enterprises. From a production point of view the prospective deregulation of the sector is viewed in a positive manner, as a result of the greater investment opportunities and the substantial reduction in supply costs of energy resources it would create. However, since it is not yet clear to what extent and on which conditions the introduction of free-market elements would lead to the desired results in terms of greater efficiency and social wealth, the position of the EU is subject to careful and critical evaluations. These doubts seem particularly justifiable in those countries where the gas industry is still in the initial phases and hardly as mature as other markets. Given the emergent character of these novel industries, many retain that an appropriate level of protectionism is needed. The option of deregulation and greater commercialization of the sector is evidently sustained with greater vigour by the newcomers as a result of the greater opportunities they imply.

The drive towards greater competition in the sector has various origins involving diverse forces and interests which are not compatible at all times. In the EU the diversity of these forces and interests has been demonstrated by the difficulty experienced in reaching agreement on the proposals of the Commission. In fact, some of these proposals have been blocked for years due to further modifications requested by the member states, and this has inevitably led to negotiations being slowed down. This restraining action exercised by the member states has reduced the efficiency of the objectives of the EU. The EU action has nonetheless gone ahead, and in various countries much progress has been made in the process of deregulation of the market.

Evidently there are strong arguments to be made in favor of the introduction of free-market elements and the deregulation of the sector. The sector is in continuous expansion and the improvement of efficiency and the reduction of costs can also be obtained by means of restructuring and institutional changes. The traditional motivations in favor of public intervention in the sector, such as the enormous financial support required for the development of the methane system and the protection of new expansion areas, have lost much of their relevance. Technical progress has contributed to the modification of the structure of the sector and some parts can be depicted as being competitive. Contemporaneously the feeling is that the government's previous general interests in the sector have become more political. Furthermore the distorting effects and the costs of a tariff system based on cross-subsidies are evident. As a result of the monopolistic character of the sector, privatization does not exclude the necessity for some form of regulation and protection from abuses, but public interest should also be guaranteed as a result of the strategic national interest of the energy sector.

In various countries the process of privatization of public services enterprises has been initiated, but the objectives stated do not necessarily coincide with those of deregulation of the market. In the countries where state-owned utilities have been abolished, this move, apart from representing a boost to the development of the capital market, represents an instrument for increasing government revenues. From an ideological point of view it can be seen as the curbing of political control of the management of the enterprises. The privatization process in the United Kingdom was not exemplary either, as the initial phases were characterized by the transferring of a monopolistic sector to the private sector, with the introduction of free-market elements only taking place afterwards.

The beginning of the privatization of the energy sector in Italy with the sale of an initial 15-17% share of the sector leader ENI (Ente Nazionale Idrocarburi) at the end of 1995, placed the emphasis on the problem of balancing state revenues and reducing public debt in accordance with the obligations of the EU. An improvement in public finances is only possible if privatization is associated with an improvement in efficiency of the enterprises. Savings in public expenditure should result from less interest expenditure and from fewer transfers to cover the losses incurred by enterprises. For the country to gain wealth from the sale of public enterprises, the market must recognize an increase in the value of the enterprises as a result of the process of privatization. Such an increase in value must occur, at least partly, during the sale of the enterprises. This means that the abolition of the former structures must be associated with the elimination of bureaucratic constraints and various obstacles that impede management and economical efficiency, thereby promoting "efficiency and competitiveness".

This work examines the guidelines and the positions expressed by the EU with regard to the deregulation of the energy market, highlighting the implications on sector organization and the role played by public intervention. A brief synthesis of the energy situation in various areas of the world relative to the distribution of resources, the supply policies adopted in various countries, and the structure of international energy exchanges will allow us to identify some important factors for a correct evaluation of the effects of the proposals made by the EU Commission.

We will attempt to identify the principal elements that currently mark the state of the energy sector in Italy, such as the ownership structure, the organization of production and distribution, and the bureaucratic and regulatory constraints, highlighting their shortcomings with respect to the proposals of the EU. Besides acting as an incentive for the development of the capital market, the privatization process underway could constitute a further step towards reinforcing the principle of competition and efficiency in our economic system. In the case of public utility enterprises, privatization consists of allowing free initiative to govern the activities without impeding the unfolding of competition. Where this is not possible, privatization must be accompanied by the formation of independent regulatory bodies that will guarantee consumer interests such as tariffs and service quality. With the institution of the electric energy and gas authority (Autorità per l'energia e per il gas) in November of 1995 these principles have been established, but much still has to be said with regard to the future organization of the sector. Particular attention has to be paid to the institutional modifications foreseen and the restructuring objectives proposed in order to ultimately introduce free-market elements and competition.

2. - Market Deregulation and EU Policies

The gas market in the EU is subject to considerable control. Despite the attempts by the Commission to open it to a more competitive supply of energy resources, the market tends to maintain a strong monopolistic connotation as far as transport, and to a lesser degree distribution, is concerned. In most of the countries of the EU the gas sector is governed by the state-owned public utility enterprises. The general trend towards regulation proposed by individual countries and the EU originates from the idea to introduce competitive elements into a market with a natural monopolistic character. The reduction of state ownership and consequent reduction of direct control by the government, necessitates the introduction of other control mechanisms to protect public and strategic national interest and defend new market players against abuses of monopolistic power. In the UK for instance, an independent gas regulator has been instituted, and in Germany an institution for the promotion of competition is in operation. In other cases the government has opted to retain control and decision-making powers with regard to crucial matters by implementing a «golden share» system. This is to prevent strategic enterprises, which are immune from the normal market constraints, from managing price levels in socially unacceptable ways. Furthermore, experience in various countries has shown that the state's role in the privatization process is crucial, as it is required to create conditions favorable for investments and projects characterized by elevated costs and enormous mobilization of capital and which are destined to produce results and profits only in the long run. The reduction of the risks coupled with these investment projects and the security of resource supply are factors of vital importance to the development of the market.

With the inter-governmental conference on the Maastricht Treaty approaching, the EU's policy with regard to energy is currently being subjected to critical revision, and a reinforcement of the Community energy policies and the examination of the articles regarding competition and the environment can be expected. The specific articles related to energy of the *Maastricht Treaty*, together with the ECSC (1952) and EURATOM (1957) Treaties provide the Commission with the necessary powers to remove all obstacles that prevent a single market for the products and services of the sector. It is obviously necessary and explicitly required that the rules of a single market are compatible with adequate criteria for security and continuity of supply.

The European Commission's action has taken place across a wide spectrum and comprises all the diverse aspects of the regulation of the sector. In the past few years this has lead to the formulation of numerous policies regarding price transparency (*90/377/EEC*), access rights to and the use of natural gas pipeline networks (*91/296/EEC* amended by *94/49/EEC*), establishment of procedure for the allocation of contracts (*90/531/EEC* and *92/13/EEC* and *93/38/EEC*), and establishment of transparent and non-discriminatory criteria for the authorization to explore for and produce fossil fuels (*94/22/EEC*). The European Commission has also proposed common rules for the establishment of an internal natural gas market and the liberalization of access to the distribution networks by third parties, and has developed guidelines for the creation of a trans-european gas pipeline network.

The introduction of the policy (*90/377/EEC*) on distribution price transparency in the *Maastricht Treaty* imposes a common procedure regarding transparency of prices charged to final consumers of industrial gas and electric energy, thereby compelling gas producing enterprises to communicate all prices charged to various categories of consumers.

The introduction of the policy (*91/296/EEC*) on the transport and distribution of natural gas between large pipeline networks represents the principal instrument used by the Commission to regulate transport and distribution. The objective of this policy is to promote the establishment of a single energy market modifying, if necessary, national legislations that interfere with the transport of natural gas, thereby establishing an integrated system of national pipeline networks. In this regard countries are required to adopt the measures aimed at facilitating the transit of natural gas between large pipeline networks in their territory. The transport of gas should take place at fair and non-discriminatory conditions that do not contain abusive provisions and unjust restrictions and therefore do not compromise security of supply and service quality. All member states are required to initiate negotiations with regard to the transport conditions and to keep the European Commission informed on the outcome of such negotiations. Failure by the parties concerned to reach an agreement for no justifiable reason, will render disputes subject to arbitration by the European Commission. This policy furthermore regulates access by third parties to the distribution networks by way of specific transit authorization. The agreement reached between ENEL (Ente Nazionale Energia Elettrica) and SNAM (Società Nazionale Metanodotti) for the transport of Algerian gas acquired directly by ENEL for its electricity plants is an example of this. This policy has been implemented by all the member states except France, Portugal and Spain.

The policy *94/22/EEC* (to be implemented by July 1995) on exploration and production of hydrocarbons aims at guaranteeing transparent and non-discriminatory conditions for the issuing of exploration and production permits, and consequently at increasing competition. Based on this policy member states will be required to abrogate all norms assigning exclusive rights to exploit a specific area to a single institution as from January 1997. This is the case of the deposits located in the area where ENI has exclusive access rights (Val Padana and surrounding areas). The contents of this policy and the change it has brought about in the position assumed by the European Commission is extremely relevant, if one considers that previously the norms contained in the mentioned treaties did not contain indications relevant to the production of natural gas.

The European Commission has made several other proposals aimed at creating an internal gas market to improve the security of supply and promote competition and efficiency in the sector. Common measures have been proposed by the European Commission in 1992, which have subsequently been amended in December 1993 (*OJ N C123/26* of May 1994). These measures have the following purpose:

a) the establishment of service obligations to be undertaken by public utilities as far as quality, prices and security of supply are concerned; and

b) the establishment of transparent and non-discriminatory procedures for the authorization of pipeline construction and the management of transport and distribution.

A significant change with respect to the past is that the issuing of new pipelines construction permits is not constrained by the existence of available pipeline capacity at fair prices. Furthermore gas companies will have the possibility to negotiate access to pipeline networks on a commercial basis in order to supply distributors and large industrial consumers of gas.

Ever since September 1992 the European Commission was intent on examining the possibility and conditions to grant third parties access to the European pipeline networks. The so-called third party access (TPA) regime, if applied, would oblige the companies who manage the gas transmission and distribution network to grant third parties the possibility to utilize available capacity on their networks at appropriate conditions. This proposal represents an instrument with which to promote competition from a supply point of view, thereby eliminating a natural monopoly. Based on this proposal the companies that own and control these pipelines cannot refuse to transport gas exchanged between third parties if they have unutilized capacity available. In its current form the proposal is not limited only to long-term agreements reached with large industrial consumers, even though the right of access to pipelines could be limited to these specific cases in a transitory period. Despite member states' opposition to the TPA rule, there is a growing experience of how it could be successful, for example, in the North Sea and even at an early stage in Italy.

The European Commission does not consider the unbundling of the various phases of the production and distribution process to be crucial. The new approach does however imply the separation of the management and administration of the successive phases, from production to distribution to increase cost transparency and income trasparency, particularly with regard to the transport phase which constitutes a natural monopoly.

As a whole the proposals related to the deregulation of the gas market would lead to enterprises being able to acquire the freedom to construct and control pipelines, liquid natural gas treatment and gas storage plants, but having to respect the criteria fixed on an objective and non-discriminatory basis by the member states. Based on the TPA, every client will be free to acquire gas from any producer within and across national boundaries and receive it through the interconnected pipeline system. The prices of gas acquired through the great pipeline networks should not be subject to regulation. The vertically integrated distribution business units will have to unbundle their accounts.

In conclusion, it must be said that if the European Commission has been successful in having its proposals on price transparency, pipeline access, and exploration and production authorization procedures approved, it has been less successful in fixing common rules for an internal gas market and greater competition in the sector. The result is that government intervention with regard to prices and investment is extensive, thus preventing enterprises from adapting to a market situation.

3. - Distribution of Natural Gas Resources and Supply Policies

The actions undertaken by the European Commission have been criticized for various reasons. First of all, since the number of potential suppliers of energy resources is rather reduced, it has been said that the function of grouping the demand for gas by European transporters/importers in the current monopolistic situation is crucial in order to clearly define the relationship between producers (external) and consumers (internal) with the greatest advantages to the consumers. Furthermore, the application of the TPA regime would weaken the position of European consumers and favour foreign producers. Also, access by third parties to European networks could compromise security of supply which is based in large part on the stipulation of long-term contracts well in advance. A more vast choice for buyers of gas can in fact cause buyers to be less willing to sign long-term binding agreements. Finally, a policy on natural gas supply at Community level would increase supply security and resource availability only if some countries had an excess of resources with which to compensate internal European scarcities of resources, and also if this led to real and greater diversification among suppliers. If this were not to happen, the liberalization of the gas market on a Community level would not significantly modify the current conditions.

The introduction of the TPA principle could also lead to undesirable price discrimination and possible cross-subsidies among large consumers, who would then have access to an unregulated market. Small new entrants would be forced to negotiate terms with a given suppliers. The result could be a Ramsey price system where clients who have less demand flexibility would be charged higher prices, and vice versa, and a subsidy system among users. In conclusion a monopolistic market setting would instead allow easier coverage of costs and make reaching the break even point easier as a result of the enormous quantities of gas handled, and in turn leading to lower prices for all consumers.

According to this interpretation, greater efficiency in the sector is mainly limited by the absence of competition between alternative suppliers of energy resources due to the existing tax distortions. Neither the application of the TPA regime nor restructuring and unbundling processes of the sector are necessary to remove these obstacles, but rather the modification of national rules. The TPA regime could instead increase the necessity for regulation.

Much of the criticism introduces arguments of validity and substance. The various countries of the EU find themselves in fact in diverse situations as far as the supply of natural gas is concerned. Of similar importance is the fact that the negotiating power of countries who have access to resources is increasing following the rise in importance and the potential demand, and certain participants maintain that there is also a problem of dependability and political equilibrium.

These criticisms fail in grasping a more general and complete view of the EU proposals which are, all together, robust and sustainable. Security of supply is not only a matter of diversification of suppliers and compensation between countries, but it is also a problem of coordination and investment as is demonstrated by the interest shown by the European Union in formulating an energy policy. The approach which suggests that the break even point is more easily reached when lower prices are charged by a single supplier, does not take into consideration the fact that in a monopoly the real market price is unknown. The proposals of the European Union for the creation of an internal market are based on interventions aimed at the promotion of competition in the market (such as those related to pipeline construction and the TPA regime), and measures aimed at greater regulation of the sector (such as the service obligations for public utility enterprises and quality and price standards).

A brief look at the distribution of natural resources in the world and the supply and exchange policies adopted in various countries would be useful to the further discussion of this topic. Between 1983 and 1993 the consumption of natural gas by the 15 countries of the European Union has increased by 40.57% (87.49% in Italy alone) with natural gas constituting 18.9% of all primary resources utilized by these countries (26.78% in Italy - see Table 1). Forecasts confirming an increase in the consumption of natural gas in Europe over the long period highlight the relevance of the role to be played by government and the EU in creating favorable conditions for investments characterized by very high initial costs and risky long-term earnings, and in guaranteeing security of supply. Further development of the market therefore depends on the creation of these conditions.

TABLE 1

OECD COUNTRIES, EUROPEAN UNION AND ITALY: ENERGY SUPPLY BY PRIMARY ENERGY SOURCE[a]

	Levels[b] 1993			Variation (%) 1983-1993			Share (%) 1993		
	OECD	EU (15)	Italy	OECD	EU (15)	Italy	OECD	EU (15)	Italy
Nuclear	472.81	206.98	–	108.91	111.73	–	10.77	15.53	–
Coal	874.06	243.64	10.79	7.02	–18.86	–12.58	19.91	18.28	6.89
Oil	1,850.93	573.16	92.66	12.21	7.99	5.19	42.16	43.00	59.17
Gas	903.46	251.95	41.94	30.13	40.57	87.49	20.58	18.90	26.78
Other[c]	288.74	57.27	11.22	28.63	17.34	43.52	6.58	4.30	7.16
Total	4,390.00	1,333.00	156.61	21.56	15.23	18.53	100.00	100.00	100.00

[a] Efficiency rates: hydro-electric plants - 100%, nuclear plants - 33%, geothermic plants - 10%.
[b] Mtoe.
[c] Hydraulic, geothermal, solar, wind, combustible renewables and waste.
Source, own elaborations from OECD [31].

The distribution of proven natural gas resources in the world [1] in 1995 indicates the positions of various countries with regard to the supply of energy resources, and also provides information with regard to the supply policies adopted (Table 2). With respect to 1970, the North American (from 23.9 to 4.7%) and the Western European (9.1 to 4.2%) shares relative to the total world resources have decreased, while the shares of Eastern Europe (31.8 to 39.3%) and the Middle East (16.8 to 30.3%) have increased. While the decrease of the Western European share can be attributed to the large amount of reserves discovered in the rest of the world, the decrease in the North American share is a result of an inclination to exploit local resources for local use and export purposes. This is also indicated by the decrease in value of the resources currently available in North America and its high share of total world production (Table 3). The relationship between available resources and production is measured in terms of the potential duration (in years of production) of the resource, which consequently indicates the supply autonomy of the country. This has been significantly reduced in the case of North America and Europe as a result of the high rate of production. In Africa, where the exploitation of natural gas sources has only commenced recently, this figure is also relatively low, yet only second to the figure of the Middle East (Table 4). A comparison of production and consumption in every area shows that almost all of the production in North America and Latin America is destined for internal consumption, while Western Europe is seen as a big importer and Eastern Europe as an exporter of natural gas.

The supply policies of Europe have to satisfy a demand estimated at approximately 400 billion cu meters for 1995 (of which at least 330 billion cu meters will come from the OECD European countries). This demand will be more than 600 billion cu meters in 2010 (more than 450 billion cu meters from the OECD European countries) (Table 5). With 1995 as a reference, about 220 of the 330 billion cu meters consumed by Western European countries will come from internal production which will be destined for local consumption or internal

---

[1] Proven natural resources consist of currently detected resources, exploitable at adequate costs on the basis of the existing technology.

TABLE 2

PROVED NATURAL GAS RESERVES IN THE WORLD
(10^9 m^3)

	Levels					Share %				
	1970	1980	1990	1994	1995	1970	1980	1990	1994	1995
North America	9,428	8,015	7,464	6,831	6,932	23.9	10.4	5.7	4.6	4.7
Latin America	1,874	4,353	7,159	7,652	7,848	4.8	5.7	5.5	5.2	5.3
Western Europe	3,583	3,950	5,598	6,228	6,292	9.1	5.1	4.3	4.2	4.2
Eastern Europe........	12,547	31,533	52,466	58,515	58,559	31.8	41.0	40.3	39.7	39.3
Africa	3,834	5,683	8,580	9,893	9,982	9.7	7.4	6.6	6.7	6.7
Middle East	6,627	18,541	37,862	44,572	45,038	16.8	24.1	29.1	30.3	30.3
Asia/Oceania	1,550	4,796	11,129	13,649	14,224	3.9	6.2	8.5	9.3	9.6
Total	39,443	76,871	130,258	147,340	148,875	100.0	100.0	100.0	100.0	100.0

Source, CEDIGAZ [9].

TABLE 3

PRODUCTION OF NATURAL GAS

	(10⁹ m³)				Share %			
	1970	1980	1990	1994	1970	1980	1990	1994
North America	651.8	624.4	611.7	685.8	62.7	41.1	29.5	31.6
Latin America	34.5	65.5	85.1	94.7	3.3	4.3	4.1	4.4
Western Europe	80.7	200.8	199.1	233.5	7.8	13.2	9.6	10.7
Eastern Europe	233.2	482.6	852.5	748.6	22.4	31.8	41.2	34.5
Africa	3.4	27.2	70.9	76.3	0.3	1.8	3.4	3.5
Middle East	19.5	44.5	102.9	132.9	1.9	2.9	5.0	6.1
Asia/Oceania	17.0	74.1	149.0	200.9	1.6	4.9	7.2	9.2
Total	1,040.1	1,519.1	2,071.2	2,172.7	100.0	100.0	100.0	100.0

Source, CEDIGAZ [9].

TABLE 4

RESERVES/PRODUCTION RATIO [a]
(%)

	1970	1980	1990	1994
North America	14.5	12.8	12.2	10.0
Latin America	54.3	66.5	84.1	80.8
Western Europe	44.4	19.7	28.1	26.7
Eastern Europe........	53.8	65.3	61.5	78.2
Africa	1,127.6	208.9	121.0	129.7
Middle East	339.8	416.7	367.9	335.4
Asia/Oceania	91.2	64.7	74.7	67.9
Total	37.9	50.6	62.9	67.8

[a] Equivalence in years of production.
Source, own elaborations from CEDIGAZ [9].

exchanges. The remainder will be imported from non-OECD countries (respectively 65 and 39 billion cu meters from countries in the CIS and Algeria). It is evident that the share obtained from internal sources is relatively large, and according to predictions the proportions of the share are not bound to until 2010. To ensure timely supplies, contracts have to be defined well in advance as is indicated by the fact in 1992 90% of the estimated Western European demand for the end of the nineties had already been agreed upon.

The position of the 12 countries of the European Union in 1995 shows it to be an importer of natural gas with respect to the rest of the world, with imports of 111 billion cu meters, slightly less than a third of the total consumption. Taking into account the 45 billion cu meters exported primarily by the Netherlands this figure goes down to about one sixth of total consumption (Table 6). The matrix of international exchanges shows that a large share of the gas exported by northern European countries is destined to other OECD European countries (Table 7). The European countries that have relevant exports and that can be considered as potential suppliers are few. A significant share of 18% can be attributed to the Netherlands and Norway alone (Table 8). It must however be said that the number of countries who need to import is also relatively limited. In particular the total demand of Belgium, France, Germany and Italy amounts to 39% of the total

TABLE 5

NATURAL GAS SUPPLY AND DEMAND IN EUROPE, 1988-2010
(10^9 m^3)

	Estimates					
	1988	1989	1990	1995	2000	2010 [a]
Demand						
OECD Europe [b]	242	250	278	320-340	370-390	450-480
Central and Eastern Europe	91	95	73	70-80	90-110	120-170
European total	333	343	351	390-420	460-500	570-650
Supply						
OECD Internal production	116	119	129	140-150	140-150	120-140
Destined for local consumption *intra*-OECD import contracts:						
Netherlands	25	30	31	31-36	31-36	31-36
Norway	27	29	26	35	32-39	37-49
OECD zone (includes other contracts and possible renewals).........	172	180	190	210-225	210-230	195-230
Imports from non-OECD countries in the OECD area						
CIS	40	46	60	63-67	63-67	63-67
Algeria [a]	25	27	28	38-40	38-40	38-40
Central and Eastern European internal production [c]	55	52	38	20-40	10-30	10-20
Imports from USSR to Central and Eastern Europe	40	44	40	40	40	40
Total supply	330	349	356	371-412	361-407	346-392
Supply contracts to be concluded	–	–	–	0-49	53-139	178-304

[a] It is assumed that as of 2010 existing contracts will be renewed, 2000 for Algeria.
[b] Includes East Germany since 1990.
[c] Includes East Germany up to 1989.
Source, OECD, *Politiques et Perspectives du Gaz Naturel*, 1992.

TABLE 6

NATURAL GAS SUPPLY IN EU COUNTRIES, 1994
(10^9 m³)

	EU (12)	Belgium	Denmark	France	Germany	Italy	Netherlands	Spain	UK
Production	199.98	—	4.88	3.50	19.59	20.64	78.41	0.18	69.96
Intra-EU imports	41.88	5.26	—	5.11	25.89	4.47	0.47	—	—
Extra-EU imports	111.49	6.61	—	26.10	40.18	25.22	2.82	7.53	3.03
Norway	26.51	2.63	—	6.95	9.98	—	2.82	1.10	3.03
CIS	55.09	—	—	11.50	30.20	13.39	—	—	—
Algeria	27.96	3.98	—	7.65	—	11.78	—	4.55	—
Libya	1.48	—	—	—	—	0.05	—	1.43	—
Australia	0.45	—	—	—	—	—	—	0.45	—
Exports	45.13	—	1.75	—	1.71	—	40.80	—	0.87
Stock variations	−3.79	−0.22	−0.12	0.02	−3.05	−0.33	—	−0.38	0.32
Internal consumption ..	304.43	11.65	3.01	34.73	80.90	50.00	40.90	7.33	72.44

Source, CEDIGAZ [9].

TABLE 7

INTERNATIONAL EXCHANGES OF NATURAL GAS, 1994 [a]
(10^9 m^3)

Importers \ Exporters	Netherlands	Norway	Other Eastern European countries	CIS	North Africa	Middle East	Asia Oceania	Americas	Total
Italy	4.5	—	—	13.4	11.7	—	—	—	29.6
France	4.5	7.9	—	11.8	8.5	—	—	—	32.7
Germany	20.3	11.2	1.0	28.9	—	—	—	—	61.4
Benelux	4.4	3.0	—	—	4.8	—	—	—	12.2
UK	—	3.2	—	—	—	—	—	—	3.2
Netherlands	—	2.7	0.4	—	—	—	—	—	3.1
Switzerland	0.5	—	1.5	0.4	—	—	—	—	2.4
Austria	—	0.3	0.3	5.0	—	—	—	—	5.6
Spain	—	1.1	—	—	6.2	—	0.8	—	8.1
Finland	—	—	—	3.3	—	—	—	—	3.3
ex Yugoslavia	—	—	—	3.6	0.4	—	—	—	4.0
Turkey	—	—	—	5.5	0.4	—	—	—	5.9
Other Eastern Europe	—	—	—	33.0	—	—	—	—	33.0
Middle East	—	—	—	—	—	10.0	—	—	10.0
USA	—	—	—	—	1.5	—	—	70.5	72.0
Rest of Americas	—	—	—	—	—	—	—	4.0	4.0
Japan	—	—	—	—	—	4.3	50.5	1.6	56.4
South Korea	—	—	—	—	—	—	7.9	—	7.9
Taiwan	—	—	—	—	—	—	3.0	—	3.0
Total	34.2	29.4	3.2	104.9	33.5	14.3	62.2	76.1	357.8

a Provisional data.
Source, SNAM [36].

TABLE 8

IMPORTS AND EXPORT, 1994 *

	Imports		Exports
USA..............	20%	CIS	29%
Germany..........	19%	Canada	20%
Japan	16%	Netherlands......	11%
France...........	9%	Indonesia........	10%
Italy.............	8%	Algeria..........	9%
Czech Republic	4%	Norway	7%
Belgium	3%	Other	14%
Other	21%		

* Total international exchange = 363 billion cu meters.
Source, CEDIGAZ [9].

imports. And it is therefore in consideration of the importance and the volume of this internal exchange among OECD European countries that the proposals of the European Commission on liberalization and integration of the market become relevant.

4. - Market Structure in Italy

In 1994 the transport and distribution sectors utilized 150,000 km of pipeline network and a distribution system of 26,000 km to distribute approximately 50,000 million cu meters, employing more than 30,000 people. The annual investments in this sector amounted to 2 billion ECU in 1993. In the same year the per capita consumption was slightly higher than the OECD average, and in Europe, signifi-cantly inferior only to that of the Netherlands. In 1994 the consump-tion of natural gas made up 27% of the total national energy consump-tion in Italy, an increase of 88% on the total volume consumed in 1983 and four times more than in 1970 (Table 9). Between 1970 and 1994 the production of natural gas in Italy has increased very little, contrary to the considerable increase in imports which have gone from marginal amounts to almost twice the national production. Of the 49.6 billion cu meters available in 1994, 29.6% billion cu meters had been imported and 20 billion cu meters constituted the internal

TABLE 9

STRUCTURE OF NATURAL GAS CONSUMPTION BY SECTOR

	Italy				EU (15)			
	1970		1994 [a]		1970		1994 [a]	
	10^9 m³	%	10^9 m³	%	10^9 m³	%	10^9 m³	%
Civil............	3.0	23.4	20.6	41.5	27.7	36.2	141.7	45.7
Industrial	6.1	47.7	19.2	38.7	27.5	35.9	110.0	35.5
Chemical	2.1	16.4	0.8	1.6	7.3	9.5	13.2	4.3
Thermoelectric	1.6	12.5	9.0	18.1	14.1	18.4	45.1	14.5
Total	12.8	100.0	49.6	100.0	76.6	100.0	310.0	100.0

a Provisional data.
Source, SNAM [36], *Metano ed energia, dati statistici, 1994, 1995.*

production. An analysis of the consumption of natural gas according to the sectors of utilization shows 41.5% being utilized for civil purposes (23.4% in 1970), 38.7% for industrial purposes (47.7% in 1970), 18.1% for electric purposes (12.5% in 1970) and 1.6% for chemical purposes (16.4% in 1970).

Italian energy policies have not undergone significant changes since the last three-year national energy plan was adopted in 1988. The principal aims are still the improvement of efficiency, environmental protection, the development of national resources, and the diversification of supply policies. The emphasis has however moved from quantitative objectives based on the dimensions of supply and demand, to a more flexible and market-orientated approach. The EU proposals aimed at increased transparency and competition on the European markets have contributed to the revision of the market regulation which in turn has led to greater ease of access to the transport networks and greater price transparency.

In 1992 ENI was transformed into a corporation in view of its future privatization. With the abolishment of the inter-ministerial price committee, the body which was responsible for regulating prices and tariffs up to the end of 1993, and the beginning of the privatization process, the institution of a regulating authority for electrical energy and gas became imperative during November 1995.

The new strategy is aimed at the privatization of energy utilities, the elimination of centralized planning, the removal of exclusive rights that are not justified by cases of natural monopolies, the promotion of competition and a clear distinction between political, economic and social objectives. ENI's privatization plan can also improve its efficiency and competitiveness, provided that the energy sector will be restructured.

ENI operates in the natural gas market through its subsidiaries, of which it holds a controlling share, and which in some cases are quoted on the stock market. The subsidiaries for their part consist of corporations and are subject to corporation law. Even though the sale of a minority share by ENI has reduced public participation by 15-17%, it has not modified, at least for the moment, the order or structure of the sector.

The production and transport phases of the gas sector are almost completely managed by public enterprises, while the distribution sector is occupied by public, private, and semi-private enterprises.

As far as production and exploration is concerned, law (L. 352/92) of 1992 states that special mining rights previously conceded to ENI, should also be conceded to the new corporation until the formulation of a new law. The thinking behind this was to predispose the sector to privatization, yet leaving the possibility of legislative changes at a later stage. Complete and self-contained legislative reference in this regard is not yet available.

A 1953 law defines the extraction of hydrocarbons as being of strategic national interest, and compels ENI to pursue these interests. AGIP (Azienda Generale Italiana Petroli) has exclusive rights to explore and extract natural gas in the Po valley and adjacent areas on the Adriatic coast. AGIP is furthermore exempted of all royalties and rent, and as far as the area in question is concerned, it has exclusive rights for the utilization of pre-existent caverns as storage areas.

The new EU policy of May 1994 regarding permits for the extraction of hydrocarbons will force Italy to stop conceding exclusive rights to ENI for the area it is making use of before January 1997 and to abolish the restrictions on exploration and production currently in place in Sicily. As an autonomous region it has its own policy according to which exploration and production can be done by non-local and foreign companies as long as they are in a joint venture with local companies. According to evaluations made by ENI the reserves in Sicily are of huge dimensions, but activity seems to have been reduced in recent years.

Exploration and production activities in Italy are almost exclusively done by AGIP. Abroad, AGIP produces gas in Nigeria, Egypt and Libya in collaboration with private companies. Edison, a subsidiary of Montedison has a minor share of the national production of gas. In 1994 the national production of gas totaled 20 billion cu meters, of this 90% came from AGIP and the remaining 10% came from Edison, ELF and other Italian and foreign operators.

Exploration for and the exploitation of deposits can be done after obtaining a concession and is usually done in joint-venture with AGIP. Exploration permits are granted to both Italian and foreign enterprises, provided that reciprocity exists between the countries. The various regional authorities in Italy have special legislative powers, independent of central government, as far as gas exploration and production is concerned, except in those areas reserved to the government.

The government also retains all storage rights, but they can be acquired by concession. Even though there are no legal barriers to entering the market except possession of the necessary technical expertise, storage is basically controlled by AGIP.

No formal or legal monopoly exists in favor of SNAM as far as importing and transport is concerned, even though SNAM has exclusive rights on the installation and management of pipelines for the transport of national production within the reserved areas. In fact SNAM is the only importer of gas and has a monopoly on the sale of gas to large industrial consumers, production stations and local distribution companies (approximately 99% of all the gas consumed in Italy is transported by way of SNAM pipelines). The reasons for this monopoly can be found in the control exercised over the pipelines and the difficulty in entering the international market. Free imports would only be possible if the liberalization of access to pipelines and the installation of liquid-gas conversion plants in the proximity of the final consumer took place, which would make naval transport possible. This aspect underlines the urgency required in clarifying the programming and the institutions responsible in the energy sector.

In 1991 limited access to the SNAM pipelines was granted to national gas producers on condition that the gas they transported was destined for their own plants or to be sold to ENEL or other electricity suppliers. As a result of the large amount of natural gas utilized for the provision of electrical power, ENEL has concluded contracts with Algeria for the importation of gas independent of SNAM, thereby obtaining limited access to the distribution network by third parties. Since the law does not require increased production capacity, transport by third parties is limited to the marginal capacity of existing plants. And furthermore, the application of a «fair» price could cause disputes, as SNAM does not distinguish between transport and other activities.

Given the natural monopolistic character of the sector and based on the considerations relative to the security of supply, the government does not seem to have intentions of restructuring the sector ahead of the privatization of SNAM.

SNAM distributes 50.2% of all natural gas to final consumers such as industries, enterprises in the electric sector and road transport services, while 49.8% is distributed through the intermediate network by distributing enterprises who furnish gas for residential use (66%), industrial use (16%), and medical use and small enterprises (18%) (Chart 1).

Graph 1

METHANE GAS DISTRIBUTION IN ITALY, 1994
(billions cu meters - 38,1 TJ/m cu)

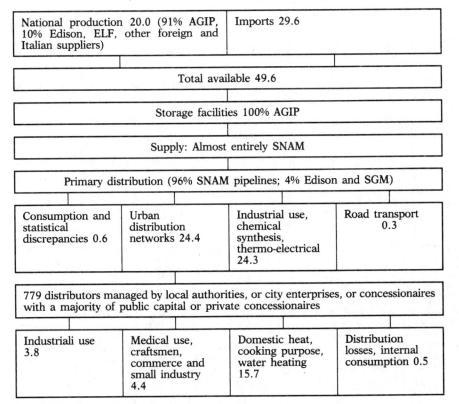

National production 20.0 (91% AGIP, 10% Edison, ELF, other foreign and Italian suppliers)	Imports 29.6		
Total available 49.6			
Storage facilities 100% AGIP			
Supply: Almost entirely SNAM			
Primary distribution (96% SNAM pipelines; 4% Edison and SGM)			
Consumption and statistical discrepancies 0.6	Urban distribution networks 24.4	Industrial use, chemical synthesis, thermo-electrical 24.3	Road transport 0.3
779 distributors managed by local authorities, or city enterprises, or concessionaires with a majority of public capital or private concessionaires			
Industriali use 3.8	Medical use, craftsmen, commerce and small industry 4.4	Domestic heat, cooking purpose, water heating 15.7	Distribution losses, internal consumption 0.5

Source, SNAM [35] and [36].

The enterprises that make up the intermediate distribution network can have the following legal status: enterprises managed directly by the local authority, normally where the limited dimension of the service required would not justify the creation of a specific enterprise; city enterprises with financial autonomy and independent of the administration of the local authority; concessions to third parties, but local authorities remain responsible for the services with the right to renew at the termination of the contract or to eliminate the service; corporations financed by a major or minor share of local public funds (mixed enterprises).

The urban distribution network consists of 459 public enterprises who serve 1,100 local authorities supplying 45% of the gas, and 320 private enterprises who serve 2,989 local authorities and supply 55% of the gas (Chart 2). The public enterprises consist of 138 city enterprises (35% of sales) and 321 enterprises managed directly by the local authorities (10% of sales). The private enterprises consist of a group of companies associated with SNAM (27% of sales), and another 307 operators (28% of sales).

In summary, it can be said that the only legal monopoly can be found in primary production and distribution in the Val Padana and surrounding areas. The organization of the market and the technical nature of the sector automatically contribute to the formation of an unregulated monopoly in the import and primary distribution areas. At the level of the distribution network for civil consumption various local monopolies exist.

GRAPH 2

URBAN DISTRIBUTION IN ITALY, 1991

Public enterprises (459 enterprises, 45% sales, 1100 local authorities - 27%)		Private enterprises (320 enterprises, 55% sales 2989 local authorities - 73%)	
138 city enterprises, 700 local authorities, 35% of sales	321 directly managed enterprises, 400 local authorities, 8% of sales	SNAM associates (Gruppo Italgas 45% SNAM), 13 enterprises, 845 local authorities, 27% of sales)	Other suppliers (307 enterprises, 2145 local authorities, 28% of sales)

Source, SNAM [35].

5. - The Privatization of the Natural Gas Sector in Italy

The laws (L. 352/92, L. 474/94 and L. 481/95) regarding privatization constitute the instruments necessary for the sale of public utilities and for redesigning the industrial order of the country. The institution of two bodies responsible for regulating the services of public utilities (one for electric energy and gas and one for telecommunications) is considered as being fundamental. The institution of the new controlling body for electricity and gas, which has made the initiation of the privatization of ENI possible, has transferred the activities of market control from ministerial level to independent authorities.

By selling 14.6% of ENI, estimated to have a total value of 50,000 billion lire, in November of 1995, the government has gone ahead with the largest public sale ever, earning more than 6,000 billion lire in the process.

The regulatory bodies in question have the task of controlling transparency and competition in the market, therefore helping to overcome a monopolistic situation and to open gradually to competitive forces. Furthermore they have the task of regulating tariffs according to technical criteria and of guaranteeing the interests of consumers by controlling the quality of services rendered. They must also verify that the unbundling of the accounts of the different enterprises of the group takes place in order to insure cost transparency and make the control of the efficiency of single enterprises possible. As far as the organization of the market is concerned, the authorities have the tasks of identifying services to be conceded or authorized, defining the condition of access to services provision, renewing authorizations and concessions and modifying the relative clauses. Furthermore the authorities must verify national distribution and efficiency of services.

The authorities fix and adjust tariffs according to the price-cap method. A maximum price limit is fixed for a period of two years according to the following parameters: the average annual variation of consumer prices for families compared to the preceding twelve months; and the variation of the annual productivity rate measured against a goal set for a minimum of three years. In determining the parameters other elements can also be taken into consideration, such as: quality gains with respect to pre-established standards, costs derived from unforeseen and extraordinary events, and legislative changes.

The controlling authorities establish and modify the basic tariff, the parameters and other reference elements including the procedure for recovering costs sustained in the interest of common good, an acceptable diffusion of services throughout the country, and the setting of general objectives of a social and environmental nature.

On the international front tariff regulation is also evolving towards a price-cap model. This method is relatively simple to administer, is easily understood by the consumer, and is capable of protecting against abuses of price policies, preventing excessive growth of the profits of suppliers, and guarantees future price change rates. It is also a useful incentive for enterprises to be more productive and allows part of the gains in productivity and efficiency to be passed on to the consumer. In principal the application of this method does not imply interference between market control and the tasks undertaken by the management of individual enterprises, while it guarantees conditions favorable to the programming of investment decisions.

The introduction of a price-cap system does however entail various problems. First of all, in a typically monopolistic market it is not easy to fix the market price of a resource. Furthermore it is necessary to reorganize the preceding price structure and level in order to avoid transferring pre-existent distortions to the price regulation rule. The determination of programmed and agreed-upon productivity increments and the duration of the reference period require complex techno-economical evaluations. If the determination and adjustment of prices were to be derived from a mechanical application of formulas, and instead were not the result of careful evaluations and decisions, the role and responsibilities of the authorities would be very much smaller.

The regulation established with the institution of the controlling authorities was not preceded by a clear definition of the structure of the sector. On a European level changes in the organization of the market will take place rapidly. Thus far the European gas industry, which maintains its monopolistic character within Italy and a oligopolistic structure on an international level, has not been influenced by the greater importance and strategic position acquired by natural gas. The liberalization of the market as required by the European Commission will inevitably lead to the revision of price formulas, currently linked to the prices of alternative competing resources, promoting the matching of social costs to prices. This will in turn affect the efficiency of allocation of resources and the programming of investments.

It is furthermore necessary to define which role the government will be required to play in the new order of the natural gas sector. In the past the government's responsibility was that of insuring the development of the pipeline system. To accomplish this the government had relieved the national producer from the payment of rental costs as long as those revenues were reinvested, and had subsidized the production and investment of primary and secondary distribution enterprises for the development of the pipeline network. As opposed to other competing forms of energy resources, natural gas resources have been protected by tax policies adopted by the government. In sustaining the distribution and the expansion of the utilization of natural gas in new areas, various forms of discrimination in the determination of prices have been applied. The government is also to clarify this occurrence as soon as possible. The transformation of public utilities into corporations followed by eventual privatization and the consequent loss of the privileges conceded to public entities could make it more difficult for enterprises to incur debt with effects on investment policies. The ownership of the corporation must in turn be made compatible with assignments and functions of the corporation which, in accordance with the law on transformation of an enterprise into a corporation, now has mineral rights and can carry out mining activities.

Various instruments can be utilized by the public shareholder to maintain control of the corporation, such as a golden share or other statutory clauses used in cases of national interest or the special-powers defined in law 474. This law grants the public shareholder a veto right on decisions regarding the dissolution, the transfer, the fusion, and the modification of the organizational objectives of the group. The public shareholder can furthermore express decisive opinions with regard to votes and can designate the CEO and a quarter of the board members, approve partners, and reinforce the limits placed on the maximum number of shares to be alloted, even if only on a temporary basis. In sectors of strategic national interest the public shareholder can place a limit of 5% on the number of shares allotted to private shareholders. This does not exclude the need for additional measures during allotment of shares. The fragmentized allotment of shares, which might be the case in Italy where important institutional investors are absent, would impede the re-organization of the management criteria of the corporation, thereby preventing the expected efficiency improvements. At the other extreme, the allotment shares to a small group of investors could lead to the excessive concentration of economic power.

Clearly the privatization process in Italy cannot be separated from the search for adequate solutions to the structural problems of our capital market. The most important of these is the structural weaknesses of our capital market, which should represent a place where firms are evaluated, allowing for balanced financial growth and risk sharing on individual investments. The sale of public utilities can contribute to this goal by promoting the enlargement of the capital market and the development of economic supervisory authorities.

BIBLIOGRAPHY

[1] ARTONI R., «Gli obiettivi di lungo periodo delle privatizzazioni», AIAF, n. 10, April 1994.

[2] AUTORITÀ GARANTE DELLA CONCORRENZA E DEL MERCATO, «Pareri e segnalazioni ottobre 1994-marzo 1995», vol. V, *Supplemento n. 2 al Bollettino*, n. 13, 1995.

[3] BARNETT A., «Natural Gas in Europe, Competing to Provide Tomorrow's Energy», London, *Financial Times Energy Publishing*, 1995.

[4] —— , «Privatising European Energy, Issues and Lessons», London, *Financial Times Energy Publishing*, 1994.

[5] BIANCHI A., «Le grandi aziende del gas europee: un raffronto di performance», *Energia*, vol. XVI, n. 1, March 1995.

[6] BISHOP M. - KAY J. - MAYER C., *The Regulatory Challenge*, Oxford, Oxford University Press, 1995.

[7] BRIOTTI M.G., «La privatizzazione dei servizi di pubblica utilità in Argentina, 1990-1992», Roma, Confindustria, *Ricerche*, n. 69, March 1993.

[8] CAMERON P., «Gas Regulation in Europe, From Monopoly to Competition», vols. I and II, London, *Financial Times Energy Publishing*, 1995.

[9] CEDIGAZ, *Natural Gas in the World, Survey, 1995*, Rueil Malmaison (France), 1995.

[10] CLÒ A., «Regolamentazione e concorrenza nei servizi di pubblica utilità; il caso del gas», *L'industria*, vol. XIII, n. 2, April-June 1992.

[11] CONFINDUSTRIA, CENTRO STUDI, *Privatizzare, una condizione per lo sviluppo*, mimeo, Roma, July 1992.

[12] DE LUCA F. (ed.), *Le tariffe del gas naturale per usi industriali*, Roma, SIPI, 1995.

[13] DE PAOLI L., *Regolamentazione e mercato unico dell'energia*, Milano, F. Angeli, 1993.

[14] ENI, «Quadro di riferimento economico ed energetico del gruppo ENI», *Studi economici*, March 1995.

[15] —— , *La congiuntura economica ed energetica*, n. 70, July 1995.

[16] EUROSTAT, «Energy», Luxembourg, *Monthly statistics*, n. 8, 1995.

[17] FONDAZIONE ROSSELLI, «I servizi di pubblica utilità in Italia», *Rapporto sullo stato e sulle condizioni di sviluppo 1993*, Torino, La Rosa, 1993.

[18] —— , «I servizi di pubblica utilità in Italia», *Rapporto sullo stato e sulle condizioni di sviluppo, 1995*, Torino, La Rosa, 1995.

[19] GOBBO F., «Privatizzazioni e disgregamento dei grandi monopoli nazionali», *Economia pubblica*, vol. XXIII, n. 7-8, July-August 1993.

[20] GRAZIOSI G., «Investimenti e tariffe nei servizi di pubblica utilità», *L'industria*, vol. XIII, n. 2, April-June 1992.

[21] INTERNATIONAL ENERGY AGENCY, *Energy policies, Italy, Review, 1994*, Paris 1994.

[22] KAHN A.E., «Regolamentazione e concorrenza nelle imprese di pubblica utilità: un "inquadramento teorico"», *L'Industria*, vol. XIII, n. 2, April-May 1992.

[23] LOMBARDO G., «Il sistema del gas in Italia alle soglie di ri-regolamentazione e privatizzazione», *Energia*, n. 3, 1994.

[24] NOMISMA, *Rapporto 1992 sull'industria italiana*, Bologna, Il Mulino, 1992.

[25] —— , *Rapporto 1993 sull'industria italiana*, Bologna, Il Mulino, 1994.

[26] OECD, AGENCE INTERNATIONALE DE L'ENERGIE, *Politiques et Perspectives du Gaz Naturel*, Paris, 1992.

[27] OCSE, *IEA Statistics, Energy Balances of OECD Countries 1991-1992, 1994 e 1992-1993, 1995*, Paris, 1995.

[28] — —, «Energy Prices and Taxes», Paris, *Quarterly*, 1995.

[29] — —, *Energy Statistics of OECD Countries 1991-1992*, Paris, 1994 and 1992-1993, Paris 1995.

[30] OECD, INTERNATIONAL ENERGY AGENCY, *Natural Gas Transportation, Organisation and Regulation*, Paris, 1994.

[31] OECD, *OCDE en Chiffres, Statistiques sur les Pays Membres*, Paris 1995.

[32] PRICE C., «Gas Regulation and Competition: Substitutes or Complements?» in BISHOP M. - KAY J. - MAYER C., *Privatization and Economic Performance*, Oxford, Oxford University Press, 1994.

[33] ROVIZZI L. - THOMPSON D., «Regolamentazione della qualità dei servizi delle imprese pubbliche sottoposte a price cap regulation, il caso della Gran Bretagna», *L'Industria*, vol. XIII, n. 1, January-March 1992.

[34] SCAN-ENERGY, *The Future Europen Natural Gas Market*, Copenhagen 1992.

[35] SNAM, *Il gas naturale in Italia*, Roma, March 1995.

[36] — —, *Metano ed energia. Dati statistici 1994*, Roma, 1995.

[37] UNITED NATIONS, ECONOMIC COMMISSION FOR EUROPE, «Gas Rates, Fundamentals and Practices», New York and Geneva, ECE, *Gas Centre Series*, n. 1, 1995.

[38] VICKERS J. - YARROW G., *Privatization: An Economic Analysis*, London, MIT Press, 1988.

Privatization and Reorganization in the Italian Public Utilities: Railway Transport

Andrea Pezzoli *

Autorità Garante della Concorrenza e del Mercato, Roma

1. - Introduction

«For a European born after the Second World War, railways are bound up with the State, not the nation: there are German, French and Italian railways, but it is just not possible to imagine two railway companies in the same nation». So wrote Marco d'Eramo [4] in the second chapter of his book on Chicago.

The objective of this paper is to verify if there is an ongoing process of transformation in the railway transport sector, and if so, to evaluate to what extent it will shake the convictions of «a European born after the Second World War». More precisely, this study examines the process of redefinition of the areas of monopoly and competition in railway transport, the need for a reconfiguration of markets and finally the changes in the relationship between state-as-shareholder and Italian railways (FS).

To this end, after having briefly examined the main economic characteristics of the sector (Section 2) and the current regulatory regime (Section 3), the study takes into consideration the main factors

---

* Andrea Pezzoli is an economist at the Autorità Garante della Concorrenza e del Mercato. The opinions he expresses in this work are his own and do not necessarily represent those of the Autorità Garante della Concorrenza e del Mercato.

N.B.: the numbers in square brackets refer to the Bibliography at the end of the paper.

contributing to the ongoing change — the needs of the public coffers and competition coming from other means of transport — (Section 4), taking special note of the push toward a new, more competitive regime imposed by the Directives and the approach privileged by the European Union (EU) with regards to rail transport (Section 5). Finally Section 6 will develop the main problems that characterize the organizational and institutional changes: the need to separate the management of infrastructure from the provision of the service; non-discriminatory access to the network; the relationship between FS and state-as-shareholder (whose role after privatising the FS into a stock company would be essentially that of regulator), and the relationship between FS and suppliers.

2. - The Configuration of the Sector

As it is currently organized, railway transport forms an incontestable natural monopoly. The size of the non-recoverable costs connected to infrastructure which are necessary to provide the service (particularly network and stations) do in fact represent an insurmountable entrance and exit barrier. If one considers, instead, the management of the infrastructure separately from the provision of the transport services, the conditions for running the service alone become significantly less demanding and one might hypothesize the introduction of competition, though this would only be limited to the provision of the service.

The existence of an infrastructure network which cannot be duplicated economically[1] but which is absolutely essential to railway transport service, the monopolistic management of the infrastructure, and the presence of a monopolistic company which provides transport services seem the distinctive features of the Italian railway transport sector.

Of the approximately 20,000 km. of national railway network, more than 16,100 km. are run directly by the FS which as a service

---

[1] See PITTMAN R.W. [12].

provider accounts for more than 97% of the national passenger and freight markets. However, it must be stressed that about 80% of the traffic takes place on less than 30% of the network. On the other hand, on one third of the network there is less than 2% of total traffic.

FS's railway transport services are integrated by services which FS has given in concession. These concessions have gone to 28 firms of varying types of corporate structure located throughout Italy, but which are mostly found in the central and southern regions. The contribution of the concessions is particularly important in transporting passengers within urban environments and for commuters. All included, however, this segment does not handle more than 3% of all passenger traffic, and an even smaller percentage of freight transport.

A characteristic which distinguishes railway transport from other public utilities characterized by an analogous market structure (telecommunications and electrical power), is that this sector, given the inefficiencies of the monopolist, generates no extra-profits. In other terms, the monopolistic rents are totally absorbed by the x-inefficiency.

The main distorsions do not come from an artificial reduction in supply or in the range of services provided or from eccessively high fares, but, more commonly, from an unjustified increase of the supply of the services supplied (and of their costs), given that such a behaviour implies larger state subsidies. Thus one must consider problems of internal efficiency together with those issues related to setting the company's finances straight and those regarding how large the government subsidies should be to cover losses.

Among the monopolists with network systems, the monopolist in the railway sector might be considered as a «poor cousin». To the inefficiencies that derive from a lack of competition one must add, on one hand, the difficulty in following the evolution of transport technology and the changing characteristics of demand and on the other, the undoubtedly high costs which derive from the need to offer a universal service. In the case of FS, however, the x-inefficiencies seem practicularly relevant. Table 1 illustrates the gap, measured in terms of technical and economic efficiency, between FS and the railway systems of other European countries.

TABLE 1

A COMPARISON OF EUROPE'S MAIN RAILWAY NETWORKS

	Italy (FS)	Germany (DB)	France (SNCF)	UK (BR)
Network size	16,066	27,079	33,446	16,584
Traffic units	68,725	107,790	114,531	49,332
Economic productivity index*....	100	122	151	94
Tecnical Productivity ...**	100	169	184	117

* Unity of traffic per worker.
** Ratio of gross tons per KML transported to average workers employed.
Source, Ministry of Transport.

Although there has been a significant reduction in FS personnel over the last decade (between 1985 and 1994, more than 70,000 were cut from the workforce, appoximately 30% of the total), FS's 140,000 current employees are still far from the final target. The inadeguacy of the effort emerges more clearly if one keeps in mind that the reduction in payroll has not been as significant as the reduction in personnel and that there has been no significant improvement due to flexibility in industrial relations.

3. - Institutional and Regulatory Aspects

A public utility can be run by any of several types of corporate structure depending on the degree of autonomy characterizing the relationship between the company supplying the service and the public administration. The service can be offered by: an «Azienda autonoma» (state-owned company) bound by general political direction and public accounting supervision; a public economic agency (whose relationship with the state would be regulated by common law, but which would be juridically autonomous in the managing of the company) or a public stock company (only subject to private law).

Over the last ten years FS has been through them all. After the passage of law no. 210 of 17 May 1985, FS went from being a traditionally state-owned company to a public agency. Going from the first to the second type of company implied enacting wide reaching trasnformation, which not only caused a reconsideration of the institutional form of the company, but also caused important organizational changes, a significant repositioning of FS on the market and above all, a redefinition of the limits of FS's mission to the public and, the modality for carrying this mission out. The transformation into public corporation in 1992 marked the third stage in the process of institutional change and undoubtedly represents an important step toward an organizational realignment in the sector.

The passage from public agency to stock company was articulated into several phases:

a) the deliberation of CIPE of 12 June 1992, at which time the process of transformation, based on a program defined by FS itself in collaboration with the Ministry of Transport, was started;

b) the approval of the transformation plan by the Cabinet in October 1992;

c) the issuing of a Ministry of Transport decree, (n. 225 of 26 November 1992) which defines the way the various activities and railway transport services which were to be ceded to the new company, *Ferrovia dello Stato-Società di trasporti e servizi per azioni.* This concession, which is to last seventy years, gives to the FS *(i)* the running of public, supplementary and substitutive rail transport with any form of land transport, over routes already served by FS and supplementary bus lines. The Ministry of Transport will have to give prior approval for new substitutive and/or supplementary services, excluding emergencies; *(ii)* the running of sea transportation connecting rail terminals; *(iii)* the planning and the construction of new lines, as well as the upgrading and renovation of existing lines;

d) the nomination of a new board and the conclusion of the «quasi-bankrupcy» management, which had started in 1985 (December 1992).

The transformation into a stock company should have facilitated the achievement of the following strategic objectives: *a)* an overall increase in transport in the next decade, the result of a two-fold increase in freight and local traffic and the boosting of the percentage of medium- and long-distance passengers attracted by the new high speed services; *b)* the reaching of a break-even point in 1995, by increasing revenue from traffic through an increase both in volume and in fares, by reducing costs (in particular labor costs and savings through out-sourcing) and raising productivity; finally by creating significant income through activities complementary to transport and the more rational use of its real estate holdings; *c)* a drastic reduction of state subsidies (estimated to reach approximately $ 90 billion by the year 2000); *d)* the completion of the high speed project; *e)* the raising of the evaluation of the company's holdings to a level coherent with an increase in capitalization of 200%.

With the transformation into a stock company, the institutional framework has been completed by the *program contract* and by the *services contract* between the Ministry of Transport and FS. In fact the new situation has made it necessary to regulate the relationship between state-as-shareholder and the company.

In particular the *program contract* regulates the economic criteria used in running the railway's infrastructure, the obligation to maintain universal transport and maintenance services, investments for network development and upkeep, plant and rolling stock development and, finally, it regulates the financial responsibilities of the State.

The *services contract* regulates the quantity and quality (fares, schedules, frequency, dependibility) of the lines used for railway transport and for supplementary transport services. However, it must be stressed that neither the program contract nor the *services contract* relate the amount of subsidies to the achievement of social goals or, at least the attainment of performance targets (Ponti, [15]).

Summing up, it seems improbable that the contractual relationship between the State and FS, as it stands at the moment, will make FS into a responsible stock company. Indeed, the undifferentiated subsidy system has been eliminated, but though it is still operating in the red, FS has suffered no consequences. Both the political controller and the public management are allowed to take into consideration parameters other than efficiency of service. There are significant inadequacies in the incentive structure in the *services contract*, which make it possible to reward not only laudable *service* to the company and its customers, but also, from time to time, to grant instead rewards to gain consensus either from the industry or from the unions in the sector.

4. - Determinants for Change

Evolution in demand and changes in technology, which have been the principal determinants for change in other public utilities, can furnish only a partial explanation for the on-going transformation in the case of railways. In fact it seems as if the main impulse derives from the public deficit crisis and the urgent need to limit and requalify the State's subsidies to the transport sector (CSC [6]). Another important contribution to the redefinition of the organization of the sector has originated from the new regulatory framework which is being put together at the European level.

4.1 *Straightening out the Government's Budget*

In 1992, the transfers of funds by the government to the transport sector exceeded $ 10 billion (more than one third of the added value of the entire sector). About $ 6 billion went to rail transport (not only FS, but also rail lines in concession, subways and trams). The ratio between subsidies and added value to cost of factors of FS was estimated at about 87% in 1991 (CSC [6]).

According to the most recent estimates (Ponti [15]) in 1994 the government sudsidies to FS have reached $ 9 billion whereas, if the entire sector is considered as a whole then the total exceeds $ 13 billion, including rail lines in concession and investments.

The comparison with other European countries shows clearly how unusually high is the level of the subsidies granted to FS: the ratio between subsidies and production costs stands at around 72% in Italy while the average in the EU is about 42%. However if one makes the comparison with the other major economies, the difference is even more marked: in United Kingdom, France and Germany, the value goes from 19% to 32%. Fares cover approximately 50% of the costs on average in Europe (reaching 60% in the UK), while in Italy they cover barely 20%.

It is thus clear that the government's financial difficulties have definitely been a particularly important stimulus in starting the current process of organizational and institutional change in the railway sector. Since over the next few years the level of subsidies for the transport sector will decrease a policy of efficiency is a necessity for FS.

4.2 *The Changes in Transport Demand*

Furthermore, even though the impulse from the dramatic public debt situation cannot be ignored, the transformation process of FS is also a partial response to the decreasing importance of railway as a means of transport. In passenger transportation over medium and long distances, which has increased rapidly during the last two decades (more than 5% p.a.), the presence of FS has decreased from more than 17% in 1970 to about 12% in 1994. Intercity bus lines have nearly 15% of the market. In the freight sector, FS has seen an analogous fall in its share from 19% in the early 1970s to just under 13% in 1994. Over the same years, the share of freight carried by motor carriers increased by approximately 50%, passing from 44% to

TABLE 2

TRAFFIC BY CARRIER - 1994
(in percentage terms)

Passenger traffic		Freight	
Air	2	Pipelines	6
Rail	12	Rail	13
Water	1	Water	19
Motor	85	Motor	62

Source, Fs.

more than 62% of the total (Table 2). In the absence of a radical transformation, it is plausible to hypothesize that rail transport risks being marginalized.

5. - The External Impulse: EU Regulations[2]

To the stimuli of demand and technology and the still more impelling one of the government's deficit one must add the slower but more tenacious ones deriving from the liberalization process sweeping the EU.

During the three decades separating the *Treaty of Rome* and the *Treaty of Maastricht*, Community policy in transportation has been mostly dedicated to the removal of obstacles to trade. Following the *Treaty of Maastricht* and the publication of the Commission's [6] *White Book*, the Community's approach to the transport sector seems to have changed. There appears to be a «global» policy. The development of a trans-Europe rail network, of high-speed trains and of intermodal transport seem to be the pillars of such a policy. The access to national networks, the definition of the limits of the public services and the method for granting rail concessions are being deeply influenced by these new prospectives.

Communitary regulation, in the attempt to make the "general interest compatible with liberalisation, is moving toward a redefinition" of the acceptable size and scope of the monopoly and of the limitis which might be imposed on the behaviour of the monopolistic provider of the service. Both the general principles of the *Treaty* and the sectorial regulations have been moving it in this direction (Rangone [16]).

There are two norms which have been especially important in contributing to the process of transformation which is sweeping the area of railway transport, and have started the erosion of the national railway monopolies. The first of these directives concerns the separation of the management of the network from the provision of the

---

[2] For an exhaustive examination of the approach followed by the EU Commission as regards railway transportation see RANGONE N. [16] and SPIRITO P. [18].

transport services (*Directive 91/440* of 29 July 1991). In a second area we find the relative definition of the obligations of public service, in which a clear separation is made between the nature of the provider and the public nature of the service (see *Regulation n. 1161/69* as modified by n. *1893/91*). Then there have been recent directives which treat the subject of licences to railway companies (*Directive n. 95/18*) and the sharing of infrastructure capacity (*Directive n. 95/16*) as well as regulations on public tenders (*Directive n. 90/531* and *n. 93/38*). All these ingredients make up the crucial impulse coming from the EU.

5.1 *Directive n. 91/440*

Though this directive only had the limited goal of liberalizing combined international freight transport, it has been instrumental in the affirmation of several general principles, which have now become part of the cultural heritage of railway companies:

a) the distinction between management of the network and provision of the service. If this is interpreted as a need to actually separate the institutions that manage the infrastructure from those that provide the transport services, then obviously it is going to redesign the natural monopoly and place limits on it, bringing together both competition concerns and society's general interests. Where, instead, this principle is translated into a simple obligation to separate accounts, its use will be merely confined to pointing out unjustified expenses which derive from the universality of the service and, as a consequence, will make it easier to identify the existence of *x*-inefficiency. By January 1993 the member states of the EC were to already have made plans for separate accounting and to have defined the method they were going to use in establishing the fares for the use of the infrastructure. Though timidly worded, the directive would seem to privilege institutional separation of the management of the network and the provision of the service, and consequently the introduction of competitive mechanisms in the railway services market;

b) railway companies can have a distinct identity from the public mission sought by the State. In this sense the service provider might feel less bound by the state-ownership and, in this perspective, the notion of public service does not necessarily correspond to public sector. The obligations of public service can be determined by contracts and thus the service can be guaranteed by any company regardless of who owns it. Furthermore, this would favour the creation of a more transparent regime of subsidies to railway companies. The State, like any private company, would limit itself to the purchasing of services that it judged of public utility, defined both by costs and characteristics, thus removing from the rail companies any possibility of unjustified expenses and making any type of "catch-all subsidy totally uncalled for". At the European level a similar system is already being used in the United Kingdom and France and it should form the basis for the *program contract* between FS and the Italian State (Ponti [15]).

5.2 *The Regulations*

The principle summarised in *b)* becomes important when the regulatory framework of the sector is considered in that they introduce a contractual definition of public service obligations and allow for a more precise definition of the area subjected to restrictions. Some of the norms appear particularly incisive: *a)* the obligation to eliminate expenses which are not strictly necessary in serving the public's interests and which might alter competition (*Regulation n.1191/69*); *b)* the requirement to define the obligations of public service to guarantee the supply of «sufficient» services (*Regulation n. 1191/69*); *c)* the definition of the negotiated origin of the public service obligation. In other words, obligations are not to be imposed unilaterally by authorities, but they are to be justified by a *services contract*; *d)* separate accounting for those parts of the business activities which are aimed at fullfilling the public service obligations so that they cannot compromise the economic integrity of the company. The financial compensation for unjustified expenses are defined by a public service contract. The logic is to move away from covering any and all losses, and towards paying for services that were contracted for (*Regulation n. 1893/91*); *e)* the normalization of the accounting of railway companies (*Regulation n. 1192/69*).

5.3 *Directives on the Sharing of Capacity and the Granting of Licences*

The two *Directives* that treat the sharing of infrastructure capacity of the railways and the granting of licences to railway companies, both approved in June 1995, bring us two steps closer to the realization of the principles of *Directive n. 91/440*. The two *Directives* are particularly important in making the liberalization of the access to the network effectively operative, through the introduction of a higher degree of competition in the market for time slots. The main instruments offered by these new *Directives* to promote both the development of the public service and the development of infrastructure with the support of private capital, are the definition of «special rights» of access to the infrastructure for certain types of services (those particularly important to the public) and the consequent structure of the public's planned contribution toward the running of the network as indemnity for losses derived from the obligations imposed on part of the infrastructure capacity.

These two new *Directives* are also relevant at the institutional level. They identify the institution which will determine how capacity will be shared and they define the characteristics which are required to be considered a railway company.

In relation to the first point, the national States will maintain their autonomy in deciding if this organization will take the form of an independent authority or if it will be the manager of the network. The diversity of the impact on the market deriving from the adoption of one or the other of these choices is evident, in particular, if the manager of the network were also one of the providers of services.

The definition of railway company leaves plenty of space for interpretation. A first interpretation considers rail companies not only those which already exist but also new subjects, established or that intend to establish themselves in a member state and whose main activity is the providing of rail transport and which have at their disposal locomotives. This does not necessarily mean that they own the locomotives nor that the personnel is theirs. A second and more restrictive interpretation would essentially deny the possibility of new entrants and identifies railway companies with the current rail authorities. The oligopolistic power of the incumbents could be maintained intact. The sympathy which FS have demonstrated for this second hypothesis does not bode well for a redefinition of the limits of monopoly and the future of competition.

5.4 *The Directives on Public Tenders*

The encouragement deriving from the EU approach is not limited to the organizational and ownership aspects. In fact one cannot help but notice the Community's attempts at pushing for a different definition of the relationship that links FS with its suppliers. Indeed *Directive n. 90/531* opened to competition contracts in sectors «excluded» from the application of the directives. Since July 1994, *Directive n. 90/531* has been integrated in the area of the public tender regulations by *Directive 93/38*, which applies to both state-owned companies and to other subjects, public or private, who enjoy special or exclusive rights and that manage railway networks aimed at the provision of public service. The railway company in a dominant position, as principle purchaser of goods and services, has behavioural obligations in its relationships with its suppliers and cannot privilege, in the absence of solid economic justifications, its traditional suppliers or national companies (EU Commission [5]). Hence market tests become a necessity, regardless of the procedure employed for choosing the winning bid[3], to ensure that in the future a railway company's purchasing policies are based on economically efficient criteria.

Summing up. Though *Directive n. 91/440* has not been as

---

[3] According to *Directive n. 93/38* the party judging the tender offers may use «open» procedure, in which any supplier is free to send in an offer; «restricted» procedure in which only invited candidates are admitted to present an offer or «negotiated» procedure in which the judging agency consults suppliers of its choice and contracts with these the conditions for the contract.

effective as might have been expected, it has brought about significant changes in the strategic configurations and in the organizative models of the railway companies of the larger European countries (EU Commission [8])[4]. It is improbable that FS would have changed into a stock company as easily and, above all, as quickly as it did without the *EU Directives*. However, the slowness and skepticism with which *Directive n. 91/440* has been accepted by the member states is not likely to make us excessively optimistic. In any case, the behavior of FS need not limit itself to passivity as regards EU legislation. On the contrary, it should attempt to anticipate the institutional framework which is currently being defined by taking the first steps toward liberalization. If the wish is to draw from the experiences of other public utilities, it can be seen clearly that a defensive attitude to liberalization processes only translates into a competitive disadvantage, particularly evident in the comparison with subjects which have not refused the logic of competition (Spirito [18]). Furthermore, unlike telecommunications and electrical power companies, railway companies have little to defend. The rents that liberalization processes might put up for grabs in other public utilities are rather more attractive than those that can be extracted from a railway transport service (Spirito [18]).

6. - New Regulatory and Organizational Framework

It is undeniable that the process of reorganization is in an advanced phase. The orientation of the EU, cautious though it is, shows clearly both the direction as well as the eventual destination (EU Commission [8]). In all fairness, however, one can still ask: how far have we really moved up to today; if FS's and the State's behaviours are adequate to the need for an institutional reorganization; and what are the main problems to tackle.

---

[4] The reception of the *Directive* in the various States has varied. In June 1995, only Germany, Denmark, the Netherlands and the United Kingdom had applied the Directive completely. The legislation is in the process of being adopted in France. In other countries, including Italy, the *Directive* has only been partially adopted.

6.1 *The Relationship between FS and the State*

If one goes on to examine the changes that have taken place over the last few years in the relationship between FS and the State [5], the only important move that cannot be ignored has been that FS has been changed into a stock company. The other changes which the transformation would have required (the requalification of the role of the stockholder, the concentration of public intervention into the arena of regulation and the privatization of at least a part of the stock company) are still nowhere to be seen. The only control institution, the Interministerial Committee for the Economic Programmation of Transport (CIPET) has been dissolved. The incentive structure in the *services* and *program contracts* appears totally inadequate. There are no penalties for default and the amount of an award is set at a fixed amount, without any effort to correlate subsidies with the fulfillment of the public's objectives or, as in the case of the French railways, with simple indices of productivity or performance. Furthermore the establishment of the regulatory authority of the sector has been deferred. The interaction between the shareholder-regulator and the regulated company is rather bland and public intervention in the sector is characterized by the lack of continuity. If this situation does not change, one finds it difficult not to share the fears of those who think FS operates in thrall to the State; in a framework that reminds us of that which characterized the so-called «partecipazioni statali» (state-owned companies), but within which both the action of «capture» and that of rent seeking are further facilitated by the almost inexistent exposure to competition and by a particularly high level of public subsidies (Ponti [15]).

6.2 *Separating Infrastructure Management from the Provision of the Transport Services*

If one looks at the progress that has been made toward separating infrastructure management from the provision of the transport ser-

---

[5] See the analysis of PONTI M. [15] inspired by the literature on public-choice and by the theory of principal-agent.

vices, up to today one notices that only the first steps toward separate accounting have been taken. The slowness with which *Directive n. 91/440* is being applied, the difficulties that are developing, not only in Italy, with the modification of article 10 of the *Directive* (which extends liberalization to freight and medium- and long-distance passenger transport) and the restrictive interpretation of the *Directive* regarding licences (in particular, the definition of a railway company) justify a certain amount of guarded pessimism as regards the possibility that in the short-term we will go beyond the simple separation of accounting. In the specific case of Italy along with the traditional fears caused by a more competitive transportation sector, there are even fears of what wider competition for public subsidies would mean if FS were to separate into different companies.

6.3 *A More Radical Model: the Privatization of British Rail*

From this point of view, the lessons we can learn from the British experience as regards to the separation of infrastructure and services risks being exclusively academic in nature.

The approach followed in the reform of the railways in the United Kingdom is significantly more radical than the one which characterizes the EU *Directives*, both as regards the separation of the network from the provision of the service and as regards the introduction of a regime of total competition. The project calls for the establishment of a public agency (*Railtrack*) whose function will be to run the infrastructure applying criteria typical of private industry; the entry of a number of companies which would produce and sell transport services with franchising contracts, and the entry of three leasing companies which have acquired the rolling stock (more than 11,000 pieces including both locomotives and coaches) for approximately $ 2.81 billion. These companies are to stipulate contracts with the providers of the services, which will last until the end of the franchising (between 8 and 15 years). The companies which provide the services are to pay *Railtrack* a rent for the use of infrastructure and a leasing fee. 25 lines are to be privatized. The first seven contracts with private managers are to be signed during the half of 1996.

However as the outcome of the British experience is still uncertain it would be rash to express a premature judgement.

6.4 *A Hypothesis of Reorganization*

All considered, the «strong» interpretation of the EU approach seems the most reasonable hypothesis to be followed for the reorganization of the sector. Both ownership and investments in infrastructure will probably remain in the public domain — a basic resource essential for all competing service providers[6]. The provision of the transportation service should, on the other hand, be open to several firms in competition, at least for the services private companies are able to provide. The remaining services (probably concentrated in local transport) — the provision of which is called for by the guarantee of universal rail transport services — would not be provided and would receive state subsidies.

Within this framework FS would be called on to run the infrastructure and the services not provided by private firms. In order to achieve this objective, based on the German experience, one might set up regional companies in order to promote yardstick competition, at any rate useful in evaluating efficiency (Vickers - Yarrow [19]). In the area subject to market discipline, a plurality of competing companies would, on the other hand, guarantee freight, medium- and long-distance passenger transport and high speed services[7] (Graph 1).

The absence of links between the companies operating in the market and the manager of the infrastructure would eliminate any incentive for FS to behave in a discriminatory fashion. In any case the

---

[6] The construction of railway infrastructure requires investments that private industry is not able to finance (KAY J: [9]). The case for financing the high speed project appears emblematic. When one looks at the private capital in the main example of project financing in Italy all one finds is loans guaranteed by the State. It is not where the capital comes from, but where the risk lies that is important (SARCINELLI M. [17]).

[7] The experience in other sectors (in particular in air transport) demonstrates the difficulties that one encounters during a process of liberalization and shows that it is bilateral agreements between the agencies of two countries that bring into being the entrance of new operators of transport services more often than a true opening up to competition.

GRAPH 1

HYPOTHESIS FOR THE REORGANIZATION OF THE ITALIAN RAILWAY TRANSPORT SECTOR

Non-market sector   Market sector

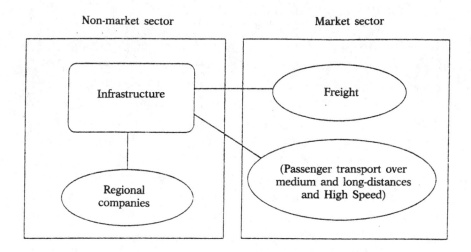

condition for access to the infrastructure should be guaranteed to all operators without any discrimination[8].

6.5 *Beyond the Tracks*

The configuration of the rail transport sector and, in particular, the hypothesis that FS will be limited to the management of infrastructure and the services the market is not willing to provide, would however seem to conflict with FS's propensity to strengthen, directly or through agreements with other operators, its presence in other transport modes (motor and maritime) with the intention of

---

[8] In the area of intermodal transport one can find interesting traces of the «temptations» that can occur when one both manages the infrastructure and provides the service. See Autorità Garante della Concorrenza e del Mercato, *Decision* of 23 July 1993, n. 1312 Fremura/FS in *Bulletin* n. 18-19/1993 and 30 November 1995, n. 3428 Italcontainer/TFC in *Bulletin* n. 38/1995.

maximizing the benefits of integrated transport services for passengers, but especially for freight[9].

From this perspective, one might be justified in interpreting FS's conduct as an attempt to take over the entire logistic and freight sectors — and granting them to a newly incorporated wholly owned company — its purchase of national cabotage currently run by Finmare, its cooperation with the main port authorities, and financial partecipation in Contship Italia (the company which manages the container terminals of La Spezia, Savona, Gioia Tauro and Salerno). The advantages of integration and the savings to be realized by coordinating services in this way must be weighed against the risks that derive from FS's extention of its dominant position in railways to contiguous sectors. Undoubtedly, privatizating the company whose job it will be to coordinate these intermodal activities will simplify the evaluation of the trade-off between gains in efficiency and market distortions. However the risks for the entire transport system might be relevant[10].

6.6 *The Relationship between FS and its Suppliers*

This is another area where it is useful to measure the progress that has been made toward a more competitive environment in the railway sector: the relationship between FS and its suppliers. In other words one should ask if and how the on-going transformation process has affected FS's behavior as a purchaser; above all when it is the only national purchaser.

Tradionally FS's purchasing policies have not incorporated efficiency as one of their main criteria (Pontarollo [14]; Autorità Garante della Concorrenza e del Mercato [1]). More often they have had other justifications: the protection of a supplier, sometimes the defence of national industry, electoral consensus, consensus from unionized labor and in a few cases illegality. In synthesis similar behaviour is

---

[9] See, for example, the article by PACI G. published in *Il Mondo*, 6 November 1995.
[10] See the opinion of the Italian Anti-trust Authority to the Ministry of Transport on the reorganization of the Finmare group, in *Bulletin* n. 1-2/1996.

what is referred to as the policy of «historical quotas», on the basis of which public procurements were attributed to various firms in proportion to their share of the market, hampering competition and favoring the creation of «lazy» cartels. The Italian antitrust authority has had to intervene in this area on four separate occasions: traditional rolling stock (*Decision of 22 December 1993, n. 1663* Consorzio Capri, «*Bulletin n. 40-41/1993*»), high speed trains (*Decision of 21 February 1994, n. 1796* Consorzio Trevi, «*Bulletin n. 8/1994*»), the infrastructure for high speed (*Decision of 21 February 1994, n. 1795* Tav, «*Bulletin n. 8/1994*» and railway equipment (*Decision of 26 May 1996, n. 1986* Fercomit, «*Bulletin n. 21/1994*»). In the case of the Capri consortium, the Italian antitrust authority considered the agreement among the companies participating in the consortium as restrictive of competition and, above all FS's purchasing policy as abusive of its dominant position, insofar its procurement policy was incoherent with the principles of competition and had the effect of blocking market access[11]. This was unusual behaviour (an abuse to damage oneself) respect to that traditionally adopted by a monopsonist. In fact, in markets controlled by a single purchaser, the prices suppliers are able to apply are usually forced eccessively low (Podestà [13]). It is rare that abuses of dominant position by the monopsonist promote the formation of inefficient cartels and allow higher prices.

The purchasing policy of FS does however seem to have been positively affected both by the EU *Regulations* on public tenders, and by the consequent obligation to hold international tenders, as well as by the Italian antitrust authority's intervention. The pressure of international competition would seem to have increased its effectivness (though foreign companies are still limited to the role of potential competitors) and the participation of the main European firms in tenders held by FS is no longer only a ritual.

Judging from the outcomes of the first international tenders held by FS, one can tend toward guarded optimism. The case of coaches for high speed trains might be taken as an example. Originally they were to be built by the Capri consortium and following the tender — won by the same companies which took part in the consortium —

---

[11] See NINNI A. [10] and D'ALBERTI S. - PEZZOLI A. [3].

they will now cost FS more than a third less (Authority [1]). Similar stories might undoubtedly be explained by technical progress, economies of scale (the procurement is for a larger number than was originally ordered) and the increasing willingness of firms to lower prices in post-«Tangentopoly» (i.e. *bribesville*) times. A fair portion of the consumer surplus (the resources saved by FS), and that anything but insignificant, can however be legitimately attributed to the purchaser applying the principles of competition.

The transformation of FS from a purchaser working against its own best interest to a monopsonist «guardian of efficiency», able to use its countervailing power when confronted with a cartel of suppliers, is an important factor in any reorganization of the rail transport sector [12]. Furthermore, if FS's behaviour as a purchaser is more «virtuous», it would also have a positive effect on the competitivness of its supply industries, thus favouring the structural adjustments necessary for much of the railway industry and relegitimizing the use of public procurement, which need not necessarily be conflictual with the principles of competition [13].

7. - Concluding Remarks

The brief summary of the determinant factors in the on-going transformation process in the railway transport sector and, above all, the steps toward a more competitive configuration that have so far been taken in this direction show us how, though we are in an inevitable process, we are probably still near the beginning. The most significant changes are those characterizing the relationship between FS and the State, but even there the main results are confined to the transformation of FS into a stock company. The principles of the EU

---

[12] The approach followed by the EU Commission for the evaluation of the concentration between ABB and Daimler-Benz is particularly interesting. Though a single subject would gain control of over 60% of the German market, the operation was allowed and this exactly because of the countervailing power that the main purchaser, the German railways, could exert on them. See EU COMMISSION [7].

[13] On the limits of public procurement as an instrument of industrial policy see NINNI A. [10].

Directives regarding the separation of the management of the network from the provision of the transport service — probably too bland right from the start — though already part of the cultural heritage of FS, are being implemented only slowly and, above all, they would appear to be in conflict, with the exception of the separate accounting issue, with the hypothesized reorganization of FS. On the other hand, it should be pointed out that some real progress in the relationships between FS and its suppliers has been made. FS's purchasing conduct now appears more coherent with a competitive environment.

It does not look like much. One cannot be sure that the changes will be sufficient to translate into benefits for consumers, for the public coffers or that they will be incisive enough to cure the financial woes of the company. Above all the changes do not seem sufficiently deep to shake the beliefs of that «European born after the Second World War» who is convinced of the impossibility of more than one railway company in any single country.

BIBLIOGRAPHY

[1] AUTORITÀ GARANTE DELLA CONCORRENZA E DEL MERCATO, *Indagine conoscitiva sul settore del materiale rotabile*, Roma, 1995.

[2] CONFINDUSTRIA CSC, *Le FS verso il risanamento. Risultati e aree critiche*, Roma, 1994.

[3] D'ALBERTI S. - PEZZOLI A., «Accordi verticali e effetti sui prezzi», forthcoming, *Rivista di Diritto del Commercio Internazionale*, 1995.

[4] D'ERAMO M., *Il maiale e il grattacielo*, Milano, Feltrinelli, 1995.

[5] EU COMMISSION, «Memorandum on the Rail Companies», *XX Report on Competition Policy*, Luxembourg, 1991.

[6] — —, «Growth, Competitivness and Employment», *EC Bulletin, Supplement*, n. 6/93, Luxembourg, 1993.

[7] — —, *Report on the Application of the Directive 91/440 on the Development of the Community's Rail and New Proposals Related to the Access of Rail Infrastructure*, Brussels, 1995.

[8] — —, «ABB/Daimler Benz, Commission Decision of 18 October 1995), *DG IV*, Brussels, 1995.

[9] KAY J., «Efficiency and Private Capital in the Provision of Infrastructure», in OECD, *Infrastructure Policies in the 1990s*, Paris, OECD, 1993.

[10] NINNI A., «L'economia dei mercati pubblici e i limiti della domanda pubblica come strumento di politica industriale», Milano, Università Bocconi, *Working Paper*, n. 9, 1994.

[11] — —, «Concorrenza per i mercati pubblici. Su due decisioni dell'Autorità garante della concorrenza e del mercato in materia di rapporti tra ferrovie dello Stato e industria ferroviaria», *Economia e Politica Industriale*, n. 86, 1995, pp. 43-53.

[12] PITTMAN R.W., «Railroads and Competition: the Santa Fè/Southern Pacific Merger Proposal», *The Journal of Industrial Economics*, vol. XXXIX, 1990, pp. 25-46.

[13] PODESTÀ S., «Quando l'acquirente pubblico domina il produttore», *L'Impresa*, n. 6, 1993.

[14] PONTAROLLO E., *Domanda pubblica e politica industriale: FS, Sip, Enel*, Venezia, Marsilio, 1989.

[15] PONTI M., «Il trasporto ferroviario», in *Rapporto della Fondazione Rosselli sui servizi di pubblica utilità*, Milano, 1995.

[16] RANGONE N., *Il servizio pubblico di trasporto ferroviario nella disciplina comunitaria*, mimeo, 1994.

[17] SARCINELLI M., *Il finanziamento delle infrastrutture e il project financing*, Roma, Cnel, 1995.

[18] SPIRITO P., *Il processo evolutivo della normativa europea e l'impatto sulla riconfigurazione delle ferrovie*, Roma, Direzione strategie e controllo ferrovie dello Stato, 1995.

[19] VICKERS J. - YARROW G., *Privatization: an Economic Analysis*, Cambridge (Mass.), Mit Press, 1988

Industrial Organization and Efficiency in Telecommunications Services

Massimo G. Colombo - **Paola Garrone**

Università di Pavia   Politecnico di Milano [1]

1. - Introduction

In recent years, information technology and optoelectronics have made new systems available to telecommunications network operators. Technological changes, such as digital lines, the development of personal communications systems and the spread of optical fibre networks, have broadened the range of telecommunications services and, at the same time, modified both providers' production structure and competition within the industry, allowing new operators to enter the market and traditional telephone providers to diversify their activity.

Stimulated by the structural changes induced by technical progress, operators and policy makers in many countries have looked very carefully at the industry's traditional organisation and assessed the extent to which it can exploit the new technologies. Various experts have subsequently proposed new industrial configurations. A valuable contribution to this debate has also come from numerous studies in the economic literature over the last fifteen years.

The present study aims to analyse the implications for the structure of the sector, on the one hand, of technological change, and,

[1] Although the article is the joint effort of the authors, the first three sections are directly attributable to Paola Garrone and the remaining parts to Massimo G. Colombo. Financial support from MURST 60% 1995 funds is gratefully aknowledged.

N.B.: the numbers in square brackets refer to the Bibliography at the end of the paper.

on the other, of the current debate on a number of important economic concepts (e.g. the notion of natural monopoly).

Section 2 describes the industrial system of communications services adopted in many countries in the past. The conceptual categories which are traditionally employed in support of this system are also highlighted. The technological innovations and the conceptual 'novelties' which emerged during the course of the economic debate in the 1980s are presented in Section 3. Section 4 claims that a new industrial structure would appear to be likely to emerge from the action of economies of scale and scope. Weaknesses in the arguments which have frequently been raised in this respect are also evidenced. In Section 5 references are made to regulatory proposals recently examined in Europe. Section 6 concludes.

2. - The Traditional Organization of the Telecommunications Services Sector

Up to the beginning of the 1990s, the system of telecommunications services generally comprised three subsystems which were distinct both from an institutional and a technological point of view: *a)* telephone and data services, *b)* telex and telegraphic services, *c)* television and radio services. The first two constitute the telecommunications sector, while the third is the radio and television sector.

This section concentrates in particular on the telecommunications sector, which in terms of investments, income and spread of services was dominated by the national public telephone network operator (Telecom). Adjacent companies cannot, however, be ignored, even if our qualitative model does not take account of television, telegraphic and telex services, which up to the end of the 1980s were only marginally affected by technological change. It should also be noted that in many countries, the demand for telex and telegraphic services is contracting (or slowing) as they are being replaced by other services such as *fax* (Morganti [28]).

With regards to the general organisation of the sector, it must also be said that various countries present some peculiarities. Italy, for example, did not have a Telecom in a strict sense for many years, while other countries, including a number in Europe, enjoyed a greater breadth of services and more complex configurations[2].

A further simplification of the reference scheme is that the role of the sector regulatory agency is not described. Consequently, the numerous differences in tariffs and in public licence and concession policies are not surveyed.

The Telecom companies, which are often state owned, provide voice connections to their subscribers over fixed lines. Dedicated infrastructures also support data services, with network redundancy as a result of the use of different technologies (packet switching and circuit switching, point-to-point lines, as well as low speed transfer via the telephone network). Other operators, from terminal suppliers to data application developers (e.g. the weather forecast or specialised legal databases), are grouped around the national operator, which in general also has its own divisions in these two sub-sectors.

The main features of the traditional organisation of the sector are *monopoly* and *vertical integration*. Indeed, the monopoly is both regional and national, i.e. access for users to national and international telephone networks and the distribution of calls in a given region are offered by a single operator and this operator is the same for all regions of the country. Long-distance services and data networks and services are operated by the national Telecom company.

As far as vertical integration is concerned, it should be noted that *(i)* the long-distance network is an intermediate *input* for the company operating the access network (or vice-versa) and *(ii)* the entire infrastructure (access and long-distance networks) is an intermediate *input* for basic (delivery of calls and data) and advanced (any processing of the transmitted signal) service providers.

2.1 Determinants of the Traditional Organization

Which are the economic categories on which a vertically integrated, monopolistic organisation is based? In the literature extensive

---

[2] For a review of the organisational forms adopted in the past for telecommunications in OECD countries, see Iccp [20]; a view of the more recent problems faced by Community countries in Wik-Eac [41].

reference is made to three concepts: natural monopoly, universal service (and, strictly linked to this, cross-subsidy) and consumption externality [3].

Although a detailed analysis of the above categories is beyond the scope of the present paper, a brief definition is given, together with a summary of the main aspects underlying their application to the telecommunications sector. It should be noted that the three categories have independent conceptual roots, even if there are obviously numerous interactions in the effects of their application.

2.1.1 Natural Monopoly

A multi-product sector is a natural monopoly when the long-term total cost function of the firms operating within the sector is globally subadditive (Baumol *et* Al. [2]). For our purposes, a number of critical elements should be underlined. First, the definition refers to long-run production choices. Second, the exit of the test of subadditivity may change with specifications of the output vector. Third, the above definition assumes that the company's technology level remains constant. Fourth, neither global nor product specific economies of scale are in themselves necessary or sufficient conditions.

2.1.2 Universal Service

Support of the obligation to provide a universal service derives from the conviction that access to telecommunications services is an aspect of the freedom of expression and communication, and, as such, must be guaranteed to all. Indeed, for disadvantaged sectors of the community, communications services often have a social value. The corollaries of this obligation are that the service offers national geographic coverage, that tariffs are independent of local traffic density (the route averaging rule) and that, more generally, the price

---

[3] A review of the 'classical' arguments can be found in ERGAS H. [13] and LITTLECHILD S.C. [24].

of the service is independent of the localisation and category of the subscriber and the tariffs for the local and residential service are equitable (CEC [5]; Granham [18]; TIAP [39]). Different regulatory practices have been derived from these principles. First, the national Telecom has been allowed to use internal subsidies, i.e. cross subsidies, of various type [4]. Secondly, cream-skimming on more profitable services has been impeded [5]. Here it should be noted that the general nature of the definition of universal service leaves a number of questions open (see Granham [18]; e.g. which services are included in the obligation to provide a universal service?).

2.1.3 Consumption Externality

The benefit to the subscriber from participating in two-way communication grows in proportion to the number of subscribers [6]. Traditionally, it has been felt that hierarchical integration was the most appropriate way to internalise these externalities. On the one hand, hierarchical integration also resulted in increased efficiency in the production structure due to economies of scale, and, on the other one, it allowed to partially internalise the obligation to provide a universal service. It must, however, be underlined, that integration is necessary only in the absence of open networks or, more generally, of conditions of equal access [7] (Hayashi [9]; Neu — Neumann [31]; Wik-Eac [41]). Furthermore, the benefit to the subscriber of participation in the network is not independent of the characteristics of the

---

[4] Cross subsidy exists when cost coverage in one product or end-user area is obtained by internal transfer from other products or users (RALPH E. [34]). The traditional argument that such practice is a function of the obligation to provide auniversal service is empirically rejected by KASERMAN D.L. *et* AL. [23]).

[5] Cream-skimming exists when a newcorner enters only product or user areas without the obligation of providing a universal service and competes with the incumbent, bound and regulated by the universal service, only on the most lucrative products. For an example of cream-skimming, see the first chapter of FUSS M. - WAYERMAN L. [15].

[6] On the importance and nature of externalities in telecommunications services see CAPELLO R. [3].

[7] Equal access pertains when interconnection to a company's facilities by other operators is not discriminatory, i.e. when an operator offers its own network services to other operators at the conditions offered to an internal unit requesting such services.

other subscribers, so that the addition of new subscribers generally enhances the value of the network in a non-linear manner.

2.2 *Characteristics of the Communications Services Sector*

The following sections outline the main arguments which have traditionally been advanced with respect to the configuration of the sector. These will be critically reviewed in Section 4.

2.2.1 Regional Monopoly in Local Telephone Services

Each individual access network (a central exchange and the lines connecting to subscribers) enjoys increasing return to scale. Duplication of the dedicated user circuit (and thus of resources dedicated to the laying and maintenance of the local loop itself) would be inefficient. Furthermore, there are minimum capacity thresholds for the primary distribution network [8] and the local exchanges, making these indivisible for technical reasons (even if it is recognised that the complexity of the connection matrices for the exchanges increases more than proportionally to the number of circuits).

The section of the network linking the access networks and urban network exchanges (so-called tandem exchanges) also benefits from scale, due to the technical indivisibility of the junction circuits (particularly laying and maintenance). Also the probability of a rationing of demand in this segment falls in function of the installed base, as a result of the greater flexibility in controlling and routing traffic. In addition, there are also organisational indivisibilities, due to minimum thesholds for a number of functions (design, planning and programming of the network, customer support, administration and billing). Other sources of economies of scale are the unique nature of maintenance teams and of safety circuits.

---

[8] The term primary distribution network refers to that part of the access network having lines shared by different users.

2.2.2 National Monopoly in the Local Telephone Services

The legal barrier to a plurality of local operators has generally hinged on two aspects of the universal service: the national geographic coverage and the practice of route-averaging. Should the national access tariff lead to a deficit for a given regional operator, the subsidy is realised by connecting a number of regional areas to the same operator and by legal barriers to skimming off entries into the sector. Furthermore, in the absence of open network systems and equal access, separate operation of the different local areas would reduce the positive consumption externalities.

2.2.3 National Monopoly in Long-Distance Telephone Services

The junction circuits in a national, long-distance network are characterised by technical indivisibility, particularly with regards to laying and maintenance, while the security systems of such networks benefit from economies of scale. For large scale networks, there may also be other organisational benefits and pecuniary economies in the purchase of network systems. Specific economies of scope in a strict sense lead to a reduction in the risk of saturation on transmission lines by virtue of the complementary nature of the time profiles of traffic generated by the different user categories.

2.2.4 Vertical Integration Between Local and Long-Distance Telephone Services

The sum of local and long-distance traffic can allow joint economies of scale resulting from organisational indivisibility to be exploited. Moreover, only with a joint operation of the two types of service can the network and local traffic be subsidised by income from long-distance services (it is widely held that *(i)* there are major differences in the price and income elasticity in the demand for the two services and *(ii)* local services have a social value). The joint operation of the two services can also be seen as a pre-requisite for the full and direct exploitation of consumption externalities.

2.2.5 Vertical Integration Between Services and Network

As far as basic services are concerned (distribution of calls), their operation by the network operator was not questioned until a few years ago, as the electro-mechanical and analog technologies combined the information transmission network and the control of traffic flow into a single phase of production. Moreover, information on the state of the network and the traffic were distributed and difficult to transfer, obliging a provider of non-integrated services to replicate the structure of the network operator.

For advanced services, their relevance in terms of income was negligible and did not prompt any alternative hypothesis of how they could be provided.

2.2.6 Monopoly in Data Services, Integration Between Network and Service, Integration Between Data and Telephone Services

The debate on the organisation of data services has been relatively limited, given that these are less widespread than telephone services. It must, however, be said that no technological economies of scale or scope in a strict sense would appear to emerge from joint ownership of data and telephone networks, given the differences in the switching and transmisison technologies used for the two types of network.

Other aspects have prompted revisions of industrial policy, but these could have influenced the configuration of public data networks only indirectly. Indeed, the development of the latter is highly dependent, on the one hand, on the growth of company networks and so-called 'closed' user groups, and, on the other, on application suppliers. The most debated points are: tariffs for point-to-point circuits leased from Telecom, the possibility of linking these to the public network, the re-sale of capacity by company users and closed groups, and incentive and tariff policies for developers of information applications. The industrial policy response to these questions has been very varied, as evidenced in the reviews in ICCP ([20]) or OECD ([32]).

2.2.7 Separation Between Radio/Television and Telephone Services

Radio, cable and broadcast TV signals could not have been transmitted via the telephone network, above all because of the bottle-neck caused by the low capacity of the so-called copper 'couple' which connects subscribers to the telephone network. The infrastructure of the broadcast radio and TV networks is also considerably smaller than that of the telephone network, while the differing determinants of demand for the two groups of service and the differing management competencies have also contributed to maintaining the division between the two sectors.

3. - Changes During the 1980s

The changes occurring in the organisation of the sector feed, above all, on the opportunities emerging from progress in transmission and switching technology. In addition, the economic debate, i.e. the analysis and testing of the concepts on which the organisation of the sector is based, also plays an important, albeit indirect, role in institutional change.

3.1 *Technical Progress*

Recent technological changes in the sector have been numerous, radical and complex, and can, in the main, be traced back to the paradigms of information and optoelectronic technologies. Very briefly, the changes can be summarised as follows:

1) the introduction of digital transmission ensures high quality standards, independently of the original format. At the same time, the

performance of the junction lines has increased considerably with the use of time-division multiplexers;

2) digital exchanges permit a potentially enormous differentiation of services, as on digital networks, the transport network and the so-called intelligent network are distinct, giving greater flexibility in the production process [9]. The transport network is responsible for basic functions involving the network hardware, i.e. the transmission and switching of signals entering the network. In contrast, the information network is in charge, on the one hand, of the routing and control of calls and, on the other, the intelligent services (processing of transmitted information giving added value with respect to the simple delivery function) which provide the user with potential access to a large number of applications. The information network includes an operating system, numerous databases, and a series of devices to connect to other networks or internal and external information suppliers;

3) the replacement of traditional copper junction cables with optical fibre systems increases the speed/capacity and the quality of transmission to an extraordinary extent, reducing the public works necessary to install line electronics (repeaters and protection systems), as well as the maintenance and cable transport costs. When these systems are linked to digital network nodes and optical fibre access lines (Fibre in the Loop), firms and, in the future, families will be able to take advantage of new, interactive services, made possible by the intelligent nodes and the considerable amount of data, telephone conversation and images which the network will be able to carry;

4) the development of personal and mobile communications services by means of both analogical and digital radio signal access to the fixed network, and, to a lesser extent, via satellite networks, satisfies previously unexpressed and unsatisfied communications needs.

What are the potential consequences of all these changes? Vari-

---

[9] On digital networks, the physical path of the call does not coincide with that of the control information and signalling (introduction of the Common Channel Signaling System). Furthermore, changes in the transmission network (a new junction line or new access topology) are reflected in the information network simply by a change in the database.

ous short and medium-term modifications already seem probable today. A brief summary is given here.

The main consequences of digital transmission and switching are as follows. First, digital systems (in combination with optical fibre junction lines) allow the telephone network to carry data services and replace dedicated data networks. Second, a wide set of new telephone services, such as call paging, a centralised answer-phone, choice of tariff mode, conference calls and freephone numbers (in Italy, the so-called 'green numbers') are possible. The network operator can interface with any type of service provider, be they providers of services or applications, operators of other fixed networks, closed user groups, private or mobile telephone networks [10]. Fourth, barriers preventing the definition of two distinct bodies — the operator of the network infrastructure and the service provider — are, at least in theory, considerably reduced [11].

The spread of mobile telephone services opens the way to competition between different technologies on different services. The mobile telephone can even replace to some extent the traditional fixed telephone. On the supply side, this is particularly attractive in regions of low population or with a limited telephone infrastructure, but is, at present, not particularly efficient in urban and metropolitan areas. Furthermore, the emergence of new operators (mobile network operators) has placed greater emphasis on interconnection as a means of guaranteeing exploration of consumption externalities, and, at the same time, on the importance of public network access policy. Finally, competition between different operators of mobile telephone networks has been admitted, even if, in the majority of countries, practice is still being defined as it depends (among other things) on access conditions to the fixed network [12].

The most important result of the installation of optical fibre lines

---

[10] The study by Wik-Eac [41] gives a critical review of the modes adopted to make connections in the major countries.

[11] Based on the concept of 'intelligent networks', Mansell R. [25] gives an interesting analysis of the prospects and the problems associated with the development of telecommunications infrastructures.

[12] Amendola G. - Ferraiuolo A. [1] provide an extensive analysis of the subject of competition in mobile services in the light of innovation dynamics in cellular systems.

to access the network is the convergence between telephone and television services. Indeed, a single user terminal will be able to feed telephone, data and television services, laying the ground for a fully multimedial network, supporting even interactive video services. Large scale implementation of a broadband access infrastructure has been hampered both by uncertainty with regard to the demand for the new services and the amount of the investments (and related financial constraints). Nevertheless, plans to cable major cities have recently been approved in many European countries [13].

Finally, it should be underlined that the convergence of video and telephone is also guaranteed by cable TV operators, who sell telephone services in those countries in which this is permitted.

3.2 *The Economic Debate on the Organization of the Telecommunications Industry: Results from the Aggregated Econometric Models*

Numerous applied studies have examined the overall production structure of the Telecom companies, in an attempt to verify the hypothesis of natural monopoly and the relationship between cost subadditivity and technical progress.

It must be said from the outset that the results of these studies are ambiguous. Measurement of economies of scope in a strict sense is fraught with difficulty; consequently most of the 'classical' evidence on natural monopoly concerns economies of scale, obtained with a mono-product approximation of the various Telecom companies. North American operators would appear to show increasing returns, while those of the European operators generally turn out to be constant (Nadiri - Schankerman [29]; Denny - Fuss - Everson - Waverman [10]; Christensen *et* Al. [4]; Elixmann [12]). A few multi-product studies have sought to verify the subadditivity of the

---

[13] Interesting studies of the economic and financial feasibility of optical fibre broadband networks have been carried out by EGAN B. [11], REED P.D. - SIRBU M.A. [36]. ONIKI H. [33] outlines the *ideal* organisation which in the long-term will characterise a communications industry based on a fully optical fibre national network, the BISDN infrastructure (Broadband, Integrated Services Digital Network).

cost function directly (Evans - Heckman [14]; Röller [37]; Shin - Ying [38]). The findings are contradictory, as the level of subbaditivity of the cost function depends on the functional form and the chosen specification (Garrone [16]).

As regards the impact of technical progress on economies of scale and subadditivity, we will look first at those models which refer to technological innovations prior to 1980. For the American Bell System, Christensen *et* Al. [4] report that the effects of scale are emphasised by technical progress affecting the network, while Nadiri and Schankerman [29] claim that technical progress is non output augmenting [14]. In constrast, Evans and Heckman [14] and Röller [37] find that technical progress reduces the scale effects for local calls but increases those for long-distance traffic.

Looking at studies on the more recent evolution of the operators, the most general model among those proposed by Elixmann [19] shows that for the German operator, technological change is non output augmenting. In a study of American local carriers Shin and Ying [38] report that the scale effects of the number of subscribers (access to the network) are greater the more advanced the network system, while both local and long-distance calls (use of the service) show lower economies of scale. In contrast, Garrone [17] finds that for the European Telecom companies, scale economies as a result of an increase in local and long-distance calls diminishes as more digital switching nodes are introduced, while economies of scale associated to a balanced growth of access and use do not experience this effect.

4. - Revision of the Traditional Organization of the Industry

In this section we will argue that a critical revision of the traditional organisational model of the sector highlights weaknesses and ambiguities. In particular, it emerges that the model does not necessarily derive from the economic categories which in the past

---

[14] Technical progress is said to be non output augmenting, when the measures of scale and subadditivity are independent of it, i.e. when the cost function is separable into outputs and technological level.

have been used in its support, nor would it seem to be robust with respect to the current prospects of change.

Is the monopolistic organisation of the industry truly dictated by the presence of increasing returns of scale in different segments of the network and by scope economies between the various services? While the economies of scale of the local loop would not appear, at first sight, to be in doubt, some of the arguments in support of the monopoly of the junction network (both the local and long-distance portions) and the integration between the various production stages are not of general validity. A number of points merit closer analysis:

1) the technical indivisibility produces density economies in filling up excess capacity in junction circuits, local exchanges and the primary distribution network, but not necessarily increasing scale returns. Only if the country and the individual regions show low and steady demand will the path of expansion result in constant reductions in average costs in the long-run as well. Indeed, because of the *lumpy* nature of the capital invested in the network, there is no radical distinction between the short and the long run. The low costs of an additional unit of service in optical fibre networks with digital nodes can also be explained by short-run density economies [15];

2) the presence of economies of scale as to discourage the presence of a variety of operators in individual segments of the network will thus depend to a large extent on organisational indivisibilities and on financial and «massed reserves» economies. In this respect, we feel that in countries with heavy traffic, the long-distance network and the aggregated local netowrks have probably passed the threshold of increasing returns;

3) as far as the effects of technical progress are concerned, over and above pecuniary economies and notwithstanding the significant downward trend in the cost of network components, a particular network size does not appear, *a priori*, to be advantaged [16];

4) the only complementary effects between long-distance and local services, between local services in one region and those in

---

[15] See MITCHELL B.M. [27], an example of an extremely detailed technical-economic study.

[16] See RAVAZZI P. - VALLETTI T. [35] on the relation between scale economies and technological innovation.

another, between the network and the services or between basic and advanced services which can be expected *a priori* would appear to be those linked to the presence of an umbrella brand name, and, even in this case, these are not such as to compensate the possible benefits of specialisation (if vertical foreclosure practices are to be excluded).

These considerations would seem to suggest that in regions with strong and growing subscriber and service demand, scale effects are not such as to exclude, first, the presence of a number of operators on some of the long-distance routes, second, the independence of different regional operators of local services, and, third, the separation of local and long-distance services. Even the integration between service provider and network operator is undermined. In contrast, on conservative assumptions and in line with the traditional model, the economies of scale which characterise the access network would seem to draw the majority of local networks into the area of increasing returns to scale, so that competition for individual users among local operators can for the time being be excluded [17].

A hypothetical industrial system compatible with the allocative efficiency and with the opportunities offered by technical progress is comprised of four 'layers':

1) the access network. By virtue of technological progress, users can access the communications network in four different ways. Local operators can connect subscribers either via the traditional twisted wire pair (first possibility) or via optical fibre (second possibility), which, in addition to the telephone, offers high speed data and interactive video services. When linked to the fixed telephone network, cable TV operators can also carry telephone services (third possibility). Finally, cellular network operators (including via satellite) guarantee standard and personal communication services to their

---

[17] In effect, this is a conservative assumption in the absence of cost-engineering models dedicated to segments of the local network other than the local loop. It should not be excluded that appropriate special network access policies allow competition on local services without necessitating system duplication. For example, in some states of the United States, the interconnectors (long-distance or mobile operators and service providers) can use the access infrastructure of local operators,in order to guarantee genuine parity of access to subscribers (special access conditions, NEU W. - NEUMANN K.H. [31]). Finally, different access technologies guarantee services which are partly replaceable.

subscribers (fourth possibility). Cable TV and cellular network operators interconnect to the local and long-distance networks.

The user will be able to choose between various cellular operators, but because of the sunk costs and scale effects, the monopoly on those users already connected to a local landline circuit (in copper or optical fibre) will persist, at least in the medium term, even if some limitation to the exercise of market power is provided by the alternative radio telephone system;

2) the long-distance network. There is competition between operators on many sections of the long-distance network. The prevalent transmission technology is optical fibre;

3) services. The definition on a given telecommunications network of a transmission network, a basic services network and a further, intelligent network dedicated to accessing and processing other information services has promoted the distinction between network operators and service providers, the latter understood as points of access, gathering, maintenance and up-dating of information applications, be they databases, video libraries or advanced telephone services. Competition between service providers (especially of the advanced type) is not excluded;

4) information content. There are specialised producers of video, audio and data applications and, although not fully part of the telecommunications system, consistute a critical pre-condition for the differentiation of services.

5. - Liberalization of Telecommunications Networks in Italy and the European Union

In the previous sections we have illustrated the reasons underlying the crisis in the monolithic organisation traditionally adopted in the telecommunications sector. However, the weakness of this model does not necessarily lead to the conclusion that for 'objective' reasons of efficiency the trend is towards a fragmented organisation of the sector. In other words, fragmentation of the industry would, at least, not appear necessary. Even if different, independent technology stages in the production *filière* have been identified, and it is recognised that the majority of these do not enjoy particular economies of scale, it must be recognized that the organisation of the communications system responds not only to concerns of allocative efficiency, but also to a complex and articulated body of objectives.

Below, the contingent nature of possible configurations for the sector (including 'sub-division') is documented with reference to the process of liberalisation underway in Europe. A preference on the part of European Union policy makers for a particular organisational solution does not emerge from the acts and recommendations which are currently available. In this respect, the range of configurations which has resulted from the recent deregulation of various industries should be remembered. In particular, it is evident that different structures are used in different industries in the same country or in the same industry in different countries [18].

In recent years, proposals to reform the regulatory framework of the telecommunications network and services industries have been advanced in numerous countries. In the United States, the administration and industry representatives are discussing the restrictions which resulted from changes to the structure of the sector introduced in the first half of the 1980s (National Telecommunications and Information Administration [30]), with the aim of attracting private investment in the networks (Information Infrastructure Task Force [12]) [19].

In Japan, too, the government has begun to look at the need for liberalization measures to promote private investment in 'telecommunications, broadcast and other areas', recognising that the 1985 deregulation only marginally affected local networks (Ministry of International Trade and Industry [26]).

---

[18] This is the case in the electricity, rail and telecommunications industries in the United Kingdom. The first two sectors have structures based on the separation of production from transport and distribution, while the latter has two vertically integrated operators (BT and, to a lesser extent Mercury), together with operators specialised in individual stages (e.g. various radio telephone network operators or the services providers). We also recall the different organisation of the telecommunications sectors in the United Kingdom and the United States.

[19] We recall that the *Modified Final Judgment* of 1984 impeded the Regional Bell Operating Companies from supplying information services, while the *Cable Act* of 1984 forbade them to programme video services and operate cable networks in regions in which they were licensees for telecommunications services. Congress is currently debating a new *Communications Act*.

In Europe, the *Green Paper* on the development of a common market in telecommunications services and systems (1987) has lead to numerous suggestions and recommendations being brought to the attention of operators in the sector. Recently, the *Bangemann Report* (Commission of the European Communities [6]) stated that the extraordinary technological change over the last years has opened up possibilities for the diffusion of new information services which could stimulate the growth and the competitiveness of the European economy. Such a development would demand communication infrastructures which have themselves to be liberalised. In order to guarantee the opening up of the European communications market, the Council and the Parliament have been asked to liberalise networks — ranging from alternative infrastructures, including cable TV networks and mobile and satellite communications, to networks distributing voice services — by 1 January 1998 (Commission of the European Communities [8] and [9]).

5.1 *Regulatory Authorities and the Move to Competition*

In the debate between industry firms' top managers, experts and policy makers, various problems have been raised with regard to the ways of opening up the market, and, above all, the role of the incumbent operator in a liberalised market. A telecommunications regulatory authority should contribute to the formulation of rules which maintain the universal service, oversee the dominant company, define and grant operating licences, ensure an adequate flow of investments into the network, define the mode of connection between networks and between the network and service providers, govern the setting of access tariffs and verify that equipment and systems to be used on the public network meet technical operation standards.

As documented by Tyler and Bednarczyk [40], there are numerous important questions concerning the regulatory agencies in the sector and their role in liberalising the market. Here, we would only underline that the National Telecommunications Regulatory Authority can serve a dual function: in an initial, transition phase, support and control of the move out of the monopoly, and, subsequently, maintenance of competition and promotion of investment. In this sense, the agency is responsible for the definition of aspects which are crucial for the move to competition, for the identification of possible solutions and, finally, for the translation of the chosen solution into institutional mechanisms.

The second part of the *Green Paper* on infrastructures displays a substantial recognition of the complexity of the move from a market which has traditionally been dominated by few operators (often by just one) to a fully competitive environment. The procedures suggested to render liberalization effective include: close scrutiny of connection agreements, joint ventures and cross or joint ownership of different networks or of networks and services; assessment of the schemes to finance the universal service, and guarantee of open non-discriminatory access by means of either structural separation or transparent accounting structures in those companies which both provide services and operate a network.

5.2 *Licences*

The assignment of licences for the installation and operation of telecommunications infrastructures is a central argument in the *Green Paper* on infrastructure liberalization, which states that it is the infrastructures and not the services which are subject to licence, and that the criteria for concession must be objective, pre-defined and not discriminatory on grounds of the nationality of the applicant. Only exceptionally may the conditions accompanying the licence regard services other than telecommunications, such as broadcast.

It is useful to recall a number of further specifications with regards to licences. Restrictions on the number of licences granted for a given public network can only be justified on the basis of so-called 'essential requirements', which include network safety, integrity and inter-operability, the protection and confidentiality of information, and the conservation of the environment. If a right of way is not granted to suppliers who have applied, the licence must be accompanied by less onerous obligations. In any case, the efficient use of resources (possibly including the introduction of schemes to share lines and ducts voluntarily or if necessary, obligatorily) is to be encouraged. Further-more, demand for connection by other networks or service providers must be satisfied and negotiated on a commercial basis.

While the *Green Paper* does not specify the nature of the agency which distributes the licences, it should be remembered that for the European cable TV networks, different situations exist. In the United Kingdom, the Department of Trade and Industry authorises com-panies responsible for the construction and technical operation of the networks, while service providers (the commercialisation of the net-work and programming of subscription terms) must respect different procedures. In France, the Ministry installs the Plan Cable network via France Telecom, while for networks outside Plan Cable, the local authorities are responsible, either directly or via private firms. Commercial administration is with mixed or private companies, licensed by the Supreme Audio-visual Council. In Germany, Telekom constructs and operates the majority of the networks, although a small part is licensed by the Ministry to private operators. However, it is the regions which are responsible for programming.

5.3 *Universal Service*

The *Green Paper* places great emphasis on the obligation to preserve the universality of a 'minimum body of services and infrastructures' and common tariffs in telecommunicaitons. Although observing that in many cases this objective is possible on a commercial basis without public intervention, it is admitted that views on how to realise this objective in a liberalised environment diverge. Indeed, the supply of basic voice services to all consumers could oblige operators to serve uneconomical or disadvantaged users.

In order to satisfy the obligation to provide universality, national regulatory authorities are recommended to define 'transparent schemes' for determining the cost of an obligatory universal service and to finance this obligation through the set-up of a national fund (rather than by increasing access tariffs). It is also stated that tariffs should be rebalanced, as traditional cross subsidies have impeded differentiation between services.

5.4 *Liberalization in Italy*

In the course of 1995, two proposals were advanced in Italy for a law to liberalise telecommunications services and infrastructures (the Gambino and Bassanini proposals). Furthermore, in November 1995, a law came into force setting up a regulatory autority in the public utility sector: electricity and gas, on the one hand, and telecommunications, on the other.

As regards the Italian telecommunications authority, the *Competition and Regulatory Norms in Public Utility Services and the Institution of a Regulatory Authority for Public Utility Services* law leaves open the possibility that the telecommunications authority may take on broader responsibilities for the entire communications system. In the functions and measures assigned to the Italian authority, the liberalization of infrastructures promoted by the Community would appear to receive ambitious support.

The letter of the law shows that the problems outlined above are significant to define the role of the new agency. With respect to equal access, the agency can control the connection mode (including prices), issue directives on accounting separation and the unbundling of network services and ensure that data is made public. As far as licences are concerned, the agency is responsible for proposing means of assignment and clauses to Parliament and the Government. Finally, the spread of services and the realisation of social objectives are defended through tariff setting. It is also interesting to underline the powers held by the authority for the exercise of its provisions: it can request information from companies, carry out controls and punish infringements with sanctions of various types.

Four specific questions would appear to be critical to the move to a liberalised environment in Italy: *(i)* the debated need to treat newcomers and ex-monopolists asymmetrically and, if this be the case, whether the advantage granted to the former be on networks, services or both; *(ii)* a balance between the two opposing needs of urgent cabling and a precise definition of guarantees for entrants; *(iii)* the alternative between accounting separation (or even separate structures) for network operation and services and the dual risk of polarising accounting and producing double marginalisation of tariffs [20]; *(iv)* the status of alternative network operators (transport, electricity, gas and water).

With regards to licences and authorisations for operators, two questions are of particular importance. Which criteria should be used to define the number of licences and the associated connection conditions? Which body is responsible for the granting of licences?

The two questions outlined above involve numerous aspects of the emerging competitive environment: *(i)* the possible definition of the local loop as a natural monopoly and effective competition in that segment of the market; *(ii)* the need to share resources such as public works sites or line trenches; *(iii)* control cream skimming practices (entry of a company only in lucrative product or user segments); *(iv)* adequacy of private contracting for the access charge; *(v)* bodies responsible for the granting of licences and co-ordination of these at national level.

While the definition of the obligations connected to the universal service and its means of finance can be examined in more detail elsewhere, it is interesting to draw attention to two implications for the competitive environment in telecommunications infrastructures: *(i)* whether the incumbent can sustain the obligation to provide a universal service and *(ii)* whether the market is such as to support the burdens of this obligation.

6. - Conclusions

In our opinion, recognition of the drawbacks of the traditional configuration of the telecommunications sector does not necessarily lead to the formulation of proposals for a fragmented organisational model. Indeed, such proposals suffer from limitations imposed by highly restrictive hypotheses which would not seem able to reproduce the complexity of current conditions in the industry.

We therefore argue that it is critical to admit the possibility of a

---

[20] Double marginalisation derives from the adjacency in the production *filière* of two stages, in both of which companies exercise market power, consequently raising prices in the end-market with respect to when the two stages are hierarchically co-ordinated.

broad range of institutional solutions, each with its relative merits. As the objectives are numerous, we do not believe that an optimum organisation for the sector can be identified. An important contribution in making the choice derives from the introduction of theoretical models based on hypotheses able to embrace the technological and institutional complexity of the sector and, in particular, analyse in terms of appropriate efficiency criteria the ownership and control structure of the firms producing services.

BIBLIOGRAPHY

[1] AMENDOLA G. - FERRAIUOLO A., «Regulating Mobile Communications», *Proceedings of the ITS Conference*, Sidney, 3-6 July 1994.

[2] BAUMOL W.J. - PANZAR J.C. - WILLING R.D., *Contestable Markets and the Theory of Industry Structure*, San Diego (CA.), Harcourt Brace Jovanovich, 1982.

[3] CAPELLO R., *Spatial Economic Analysis of Telecommunications Network Externalities*, Hants., Avebury-Aldershot, (UK), 1994.

[4] CHRISTENSEN L.R. - CUMMINGS CHRISTENSEN D. - SCHOECH P.E., «Econometric Estimation of Scale Economies in Telecommunications», in COURVILLE L. - DE FONTENAY A. - DOBELL R. (eds.), *Economic Analysis of Telecommunications: Theory and Applications*, Amsterdam (NE), North-Holland, 1983.

[5] COMMISSION OF THE EUROPEAN COMMUNITIES, *Livre Vert sur le Developpement du Marché Commun des Services et Equipments des Telecommunication*, Brussels, DGXIII, 1987.

[6] — —, *Europe's Way to the Information Society: an Action Plan.*, COM(94), 247 final, Brussels, DGXIII, 1994.

[7] — —, *Green Paper on the Liberalisation of Telecommunications Infrastructure and Cable Television Networks. Part One*, COM(94), 440 final, Brussels, DGXIII, 1994.

[8] — —, *Green Paper on a Common Approach in the Field of Mobile and Personal Communications in the European Union*, COM(94), 140 final, Brussels, DGXIII, 1994.

[9] — —, *Green Paper on the Liberalisation of Telecommunications Infrastructure and Cable Television Networks. Part Two*, COM(94), 682 final, Brussels, DGXIII, 1995.

[10] DENNY M. - FUSS M. - EVERSON C. - WAVERMAN L., «Estimating the Effects of Diffusion of Technological Innovations in Telecommunications: the Production Structure of Bell Canada», *Canadian Journal of Economics*, n. 14, 1981, pp. 24-43.

[11] EGAN B.L., *Information Superhighways: the Economics of Advanced Public Communication Networks*, Boston (Mass), Artech House, 1991.

[12] ELIXMANN D., «Econometric Estimation of Production Structures: the Case of the German Telecommunications Carrier», *WIK Diskussionbeiträge*, 57, 1990.

[13] ERGAS H., «Regulation, Monopoly and Competition in the Telecommunications Infrastructure», in ICCP (ed.), *Trends of Change in Telecommunications Policy*, Paris, OECD, 1987.

[14] EVANS D.S. - HECKMAN J.J., «A Test for Subaddittivity of the Cost Function with an Application to the Bell System», *American Economic Review*, n. 74, 1984, pp. 615-23.

[15] FUSS M. - WAVERMAN L., «The Regulations of Telecommunications in Canada», *Economic Council of Canada Technical Report*, n. 7, 1981.

[16] GARRONE P., «Imprese di gestione delle reti di telecomunicazioni: modelli econometrici della struttura di costo», *Rapporto interno CIRET WP 94.01*, Milano, Politecnico di Milano, 1994.

[17] — —, «Network Subscription and Services Usage in European Telecommunications Industry», *Information Economics and Policy*, forthcoming, 1995.

[18] GRANHAM N., «Universal Service in European Telecommunications», in ICCP (ed.), *Universal Services and Rate Restructuring in Telecommunications*, Paris, OECD, 1991.

[19] HAYASHI K., «From Network Externalities to Interconnection», in ANTONELLI C. (ed.), *The Economics of Information Networks*, Amsterdam (NE), North-Holland, 1992.

[20] ICCP, *Trends of Change in Telecommunications Policy*, Paris, OECD, 1987.

[21] — —, *Universal Services and Rate Restructuring in Telecommunications*, Paris, OECD, 1991.

[22] INFORMATION INFRASTRUCTURE TASK FORCE, *The National Information Infrastructure: Agenda for Action*, Washington (DC), National Telecommunications and Information Administration, 1993.

[23] KASERMAN D.L. - MAYO J.W. - FLYNN J.E., «Cross-Subsidizitation in Telecommunications: Beyond the Universal Service Fairy Tale», *Journal of Regulatory Economics*, n. 2, 1990, pp. 231-49.

[24] LITTLECHILD S.C., *Elements of Telecommunications Economics*, Stevenage (UK), Peter Peregrinus, 1979.

[25] MANSELL R., «Rethinking the Telecommunication Infrastructure: the New «Black Box», *Research Policy*, n. 19, 1990, pp. 501-15.

[26] MINISTRY OF INTERNATIONAL TRADE AND INDUSTRY, *Program for Advanced Information Infrastructure*, Tokyo, 1994.

[27] MITCHELL B.M., *Incremental Costs of Telephone Access and Local Use*, R-3909-ICTF, Santa Monica (CA.), RAND Corporation, 1990.

[28] MORGANTI F., *Le telecomunicazioni*, Roma, SIPI, 1990.

[29] NADIRI M.I. - SCHANKERMAN M., «The Structure of Production, Technological Change, and the Rate of Growth of Total Factor Productivity in the US Bell System», in COWING T. - STEVENSON R., (ed.) *Productivity Measurement in Regulated Industries*, New York (NY), Academic Press, 1981.

[30] NATIONAL TELECOMMUNICATIONS AND INFORMATION ADMINISTRATION, *White Paper on Communications Act Reform*, Washington (DC), 1994.

[31] NEU W. - NEUMANN K.H., «Interconnection Agreements in Telecommunications», *WIK Diskussionsbeiträge*, n. 106, 1993.

[32] OECD, *Communications Outlook 1993*, Paris, 1994.

[33] ONIKI H., «Japanese Telecommunications as a Network Industry: Industrial Organization for the BISDN Generation Technology», Osaka, Osaka University, *ISER Discussion Paper*, n. 324, 1994.

[34] RALPH E., «Cross-Subsidy: a Novice's Guide to the Arcane», *Proceedings of the BellCoRe - Bell Canada Conference*, San Diego (CA), 5-7 Apr. 1989.

[35] RAVAZZI P. - VALLETTI T., «Innovazione nelle reti e nei servizi di telecomunicazione», Roma, *Atti Convegno AiIG*, 1993.

[36] REED P.D. - SIRBU M.A., «An Engineering Cost and Policy Analysis of Proposed Fibre Optic Telephone Networks in the Residential Subscriber Loop», in ELTON M.C.J., (ed.) *Integrated Broadband Networks. The Public Policy Issues*, Amsterdam, North-Holland, 1991.

[37] RÖLLER L.H., «Modelling Cost Structure: the Bell System Revisited», *Applied Economics*, n. 22, 1990, pp. 1661-74.

[38] SHIN R.T. - YING J.S., «Unnatural Monopolies in Local Telephone», *The RAND Journal of Economics*, n. 23, 1992, pp. 171-83.

[39] TIAP, «Apples and Oranges: Differences between Various Subsidy Studies», *NARUC Meeting*, Reno (Nevada), 1994.

[40] TYLER M. - BEDNARCZYK S., «Regulatory Institutions and Processes in Telecommunications. An International Study of Alternatives», *Telecommunications Policy*, December 1993.

[41] WIK-EACH, *Network Interconnection in the Domain of ONP. Study for DGXIII of the European Commission*, Bad Honnef, WIK, 1994.

Privatizing the Italian Postal Services Governance Structure, Property Rights and Monopoly Rents

Vincenzo Visco Comandini *

Istituto di Studi sulle Regioni - CNR, Roma

1. - Introduction

The view that public service monopolies only serve to permit the exploitation of the rents that derive from the exclusive nature of the licence granted is increasingly accepted by economists and the public in the main industrial countries. Perhaps more than any other, the postal monopoly has allowed interest groups to benefit directly or indirectly, and sometimes very considerably [1]. However, the evidence of serious operational inefficiencies — a normal consequence of the exploitation of monopolistic rents — does not mean that the problem can be overcome simply by turning the service over to the market on the assumption that, unlike the public operator, private firms will be subject to a set of internal and external incentives that will result in the efficiency loss being made good. Nor is there any good reason why the interest groups that have acquired significant rent positions should disappear in this post-monopoly scenario. Rather, they can be ex-

* The author is a research economist at Istituto di studi sulle regioni.

The Author wishes to thank Enrico Buglione, Mauro Marè and Diego Piacentino for their useful suggestions offered during the drafting of this paper; Giampiero Galli and Vincenzo Martini of Ente Poste for the information and data kindly supplied. Naturally, the author bears sole responsibility for the contents of the paper.

[1] The problem is not restricted to Italy but arises in more extreme form in the countries where the postal service played a strategic role in promoting economic development and ensuring national cohesion (LEVINE M. [15] and PRIEST L. [20]).

N.B.: the numbers in square brackets refer to the Bibliography at the end of the paper.

pected to adapt to the change in the institutional setting and focus their attention on the many opportunities to establish rent positions that exist independently of the extent of the reserve. These include: the setting of charges in the public service that permit the survival of productive inefficiencies and cross-subsidization; the scope for private operators to cherry pick while leaving the public operator to provide a universal service, as they already do today, sometimes by trespassing on the monopoly; protected markets for the supply industry with exclusive access to tenders and contracts for the running of highly specialized equipment; and the possibility for organized groups of users to continue to benefit from preferential prices by ensuring the maintenance of conditions of service that match their requirements or the inclusion of their products in categories subject to low charges. The key to the problem thus becomes the fundamental issue of regulation.

In Italy the institutional setup of the postal service has recently been reformed with a view to its inclusion in the private sector of the economy. Law 71/1994 provided for the post office to be turned from an autonomous government agency responding directly to the Minister of Posts and Telecommunications into a public organization (Ente Poste Italiane; EPI) operating under its own bylaws and subject to only a few public rules, with the intention of proceeding in 1996 to its definitive transformation into a public limited company (*società per azioni*). The change in the organizational model adopted for the postal service is the consequence, on the legal and institutional plane, of the collapse of the foundation on which the old postal administration had rested, the equilibrium between the interests of three main actors: politicians, which assigned the agency the task of supporting employment and earnings and frequently of channelling resources and capital spending to electoral fiefdoms; industry, which benefited from the monopoly in various ways, ranging from protected markets to services at preferential prices; and the trade unions, at both the national and the local level, since they were allowed to have a considerable say in the running of the agency and hence in the organization of internal consensus.

The post office is now in a delicate transition phase, since the achievement of a stable governance structure — a necessary condition if the recently initiated process of improving the quality of service is to be continued — is threatened by the urgent need to reduce EPI's losses, which are largely the consequence of the policies adopted in the past. The aim is for EPI to break even in 1996, excluding the subsidy paid by the Treasury Ministry, and this appears to be the *sine qua non* if the autonomy provided for by law 71/1994 is not to be vanified. Inevitably, as long as EPI is not financially self-sufficient, it will remain dependent on the decisions taken annually by the Government and Parliament, and thus remain exposed to the risk of having to perform functions extraneous to its objectives. However, eliminating the organization's losses has a heavy cost in terms of employee consensus; this conflicts with the need to increase both the quantity and the quality of the services provided, another priority objective that the public has been demanding for a long time and which is now embodied in EPI's *Programme Contract*. This document, agreed at the end of 1994 between EPI (as the public operator) and the Ministry of Posts and Telecommunications (as the regulator), defines the relationship between the two bodies through a series of mutual obligations, of which the most important concern service standards and criteria for determining charges.

To a large extent the situation reflects the opposing requirements typically found in enterprises that are being privatized, in the broad sense of reducing the constraints on the use of resources. A new equilibrium can be reached if the allocation of property rights and the consequent renegotiation of interests are rendered compatible with improving efficiency.

Can the reform of the institutional framework be considered adequate with respect to the well known operational and quality shortcomings of the service or is it merely a formal change with no effect on the structure of incentives? Will the experience of other parts of the economy in which the state has intervened be repeated and the importance of the postal monopoly decline gradually owing to technological and other factors? What are EPI's prospects in the light of external economic and institutional factors and technological development?

This paper seeks to contribute to the analysis of these issues by examining the economic aspects of postal markets and the possible relationship between the institutional framework and the efficiency of the service.

2. - Institutional and Economic Issues

The existence within the postal service of conditions of natural monopoly [2] justifying the maintenance of a statutory one is no longer universally accepted. Some economic factors appear to negate the existence of such conditions, notably the presence of numerous operators in several markets, while others appear to confirm their existence, especially the efficiency gains associated with a single delivery network for basic postal services, which some argue is the only segment that can be considered a natural monopoly (Crew - Kleindorfer [6]). A good definition of the postal service is that of an «unnatural monopoly», in the sense of a combination of economic characteristics that point to the need for effective regulation of charges, the establishment of criteria for the liberalization of markets and protection of the universality of the basic postal postal system (Estrin - De Meza [10]). By contrast, there is broad consensus on the existence of a public interest in the postal service being run efficiently and in its being of good quality and accessible to everybody at equitable prices. The European Union has recently approved a direct-ive [3] on the postal services of the member states that defines the principles applying to the postal service: universality (minimization of the exclusion of citizens for reasons of accessibility, price or informa-tion), equality (equal treatment for citizens of the member states in comparable circumstances), neutrality (the treatment of suppliers should be independent of their legal and institutional status) and confidentiality and adaptability (to technological developments in communications). These general principles, which refer only to tradi-

---

[2] An industry can be considered a natural monopoly when its technologies are characterized by subadditive production costs, i.e. when the total cost of producing a given service by a firm that covers the whole market is less than the sum of the costs of several firms that divide the market among themselves.

[3] 1995 Council *Directive* on common rules for the development of Community postal services and the improvement of the quality of services, Brussels, July 1995.

tional postal services in the directive, can be adopted to establish positive criteria defining the characteristics of the markets in which the postal service operates. It is only by analyzing the working of these markets that the question of whether a postal monopoly is preferable can be answered, bearing in mind that in a growing number of cases the factor determining the level of competition is the advance of telecommunications technology and, more generally, the development of the services sector, rather than single policy choices, whose role becomes that of fostering (or sometimes of hindering) trends that are already under way (Noll [16]). In fact, the main function of the postal service in the industrial countries is no longer as a communications network linking individuals, but as a complement to other systems for the transport of physical goods and information associated with the activities of other services such as banking and finance, mail order, subscriptions to magazines and newspapers and advertising campaigns, which generate a flow of mail that increases with national income [4].

Each postal, PO bank and telecommunications service can be included in one of the categories formed by the possible combinations of the presence of universality, reserve and competition, each of which gives rise to particular problems of regulation. Universality and monopoly are the direct consequence of public intervention: the European Council, and the national parliaments required to transpose its provisions, have recognized the existence of a public interest in the general provision of services of this kind independently of their profitability. According to the guidelines set out in the European Commission's *Green Paper* of 1992, which will have to be given effect by national parliaments, universal services are to be considered as including: letter mail (ordinary letters, postcards, registered letters, insured letters and printed matter), parcels [5], money orders, current accounts, savings books, savings certificates and collection services on

---

[4] No more than 20-30% of mail is between individuals in Europe (10% in the United States); the rest is between firms and individuals or between firms (EEC [9]). The share of mail between individuals decreases as the importance of the services sector in the economy increases.

[5] For parcels, it is recommended that the service should be extended as widely as possible, but there is not an actual obligation to do so as for the other services.

behalf of the government. Reserved services are a subset of the universal services, where the reserve — in force today in Italy only for mail weighing up to 2 kg [6] and for telegrams — is granted by the authorities exclusively in view of the need to cover the costs arising from the universality requirement, a rebalancing that would be impossible if private operators were allowed to cherry pick in the market, leading to competition in the profitable segments, with the public operator left to meet demand in the unprofitable ones. In certain circumstances private operators may provide the whole of a reserved service or perform just a part of the productive cycle. In this case a licence has to be obtained from the public operator, the cost of which should in theory be equal to the loss incurred as a result of the diminution in traffic. For telegrams the reserve is due to EPI's possessing a physical network for the transmission of telex messages, which is considered of vital importance for the state's national security and kept alive in this way despite its being utilized only to a very limited extent.

The third element is the presence of several firms in the same market, which can occur for universal services but, at least in theory, not for reserved services. In this case it is important to refer exclusively to positive categories: a service belongs to the group of competitive services only if several firms are found to be actually providing it or if there is a real threat of their doing so. It should be noted, moreover, that a series of factors not necessarily attributable to opportunistic behaviour sometimes result in there being competition in reserved postal services.

The overall picture is shown in Graph 1, where five categories of service are defined. Category *A* (monopoly) and category *D* (unrestricted competition) are the extreme cases. Although in theory these two categories are mutually exclusive, in practice there is a small overlap, represented by category *E*, which includes the internal mail of large organizations and, at the international level, remail. Both these cases are due to the existence of factors that permit the segmentation of the

---

[6] The reserves provided for in 1995 *Directive* are as follows: national mail up to 350 gr (or 5 times the standard charge), inward cross-border traffic and advertising material (the latter until 31 December 2000).

GRAPH 1

PROVISION, MONOPOLY, AND COMPETITION IN POSTAL SERVICES

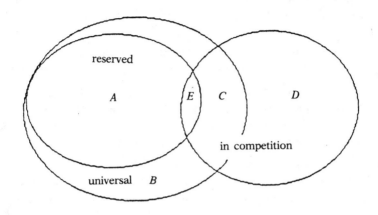

Legend,
  A = universal and reserved service;
  B = universal, non reserved service, but without competition;
  C = universal service in competition;
  D = service in competition;
  E = reserved service in competition.

relevant markets; if this is permitted or at any rate condoned, there will always be someone in a position to benefit. Many large firms and organizations establish communications links between their establishments. If the matter to be transmitted consists of letters and the quantities are very large, they may seek to reduce their postal costs by performing the service in-house (if they have the necessary resources and expertise) or by contracting it out to a third party. The legal monopoly is not violated provided the latter has a specific licence. From the regulator's point of view, the significant factor in this case is the level of the fee charged for the licence. In practice this hardly ever reflects the loss incurred by the public operator and is usually much smaller or merely symbolic, so that monopoly and competition coexist in the same market.

Remail occurs when the rate differences between countries make it profitable for private operators (or national public operators acting as pirates) to transport mail to the country charging the lowest rate and send it from there [7]. Recourse to such behaviour is frequent today in Italy for parcel mail, where is perfectly legal. In both cases the transaction cost of discovering and, if illegal, curbing such behaviour may be so high as to make the risk appear minimal to opportunistic operators.

Regulatory problems are not restricted to category *E*, which is an extreme case, but arise mainly in connection with non-universal competitive services, which are those with characteristics most closely resembling those of a private good, (category *D*). The 1995 directive reaffirms the well known rule that operators providing such services while simultaneously holding a licence for reserved universal services should not subsidize the former with income from the latter, while it permits and explicitly encourages cross-subsidization in the opposite direction. EPI is present in this category with its domestic and international Postacelere express mail service and its electronic postal service (Postel); the former is aimed at the lower part of the market (the general public), which offers considerable growth potential.

The most serious problems arise, however, in connection with the *C* and *B* categories, which consist of unreserved universal services in which private operators respectively do and do not compete. The only difference between the two categories of market concerns the rates charged at present. In the first case they are close to market equilibrium, while in the second EPI is the only operator because the rates imposed by the authorities make it impossible for other operators to cover even their marginal costs. It follows that the transition of a service from one category to the other can be very rapid and that if the division of a market into a profitable and an unprofitable segment is permitted, the same service may belong to both categories at once. At present category *B* services (no competition) include printed matter at subscription rates, while category *C* services include other printed matter, commercial invoices, mail order and all the main PO bank services (which compete with the banking system). Parcels fall into both categories. Private parcel carriers offer a high quality service, at a correspondingly high price and with strict geographical limitations, with the aim of building up a customer base of regular business users.

---

[7] For an analysis of the various configurations of the problem and of the possible solutions see EEC [9].

By contrast, EPI serves the occasional demand of the general public on a nationwide basis and the lower end of the demand of firms, whose associations lobby against increases in charges, with the result that those in force for this service are among the lowest in Europe.

Thus, while the presence of a good number of private competitors in the various postal markets (excluding those in which preferential prices are charged but not those subject to reserve) suggests that conditions of natural monopoly do not generally exist in postal services, the opposite is true for economies of scale, whose existence, in theory, is a sufficient but not a necessary condition. It can therefore by postulated that the economies of scale clearly achievable in some services are of a local nature, i.e. characteristic of only a part of the production curve and not all-inclusive as the condition of natural monopoly would require.

For public operators the problem appears all the more important because they have often seen cherry picking by private operators reduce their traffic volumes. Even in the absence of econometric analyses or market research, public operators tend to argue that returns to scale tend to rise and, above all, fall with the volume of traffic, because the size of the network and the related operating costs should be considered substantially fixed owing to the public nature of the service [8]. This calls, unless public enterprises are simplistically written off as useless, not only for careful analysis of the various postal markets in order to identify possible opportunistic behaviour on the part of operators but also for caution in liberalizing postal services and in establishing the criteria and procedures for determining and approving the charges of the public operator.

3. - The Regulation of Postal Services in the European Union

Each of the categories into which postal service has been divided requires a different type of intervention by the regulatory authority,

---

[8] This is the situation depicted in the documents drawn up by EPI justifying the changes in charges submitted to the Minister of Posts and Telecommunications for approval. In the same vein, the head of the Royal Mail (TABOR R. [23]) argued that the scale elasticity tended to rise when postal traffic diminished.

today the Ministry for Posts and Telecommunications and tomorrow perhaps the Telecommunications Authority. This is a field in which the regulatory authority has wavered between applying the traditional cost or «cost-of-service» method based and the theoretically simpler and more transparent price-cap method, which has been adopted with success for the postal services of Canada, the Netherlands and New Zealand [9]. In the first case the charge for a service is determined using the formula:

$$P(t) = F_t \left[P(t-1), \left(\frac{C(t-1)}{X(t-1)} \right) \right]$$

where:

$$
\begin{aligned}
P(t) \quad &= \text{ charge in period } t \\
C(t-1) &= \text{ total costs in period } t-1 \\
X(t-1) &= \text{ production of the service in period } t-1 \\
F_t \quad &= \text{ the procedure used by the regulator to determine} \\
&\quad \text{ the charge in period } t
\end{aligned}
$$

The charge P_t approved or set by the regulator using the procedure F_t depends on the charge and the average cost of the service in the previous period $(t-1)$. The procedure used by the regulator to determine charges is not neutral with respect to the efficiency of the organization subject to regulation. A procedure that took a long time to approve charges would impose a high cost on the public operator that would increase with the importance within the price-setting exercise of charges for reserved or universal services (on which the public operator can earn rents) and of those for competitive services (where changes in charges are a reflection of the market strategy adopted and therefore need to be implemented rapidly) (Crew - Kleindorfer [6]). Moreover, the cost method has the disadvantage of requiring knowledge of a large quantity of detailed information on

---

[9] For a summary outline of the problem, see BRAEUTIGAM R. - PANZAR J. [2]. For a detailed analysis of the issues involved in the regulation of the postal service, see CREW M. - KLEINDORFER P. [6].

each individual service, which may well not be available or strategically altered by the operator subject to regulation [10].

With the price-cap method, by contrast, the regulator simply determines the rate of increase in charges, normally setting it equal to the rise in the consumer price index less a given percentage to take account of increases in productivity, i.e. *RPI-X*. The fundamental difference between the two methods lies in the incentive effects they produce: whereas with the cost-of-service method the regulated operator is not stimulated to increase its efficiency (charges are basically set to cover costs and approved individually for each service), with the price-cap method the operator is continuously spurred to improve its performance since the method results in a reduction in charges in real terms, so that part of every efficiency gain achieved by the operator is transferred to users. In order to achieve this result, it is necessary to know the minimum cost of the service (or of the services) in the base year and then leave the mechanism to operate for a number of years (typically 3 or 5) to give the operator a chance to recover the cost of the specific investments it makes. It is worth noting that the price-cap method only requires two indices to be considered: one for the reserved services and the other for the competitive services. The postal operator is left free, however, to determine the most appropriate mix of rate changes for individual services. In Italy's case, analysis of ETI's *Programme Contract*, which lays down in detail how charges are to be determined [11], reveals a mixture of the two methods since provision is made for the notification of figures on costs, capital spending and traffic quantities, suggesting that cost-of-service is the main method, but it is also stated that charges should only rise in line with prices once it is fully operational.

In the case of reserved services, it is important to keep charges under control in order to limit the extraction of rents, but also to allow

---

[10] The methods used to determine the unit costs of different services become of considerable importance, notably those used to allocate expenses that are not directly attributable to a particular service. For an analysis of US experience, see SCOTT F. [21].

[11] In the case of competitive services it would probably be more correct to talk of prices. The reason this term is never used in official documents is the not unfounded fear that it would result in such postal services having to be subjected to VAT, whereas they are currently exempted under a Ministerial Decree. Such a move, however, would imply a tax break for monopoly services that would be hard to justify.

the licenced operator to cover its costs (the *Programme Contract* refers to the determination of «technical and economic» charges) while minimizing cross-subsidies and ensuring compliance with the service standards established. In the case of unreserved universal services, the criterion of short-term financial equilibrium could prove insufficient because it might result in the public operator being put at a progressively greater disadvantage compared with its private competitors. On the other hand, it is necessary to avoid the opposite risk of discouraging product innovation and diversification, which often bring concrete benefits for users.

An additional problem for regulators is the difference between single and multi-product operators as regards the manner of setting charges for certain by-products, where competition is often extremely fierce because the fixed costs associated with their production are very low. Multi-product operators can set the charges for such complementary services (e.g. intracity commercial invoices) on the basis of their marginal cost, which in many cases is likely to be close to zero because all the costs of the network are already covered by the receipts from other services. They thus have a competitive advantage over single-product operators, which must base their charges on average costs, including a return on the factors of production they employ. In itself, however, this does not violate the rules of competition since multi-product operators may be able to achieve economies of scale and/or scope that will be of social utility if they are reflected in charges.

When addressing the question of the control of public service charges, it is necessary to establish clearly whether the regulatory body is simply responsible for monitoring them or is also empowered to set them. Law 71/1994 introduces a clear distinction: EPI's board of directors is exclusively responsible for setting the charges for all services, while the Ministry for Posts and Telecommunications is responsible for their approval and may only suspend their application temporarily.

In addition to the general functions of regulation, there are those concerning specific sectors, which are equally delicate from the distributive point of view because organized interest groups are involved. Notable in this connection are the procedures for granting discounts to individual users. The most important case is the extension of the large discounts for newspapers and magazines. The intention was to distinguish between publications according to their cultural merits, but in practice such discounts have been the means of subsidizing the whole of Italy's publishing industry. On the basis of the situation in the first half of 1995, only 0.2% of the 1.7 billion items sent annually did not benefit from a discount of any kind and discounts were equal on average to 74.5% of the charge, with the result that the amount paid per item was equal to 158 lire, compared with a theoretical charge of 621 lire (the base rate beeing 500 lire per item) [12]. It would appear preferable to relieve the public operator of the postal service of this highly discretionary administrative task, not least in view of the new criteria for financing the postal service designed to support the publishing industry recommended in 1993 by the group of experts making up the Technical Committee on Public Expenditure at the Treasury Ministry [13]. The principle that needs to be established is that postal charges cannot be considered a legitimate means of financing particular categories of beneficiary but have to be seen simply as an instrument permitting an efficient licenced operator to cover all its operating costs. The discounts granted to publishers should therefore be transformed into explicit subsidies, to be awarded to each firm by an independent committee made up of representatives of government departments and the publishing industry. it would be illusory, however, to expect that such a change in the procedure for distributing subsidies would on its own solve the problem of the «right» postal charge for newspapers and magazines. The problem concerns most of the OECD countries, including those in which the postal service is efficient [14], because the granting of public aid inevitably distorts competition in the markets for the subsidized goods,

---

[12] In 1994 ETI applied to the Treasury for 607 billion lire to compensate for the loss of income in 1994 in respect of subscription rate traffic. In order to calculate the full amount of subsidies received by the publishing industry, it is necessary to add another 120 billion in connection with the existence of other types of discount, which were cumulable and equally unrelated to any real advantage that the public postal operator stood to gain.

[13] See COMMISSIONE TECNICA PER LA SPESA PUBBLICA [4].

[14] The increase in subscription rates in Switzerland in October 1995 was the object of a violent press campaign orchestrated by the publishing industry.

including in this case the market for daily newspapers (Stumpf [22]).

With the publication of its *Green Paper* on postal services (EEC [9]) and then the issue of 1995 *Directive*, the European Union has become the most important forum for the regulation of member states' postal services. When analyzed from a European standpoint, the very concept of competition changes since it is no longer restricted to the relationship between public operators and the private competitors that are winning a growing share of their national markets but includes competition between the public operators themselves. On the one hand, the latter are extending their competition (and strategic agreements) with private operators beyond their national boundaries; on the other, they are beginning to compete among themselves (as is shown by the growth of remail) both in the market for cross-border mail and within individual national markets [15]. In this scenario the policies of national regulatory bodies have become interdependent; for example, a decision to reduce the extent of reserved services in one country will have spillover effects in the markets of other countries. Italy's attempt to defend the extent of its statutory monopoly (a battle that it has lost since the upper limit set for letters at the EU level is 350 gr, compared with the 2 kg envisaged by Italian law) has resulted in its being criticized by the Community and in its running the risk of being in a weak bargaining position in the negotiation of the new rules compared with countries such as the Netherlands and the United Kingdom, which have efficient and aggressive public postal operators that are ready to enter the profitable segments of other countries' national markets. One of the accusations leveled against Italy is that in some services there are unjustified charge differentials between different weight classes. According to the *Green Paper*, this is an indication of the excessive extension of the statutory monopoly, but it is really evidence of how the distorted use of administrative pricing has had unforeseen detrimental side effects in the absence of effective regulation. These

---

[15] A similar pattern is to be found in telecommunications, where fierce competition is developing among national operators for large customers in other countries. A recent example is the agreement for British Telecom to supply BNL with internal communications services.

excessive differentials, which are undoubtedly much larger than the corresponding differences in costs, are in fact the undesired effect of the procedure used until now by ISTAT (the Italian statistical office) to determine the cost-of-living index for blue- and white-collar households, for many years the yardstick for the payment of *scala mobile* cost-of-living allowances. The basket of services used to calculate this index included the charges for the lower weights of several postal services, which were consequently held down artificially. The postal administration was forced to increase the charges not included in the basket more than proportionally to limit the damage to its accounts of the failure to increase the standard charge in line with inflation. The problem is on its way to being resolved since EPI is restructuring its charge schedules and, in conformity with the practice of private operators, is reducing both the number of charge levels and the differences between them [16].

4. - EPI's Performance

For some twenty years now Italy's public postal service has been caught up in a vicious circle of falling traffic (all the more rapid since competition emerged in some services), overmanning, declining labour productivity, a mismatch between capital equipment and the pursuit of efficiency, an irrational distribution of staff not only in geographical terms but also between services and shifts, poor quality and large losses despite the high charges for monopoly services [17]. These factors tend to interact and will therefore make it hard for the new operator created by law 71/1994 to carry out its plans for the reorganization of its operations. One way of assessing the chances of these being implemented successfully is to conduct a comparative

---

[16] For its part Istat is studying a new procedure for the calculation of its price indices (as regards all the main public services and not only the postal service) that will take account of all the different services and charge levels and thus provide an indication of the overal situation. This new index could serve as one of the key parameters for the calculation of an eventual price cap.

[17] See ONOFRI R. - PATRIZII V. - ZANGHERI P. [17], PATRIZII V. [18], GIARDA P. [13], COMMISSIONE TECNICA PER LA SPESA PUBBLICA [5] and VISCO COMANDINI V. [24].

analysis of its governance structures (Cheung [3]; Williamson [25]), with reference to those of the former autonomous government agency and those emerging with a view to the creation of a limited company. Even if two different institutional models can be expected to produce different results in terms of cost and quality of service combinations (a plausible hypothesis in the case of postal services), this does not mean that one is unambiguously preferable to the other. Both may be «efficient» in relation to their internal constraints and the choice between them depends on how preferences are transmitted and expressed through the political market (De Alessi [7]). If the criteria a society uses to assess the efficiency of an organization change, a solution that was previously accepted without question may be threatened, just as a new institutional arrangement that was judged preferable to the previous one may be abandoned in the following period owing to its inability to create the consensus needed to keep it in equilibrium. The choice of the «best» governance structure thus depends on the coalition of the many economic agents making up the organization, of which some receive a share of the quasi-rents arising from the specific nature of the investment or, in the case of public services produced under licence, from the monopoly (Klein - Crawford - Alchian [14], Dow [8]). The key issue is the link between efficiency and redistribution [18]. In every economic organization there is always someone performing the function of residual claimant, if not of the profit, of the quasi-rents arising from the function of redistributing the benefits associated with the exercise of control. Consequently, the possibility of reconciling their distribution depends on the structure of the (*ex ante* or *ex post*) incentives in force. Efficiency can be achieved if it proves possible to form, and maintain, a coalition of interests based on acceptance of the common objective of improving the performance of the organization. Each group in the coalition will be willing to renounce the short-term exploitation of the rents it has created within the organization and to «cooperate» in its operational rehabilitation if it expects the benefits from the valorization of the common good represented by the organization (hence the importance

---

[18] For an interesting treatment of contracting in heath care, relating markets, transaction costs, and redistribution see BARILETTI A. - FRANCE G. [1].

of the incentives) to exceed those it has obtained in the form of rents, taking account (if it is rational) of the risk that these will diminish as a result of the strengthening of the internal hierarchical order (fiat) envisaged by the 1994 reform.

In order to determine whether the reform has really modified the situation, it is necessary to examine the changes in the structure of property rights (Furoboth-Pejovich [12]), especially as regards the possibility of disposing of assets and the control of the organization producing the service (Picot - Wolff [19]). The first of these rights is particularly important in the case of the postal service because an efficient use of resources would almost certainly require the sale of all or part of the networks of services judged not to be strategic, or at any rate a diversification of the ownership of assets that are entirely in public hands today. From this point of view the legal form of a limited company undoubtedly appears the most efficient solution, though attracting private investors will require the elimination of the losses of the present organization, a difficult but not impossible objective as Table 1 shows.

The table distinguishes the result for the year based exclusively on sales revenues from that, of greater interest to taxpayers, obtained by summing the operating loss and the amounts paid by the Ministry of the Treasury to compensate EPI for engaging in uneconomic activities, such as granting large discounts to the publishing industry and maintaining its network of small and unprofitable post offices. These

TABLE 1

RESULTS OF ENTE POSTE ITALIANE
(profit and loss account reclassified by value added; billions of lire)

Year	Loss for the year	Treasury Ministry contribution	Total
1993	4,530	0	4,530
1994	684	968	1,652
1995*	751	167	918
1996*	0	143	143

* Forecasts.

subsidies are forecast to decline significantly from 1995 onwards. EPI expects to break even on its operations in 1996, the year planned for its transformation into a limited company.

As regards the second type of property rights, the 1994 reform, which put the postal service on a private-law footing, certainly strengthened the control of the governing bodies over the organization by increasing their powers to reallocate the resources available. It should not be forgotten, however, that the postal service was an integral part of the public administration and that it will be difficult to bring about a radical change in its objectives and culture. For instance, the internal information system is still largely based on the procedures inherited from the autonomous government agency and designed primarily to ensure formal correctness, to the detriment of the timely transmission of data and operational efficiency.

EPI's main problem is the control of its labour costs, something that was precarious in the past and now made more difficult by the fact that the strengthening of the internal hierarchical order has been accompanied by a tightening of financial constraints that leaves little scope for committing the resources needed to obtain agreement on the institutional changes introduced. This state of affairs has highlighted the factors that contributed in the past to the inefficiency of personnel management (hirings based on political favouritism, but above all unrelated to productive needs and marked by low levels of motivation [19], justified through the use of obsolete parameters of manpower requirements that failed to take account of automation). The only way to reduce losses in the short term was to impose a freeze on hirings, which was also a logical response to the manifest overmanning in the postal service [20]. In fact, total employment fell from 237,000 in 1990 to 192,000 in the middle of 1995.

Table 2 shows the average annual percentage decreases in staff numbers by geographical area in the periods 1990-1993 and 1993-

---

[19] Most of the hirings effected by the postal administration in the last years were in response to a demand for employment that was met by the political market: it was not generic but aimed, especially in the South, at obtaining a stable job in the public sector, with working hours similar to those of civil servants.

[20] Recent studies in Giarda P. [13] estimated the number of redundant workers in the postal service at between 20,000 and 50,000.

TABLE 2

AVERAGE ANNUAL PERCENTAGE CHANGES IN PO EMPLOYMENT
(by geographical area and year)

Geographical area	1990-1993	1993-1995*
North	− 2.6	− 5.2
Centre...........................	− 2.5	− 6.1
South	− 1.6	− 5.2
central administration in Rome	− 2.8	− 5.2
Italy.............................	− 2.3	− 5.4

* At 30 June 1995.

1995. The pace of the decline accelerated significantly following the creation of EPI and its geographical distribution also underwent a change between the two periods. In the first, the southern regions received more favourable treatment than those of the Centre and North, whereas in the second the difference was much less pronounced.

Labour productivity in the public postal service is a structural problem. After declining in the seventies and eighties (as a result of net hirings exceeding the growth in traffic), it has improved in the last three years. For a long time the postal administration measured output by aggregating the flows of the different services using questionable methods that make it difficult to verify the results obtained. Accordingly, the measure of productivity shown in Table 3 is that of output per employee, which is better suited to organizations producing market services.

The index of productivity at constant prices rose at an average annual rate of 3.8% between 1990 and 1994, which indicates a significant improvement in management performance. It is nonetheless worrying that the 38.6 million lire of output per employee in 1994 was still not enough to cover the average unit cost of labour.

Another serious problem, which is related to that of productivity and has important implications for quality, concerns the organization of the production cycle. If the postal service is to be efficient, the workload must be unevenly distributed over the day. In theory every

TABLE 3

SALES REVENUES PER EMPLOYEE
(milions of lire)

	1990	1994	Avg. annual productivity gain
at current prices	33.5	45.3	8.9
at constant prices*	33.5	38.6	3.8

* Deflated using the consumer price index for services.

letter could be delivered the day after it is posted if: 1) postboxes were emptied and mail taken to post offices by the late afternoon; 2) sorting began immediately afterwards, with the preparation of the sacks for shipment to all the various localities being completed by midnight; 3) each sack was consigned during the same night to the carrier responsible for taking it to its destination and, on arrival, its contents were divided out among the different delivery rounds; and 4) postmen delivered the letters the next morning.

The system, which is common to all countries, requires that backlogs should not be allowed to build up at any stage of the cycle and that staff should be distributed so as to optimize traffic flows [21]. The scope for automation is limited in some phases of the cycle, especially delivery, and the majority of staff are employed there. In other phases, by contrast, the crucial factor is the correct allocation of staff to the various shifts; for example, the peak workload in sorting occurs between 5 pm and midnight. The main problem affecting the Italian postal service today is its imbalanced distribution of labour; this is clearly revealed in Table 4, which is based on internal data on the cost of services in 1993 [22].

The root of the problem is the overmanning in sorting, the most

---

[21] In view of the importance of flow management, CREW M. - KLEINDORFER P. ([6] ch. 3) examined the scope for peak-load pricing in postal services.

[22] The analyses suffer from a number of methodological weaknesses that undermine their reliability, especially at the level of individual services. However, the possible measurement errors are likely to be of a systematic nature and distributed normally among the various phases of the cycle, so that the percentage breakdowns shown in Table 4 should be fairly significant.

TABLE 4

PERCENTAGE BREAKDOWN
OF THE OPERATING COSTS OF THE MAIN MAIL SERVICES IN 1993

	Collection	Sorting	Transport	Delivery
Ordinary letters	2.0	51.9	1.1	45.0
Registered & insured letters	6.1	69.9	0.3	23.7
Express letters	0.4	9.6	0.2	89.8
Postcards	2.0	52.3	0.4	45.3
Commercial invoices	1.9	51.8	1.4	44.9
Printed matter	1.9	50.0	4.8	43.3
Printed matter at subscription rates	0.0	41.7	14.2	44.1
Total	3.5	58.2	3.8	34.5

Source, Based on EPI data.

sought after work within post offices, to the detriment of final distribution, which should account for a larger share of the total cost [23]. If early retirement is to be encouraged, priority should be given to sorters since a reduction in their numbers would almost certainly not prejudice the quality of the service.

The capital spending of the postal service also reveals a long tradition of inefficiency, sometimes attributable to the distortions produced by interest groups (notably as regards decisions concerning the location of plants, often serving more to satisfy electoral requirements than to improve the efficiency of the network) but in other cases the result of unhappy technical and operational choices. A good example is the policy, pursued in the sixties and seventies following the example of large firms seeking economies of scale, of channelling flows of mail for sorting into large plants that were only cheaper than manual methods if they handled very large volumes of traffic. This made it necessary to reorganize the network in a way that resulted in its being more rigid, led to inefficiency at bottlenecks, slowed down the system as a whole and provided opportunities for local interest

---

[23] The European Commission's *Green Paper* (EEC [9]) indicates that a postal service needs to have between 50% and 60% of its staff working as letter carriers if it is to be efficient.

TABLE 5

SALES REVENUES BY SECTOR OF ACTIVITY
(billions of lire)

	1990	1994	% change	
			current price	constant prices
Mail..................	4,524	5,048	11.6	− 5.2
Telegraph	610	237	−61.1	−66.9
PO bank..............	2,809	4,272	52.1	29.3
Total	7,943	9,557	20.3	2.3

Source, Based on EPI data.

groups (suppliers, subcontractors and trade union locals) to extract rents. In this respect the proposed diversification of the ownership structure should prove an effective incentive to make better use, if necessary through drastic changes in use, of the large volume of often underutilized fixed assets.

Stimulated by the far-reaching product and process innovations under way in the services sector, the Italian postal system is modifying the composition of the services it supplies. Table 5 shows the sales revenues of the main sectors of activity in 1990 and 1994. In real terms there was an overall increase of 2.3% over the period but there were large sectoral differences: the share of the postal sector fell by 4 percentage points to 53%, while that of PO bank services rose by 10 points to 45% [24]. Telegraph revenues declined very sharply and this sector is likely to disappear or at any rate to be put to a new use.

In order to assess the operating results of the various services, reference was made to the estimates for 1993 prepared by the postal administration using methods that leave much to be desired in view of the importance of the figure. The results, shown in Graph 6, thus only provide a rough indication of the situation [25].

---

[24] EPI forecasts that the turnover of the PO bank sector will overtake that of the postal sector in 1995.

[25] The total operating loss for 1993 shown in Table 6 is about 300 billion lire larger than that shown for the same year in Table 1. The divergence is entirely attributable to the different methods used to calculate the figures.

TABLE 6

RESULTS OF THE MAIN MAIL SERVICES IN 1993
(billions of lire)

	Profit/loss	% covered by charges	% of total loss
Letters	− 208	91.4	4
Postcards	− 90	57.9	2
Manuscripts	40	152.0	− 1
Pockages and samples	1	103.3	0
Commercial invoices	− 240	47.0	5
Printed matters	− 363	50.2	5
Registered letters	131	114.6	− 3
Insured letters	− 21	92.1	0
Express mail	− 46	62.7	1
Print. matter at subscription rates	− 1,141	33.3	24
Parcels	− 566	37.0	12
Money order	− 702	12.8	15
Current acc. payments	− 558	47.5	12
Telegrams	− 868	19.6	18
Telex	− 280	46.7	6
Total	− 4,810		

Source, Based on Epi data.

In 1993 five services accounted for 80% of the total loss for the year: printed matter at subscription rates, parcels, money orders, current accounts and telegrams. The large loss incurred in 1993 makes it impossible to determine whether a deliberate policy of cross-subsidization was being pursued, although, as Faulhaber [11] has demonstrated, cross-subsidies are inevitable in a multi-product enterprise. However, improved operating results would probably cause this problem, which is common to all public postal operators, to take on greater importance for public opinion and above all for the regulator.

The most striking aspect of the postal service in Italy is undoubtedly its poor quality and the deterioration that occurred during the years in which the factors of inefficiency described above were at work (above all the poorly implemented automation of the various services), especially as their detrimental effect on quality tended to be multiplied by the organization of the system as a network. It can plausibly be argued that the strongest incentive for private operators to enter the postal market in Italy was the poor quality of the public service, which made it easier for them to establish themselves in the most profitable segments [26]. Italy's postal service offers an eloquent example of how merely changing the ownership of an economic organization without modifying its manner of operating in the market is not a sufficient condition for improving the performance of a public service. In 1991 the postal authorities granted a company called Senditalia an exclusive licence to operate the profitable sector of delivering express letters in large cities. Initially, there was a substantial improvement in quality, measured by the average time taken to effect delivery, but within two years it had been completely eroded because there was no incentive for the private operator to improve the service nor any way of verifying its productive effort [27].

The main quality factors of a postal service are rapidity or delivery time and reliability, measured in terms of both the risk of a fail (the percentage of undelivered letters) and the certainty of delivery within a given time (the variance of delivery times). The efficiency and quality of the service are closely related, but changes in the former tend to be reflected in the latter with a lag. The creation of EPI was accompanied by a deterioration in the quality indices of the various services, partly owing to the sharp fall in the number of employees. However, the reorganization programme implemented by the new public operator and the creation of a task force charged with constantly monitoring the flow of traffic has allowed the ground lost to be made good and further significant improvements to be made.

Table 7 shows the service standards for ordinary letters established in the *Programme Contract* for the end of 1995 and 1996 and the values found in 1995 before and after the reorganization. The indicator adopted is the percentage of mail delivered in the x days following that on which it is sent $(J + x)$, which provides a summary measure of both rapidity and reliability. Two standards are envisaged,

---

[26] For an analysis of the way in which private postal operators use the poor quality of the public service to enter the market, see VISCO COMANDINI V. [24].

[27] The licence was accordingly not renewed when the contract expired.

TABLE 7

PROGRAMME CONTRACT AND ACTUAL SERVICE STANDARDS
(J = mailing date)
percentage of letters delivered on time

Target	Intraity	Interregional	National average
For 31 December 1995	85% in $J + 2$	85% in $J + 3$	85% in $J + 3$
Actual in April 1995 ..	85% in $J + 2$	61% in $J + 3$	80% in $J + 3$
Actual in October 1995	98% in $J + 2$	81% in $J + 3$	93% in $J + 3$
For 31 December 1996	85% in $J + 1$	85% in $J + 2$	85% in $J + 2$

Source, Based on EPI data.

one for intracity traffic and the other for interregional traffic. The *Programme Contract* provides for 85% of intracity mail to be delivered within two days of being sent by the end of 1995 and within one day by the end of 1996. On the basis of EPI's own figures, it can be seen that this standard for 1995 had not been reached in April but that in October the intracity performance was well above standard. Nonetheless, there were still problems with interregional mail, presumably in connection with the system's automated plants, which mainly handle this type of traffic. Since the public is probably most interested in the performance of interregional traffic, where a large proportion of the mail between individuals is almost certainly concentrated [28], EPI risks seeing its efforts to improve the organization's image made futile unless it also succeeds in upgrading this part of the network.

5. - Medium Term Strategies

The analysis conducted here suggests that the issue of monopoly is not of great significance for postal policymaking, notwithstanding its theoretical interest. In the first place, the experience of countries

---

[28] See footnote 4.

such as the United Kingdom, Sweden, Denmark, France and the Netherlands shows that a limited reserve accompanied by clear rules governing the behaviour of all operators to coexist with the public operator and both to be highly efficient. Secondly, postal services are marked by considerable complementarity and substitutability with respect to telecommunications services in general, so that postal market conditions are often determined by changes in the technologies and prices of such services and products. Thirdly, responsibility for deciding which services are to be subject to reserve is now at the European level and can thus be considered a fact, at least for the time being. Of greater interest for postal policymaking are thus the manner in which national regulators are required to perform their control functions aimed at protecting users, ensuring a level competitive playing field across markets and stimulating technological innovation. There is scope today for further automation in many services (e.g. bar-code readers), which could lead to the entry of new private operators with specialized know-how into the phases of the cycle other than delivery, the only one considered to meet the conditions for a natural monopoly. Accordingly, the scenario for the postal system could be similar to that now under discussion in Italy for the electricity industry, where there are good grounds for preferring competition in some phases of the cycle (generating) and just one operator in others having the characteristics of a natural monopoly (transmission). In the case of the postal services, delivery would be entrusted exclusively to the public operator, while in the other phases (notably sorting, which is particularly inefficient today) there could be competition. The crucial condition in this case would be for private operators to have access to the delivery system.

Letter mail services have to compete with other methods of communication, at present primarily telefax (which has a lower marginal cost for local services) but in the future probably also Internet. It is too early to estimate the substitution effect, owing to the limited diffusion of the alternative equipment, but innovation in postal products and services will be necessary to offset the effects of these trends.

EPI is learning to live with the competition that emerged in the recent past as a result of the inefficiency of the public service and, in response to the erosion of many of its profitable market segments, is redefining its strategy with the aim of maximizing revenues. As part of this new course EPI plans to enter markets that have so far been dominated by private operators (such as junk mail) where it can customize charges and exploit its comparative advantage with respect to smaller operators in terms of marginal costs.

As regards other services, especially those of a universal and competitive nature that benefit from subsidies, the gradual elimination of preferential pricing will inevitably involve a reduction in traffic in the long run, not least because many small publishers will no longer find them economically advantageous. Even if these services are loss-making, such a decline in traffic will be detrimental owing to the high fixed costs of the postal network. It will therefore be necessary to find ways of increasing its utilization. One possibility would be for EPI to reach agreements, including joint ventures, with other carriers such as the state railways with a view to creating scope for complementary network reorganization [29]

The problem of the efficiency of the network is macroscopic for the telex network, which at the moment only serves the public postal operator and is seriously underutilized, with the result that unit costs are extremely high. One can envisage EPI setting up a company to lease the network to third parties. Alternatively, it could reach agreements or enter into joint ventures with large private firms to provide specific services. The internationalization of postal markets makes it possible for large operators to compete in a national market while cooperating in markets abroad. For example, in the international express delivery market, where a high qualitative standard is required, EPI could use the distribution network of a large private firm such as DHL or TNT, or those of public operators, in exchange for exclusive mail distribution rights for the whole or parts of Italy.

Such strategies depend on the fulfilment of three closely interrelated conditions: 1) achieving break-even in the near future, so as to make the postal networks and services an asset attractive to private

---

[29] The flow of traffic of printed matter at subscription rates is mostly from North to South and the articulated trucks that carry the bulk of this mail often make the return journey empty. In some cases (fruit and vegatable products, for instance) the flow on the railways is in the opposite direction.

investors, coupled with the immediate separation of the accounts of the various services for management and regulatory purposes and to allow some to be hived off as independent entities; 2) improving the quality of the existing services, and especially the ordinary letter service, which is the hallmark of the postal system and, despite technological progress in telecommunications, will remain decisive in determining the image of the public operator for a good many years; and 3) transforming EPI into a limited company, thus opening the way to the creation of companies specializing in specific aspects of the business and the possibility of adopting different ownership structures matching the needs of the strategies adopted.

BIBLIOGRAPHY

[1] BARILETTI A. - FRANCE G., «Transaction Cost Economics and Efficiency in Health Reform: the Case of Italy», paper presented at *Third European Conference on Health Economics*, Stockholm 20-22 August 1995.

[2] BRAEUTIGAM R. - PANZAR J., «Effects of the Change from Rate-of-Return to Price-Cap Regulation», *American Economic Review*, vol. n. 83, n. 2, 1993, p. 191.

[3] CHEUNG S., «Economic Organization and Transaction Costs», in EATWELL J. - MILGATE M. - NEWMAN P. (eds.), *The New Palgrave: A Dictionary of Economics*, vol. II, 1987.

[4] COMMISSIONE TECNICA PER LA SPESA PUBBLICA, «Riordino e razionalizzazione delle tariffe postali», *Raccomandazioni*, Roma, Ministero del Tesoro, June 1993.

[5] COMMISSIONE TECNICA PER LA SPESA PUBBLICA, «Servizi di pubblica utilità: trasporti e poste», in MINISTERO DEL TESORO, *Il controllo della spesa pubblica, interpretazioni e proposte*, Roma, Istituto poligrafico e zecca dello Stato, 1994, p. 207.

[6] CREW M. - KLEINDORFER P., *The Economics of Postal Service*, Boston, Kluwer Academic Publishers, 1992.

[7] DE ALESSI L., «The Effect of Institutions on the Choices of Consumers and Providers of Health Care», *Journal of Theoretical Politics*, vol. 1, n. 4, 1989, p. 427.

[8] DOW K., «The Appropriability Critique of Transaction Cost Economics», in PITELIS C., *Transaction Costs, Markets and Hierarchies*, Oxford, Blackwell, 1993.

[9] EEC, *Green Paper on the Development of a Single Market of Postal Services*, Brussels, 11 June 1992.

[10] ESTRIN S. - DE MEZA D., «Unnatural Monopoly», *Journal of Public Economics*, n. 57, 1995, 471.

[11] FAULHABER G., «Cross-Subsidization Pricing in Public Enterprise», *American Economic Review*, vol. 65, n. 5, 1975, p. 966.

[12] FURUBOTH E. - PEJOVICH S., «Property Rights and Economic Theory: a Survey of Recent Literature», *Journal of Economic Literature*, n. 10, 1972, p. 1137.

[13] GIARDA P. (ed.), *Produttività, costi e domanda dei servizi postali in Italia*, Bologna, il Mulino, 1993.

[14] KLEIN B. - CRAWFORD R. - ALCHIAN A., «Vertical Integration, Appropriable Rents, and the Competitive Contracting Process», *Journal of Law and Economics*, n. 21, 1978, p. 297.

[15] LEVINE M., «Regulating Airmail Transportation», *Journal of Law and Economics*, n. 2, 1975, p. 317.

[16] NOLL R., *Economic Perspectives on the Politics of Regulation*, in SCHUMALENSEE R. - WILLING R. (eds.) «Handbook of Industrial Organization», vol. II, Amsterdam (Ny), North Holland, 1989, p. 1254.

[17] ONOFRI R. - PATRIZII V. - ZANGHERI P., *Analisi della gestione e del funzionamento dei servizi dell'amministrazione delle poste e delle telecomunicazioni*, Roma, Commissione tecnica per la spesa pubblica, Ministero del Tesoro, 1987.

[18] PATRIZII V., «Il servizio postale: concorrenza e monopolio», *Economia Italiana*, n. 2, 1991, p. 163.

[19] PICOT A. - WOLFF B., «Institutional Economics of Public Firms and Administrations. Some Guidelines for Efficiency-Oriented Design», *Journal of Institutional and Theoretical Economics*, vol. 150, n. 1, 1994, p. 211.

[20] PRIEST L., «The History of the Postal Monopoly in the United States», *Journal of Law and Economics*, n. 18, 1975, p. 33.

[21] SCOTT F., «Assessing USA Postal Ratemaking: An Application of Ramsey Prices», *Journal of Industrial Economics*, n. 3, 1986, p. 279.

[22] STUMPF U., «Postal Newspaper Delivery and Diversity of Opinion», in CREW M. - KLEINDORFER P. (eds.), *Competition and Innovation in Postal Services*, Boston, Kluwer Publishers, 1991, p. 179.

[23] TABOR R., «Can Competitors Pass "Go" With a Natural Monopoly?», *Public Finance and Accountancy*, 8 May 1987.

[24] VISCO COMANDINI V., «The Postal Service in the European Union. Public Monopoly or Competitive Market?) A Transaction Cost Approach», *Annals of Public and Cooperative Economics*, n. 1, 1995, p. 7.

[25] WILLIAMSON O., «Calculativeness, Trust, and Economic Organization», *Journal of Law and Economics*, n. 36, 1993, p. 453.

Index